I SPY WHY *Rich* PEOPLE MAKE IT

LAINE E. LEADS

Acknowledgments

First, thank you Dad for the fun conversation we had when you used the word "copacetic." It was an ah-ha moment for me because I couldn't find the right words to title Chapter Two, but when I heard you say it, I instantly knew what it would be. Second, thank you Mom for your encouragement, and after reading my draft, sharing your perception of wealth from your farm girl childhood. A story I never would have known if I did not write this book.

Thank you to the many editors, and Kay, for your support and valuable feedback in your editing, it was great working with your joyful spirit.

And to my former employers, if you ever find out about this book, I hope you find these stories honoring. I truly appreciate all you taught me when you did not know you were teaching.

~ Laine

Acknowledgments

Table of Contents

Table of Contents

INTRODUCTION:

No Longer A Secret

WHAT ARE THEIR SECRETS?
HOW DO THE WEALTHY MAKE MONEY?

I am an insider, Pepper the Personal Assistant, I work in the private lives of self-made millionaire and billionaire families or "M&Bs."

In this book, I present fourteen years of observations and analysis of M&B subconscious behaviors that drive them to become prosperous. I will share subconscious wealth-building practices never identified by those who study the wealthy from afar. How can I claim this? Because none of those who "studied" them *really* studied them. To do so requires observing their behaviors during personal, unplanned incidents. This involves hours, days, and years of consistent observation—while they're unaware. No one has done this until now.

In the following chapters, I will expose where the wealthy derive their stability and resolve. *Secret: it isn't in having money.* I will also answer these questions and more: How did they make their money? What is their money mindset? How do they produce results day after day? Can I do it too?

With practice, the habits you read, you can learn. This book is designed to provide a unique type of mentorship through the real-life, uncensored stories of self-made M&Bs. Let them teach you how to reason and make decisions the way they do.

Get ready to engross yourself in a rare mentorship opportunity with the never-before-seen 5 Ps of M&Bs; The method to producing prosperity in life, finances, and relationships.

WHAT DO THEY HAVE THAT I DON'T?

Like a sleuth, I studied them. Then I compared their behaviors to my own and learned the differences between us—the ones that made them ultra-wealthy. They are behaviors I didn't know until I immersed myself in their worlds.

I then synthesized their behaviors into 5 Ps to help me promote a more prosperous lifestyle. By reviewing my judgments and plans with the 5 Ps in mind, I now make better decisions. Later, I shared these concepts with a few friends who struggled in business. When they implemented the principles, they experienced benefits. Now they're happier and more confident.

Because of the results I've seen in my life and friends' lives, I chose to write this book to share the practices with others who want to adapt to a prosperity-building lifestyle.

WARNING. Results are limitless and can happen quickly. After implementing one principle from the 5 Ps for less than a month, a friend's life flourished.

HOW THIS BOOK CAN CREATE IN YOU PROSPERITY-BUILDING SKILLS

At the beginning of each chapter you will find quotes from billionaires to inspire you, definitions, SYNONYMS and most impactful, ANTONYMS. Sometimes when we learn an antithesis, it's easier to understand a definition. And, at the end of each chapter is a RECAP with questions, strategies, or suggestions to challenge you.

Implement~

At the end of the book is a 5 Ps and a 13 Cs tear sheet. Post them where they will remind you of your new lifestyle. You can also find them at www.LaineLeads.com.

Create and use 5P flash cards to stay mindful of your new M&B mentality.

And, to reinforce your new mentality during difficult times, ask yourself this question: "What Would Pepper's Clients Do?" Why? Because Pepper's clients are your new mentors. Their choices can help you make similar, prosperity-focused decisions.

Your new mentors want you to role-play. They do it. And, they always role-play a hero. (You'll learn about this later.) To start a role-play, ask yourself what an M&B from this book would do in your circumstances. Practicing this helps you evolve into what you want to become.

If Pepper's M&Bs make a decision a certain way, then so can you. Do what they do. If you practice their skills in this book, you will increase your chances of thinking, deciding, and building like an M&B. This will greatly increase your ability to live like one.

Challenge yourself~

Which of the 5 Ps do you lack, and how can you change that? How can you add missing Cs to your daily life? And, what can you relate to in the M&B stories? What did you learn, and how can you implement it now?

Self-made M&Bs understand decision-making is where wealth building begins, thus why every decision matters to every one of them. Period. No effort goes unnoticed by an M&B. This book will teach you how to identify and encourage yourself to feel good about any progress you make. Learn to treat yourself like an M&B treats him or herself; by celebrating good decisions made.

Start now! Celebrate your choice to learn and practice prosperity-building skills.

Roll like an M&B in thought and deed~

For an M&B wealth is about movement: Keep moving forward. In this book you'll learn how to roll like an M&B; like a snowball, down a lifelong, snow-laden hill building up your prosperity.

ROLL ON RIGHT NOW! Read on prosperity seeker and become a prosperity maker!

~Laine E. Leads

MY DISCLAIMER:

Types of M&Bs and Me

This writing is a compilation of my research, presented for application purposes only, for those who desire an abundant lifestyle filled with prosperity-building practices. My intention is to help others learn a better way of life.

I've never had to sign an NDA, so my writing is not out of defiance or to disparage clientele. This is why I created the term "M&B," changed names, some facts and some genders, to protect the identities of those I served. The essence of their stories, reactions, and decisions are as accurate as I can remember. To the best of my ability, I concealed their identities while preserving pertinent content for educational purposes.

I am not a Personal Assistant to talented artists. The only ones I've known were stock market "geniuses" who proved to be nothing more than scam artists. They had ridiculous amounts of money. They blew through it like it was nothing, and that is what they have now: nothing. And "nothing" keeps them company inside their prison cells.

The millionaires and billionaires I've associated with operate in the pharmaceutical industry, technology, hedge funds, estate planning, real estate, fitness, financial planning, land development, grocery, and retail. I work for people who generated millions from small beginnings. They didn't achieve momentary success but are consistent producers of millions of dollars.

I've not worked with famous musicians or movie stars; therefore, I cannot assess how these groups of people created and manage their wealth.

CHAPTER ONE:

How did I get here?

~Lies bind and blind, judgments deceive, but truth empowers and sets us free ~

Laine

I certainly didn't plan a career working for M&Bs. I never heard of the Personal Assistant profession.

Because I grew up in a low-income, and many times penniless, home, I didn't know how "wealthy" wealthy could be. My first introduction to it was a small, yet awe-inspiring moment.

I was six years old. We moved into an older community and a neighbor invited me to her house. Since her children were grown, she welcomed me to play with their board games any time.

She walked me into her storage room, a long room with shelves from floor to ceiling on one side. On these shelves sat hundreds of games—so it seemed, to my six-year-old mind. I stood there stunned, wondering how she got so many. What she had, that I didn't, dazzled me. She was rich—I wasn't.

As I grew older, I assumed wealth possibly happened to people because of pure luck, or maybe because of inheritance, or more education. I even wondered if it was genetic.

My first lesson on making money was in high school when an instructor taught basic stock investing. He instructed students to look at stock tables in a week-old newspaper and choose company stocks. It was limited teaching. Sadly, we received a grade on these random investments.

I recall one of my investments decreased in value week after week, I wanted out. I told him I wanted to sell my shares to stop the loss. He said, "No." He only allowed us to buy or sell once a quarter. I couldn't believe he wouldn't allow me to sell a declining stock. I remember reasoning if I bought it so fast, why couldn't I sell it as fast?

That negative experience, and every one after, compounded my disillusionment. There didn't appear to be a real cause and effect. Wealth was not *of* the wealthy, it only happened to them. So, I determined it magically appeared to passive people.

EARLY MONEY LESSONS

By the age of eleven, I did my best to build income. I babysat for neighbors and saved every dollar. I learned about compounding interest and wanted to start multiplying my cash by opening a savings account.

My mother took me to the bank to open the account. The branch manager sat across from us, and he helped me complete the application form. I asked him if his savings accounts used simple or compounded interest. He paused, with eyebrows raised and asserted, "Compounding." I was a serious investor.

When I turned fifteen, I started my first official job, but my boss only paid me half the minimum wage. He quipped he had the right to do this because he was a small business owner. He said if I wanted the other half, I had to apply for it at the social security office. It was a discouraging experience.

After this incident, no one taught me life could be different from low-income wages, so I quit caring about building income for myself. I did what adults told me to do and worked for whatever they told me I was worth.

MY FIRST ESCAPE

The small town where I grew up had one stoplight, and no opportunities to gain a meaningful future. I escaped to college to learn about business. While there, I took an executive development class. We studied high-performers and successful business leaders. The biographies and autobiographies provided real-world lessons for me.

I enjoyed reading the books, they were great stories, but I couldn't relate to their CEO-level business deals. And they didn't teach me how I might begin to gain wealth. I still wondered how prosperity happened to some and not to others? What was the secret, or the catalyst, to their success?

PECULIAR COINCIDENCE?

It wasn't until a few years out of college a fluke forced me into a new work environment where I would discover answers to my questions. I quit my corporate job (because my paychecks bounced three months in a row), and I needed to pay my bills fast. I networked to find another job. With a friend's insistence and connections, I eventually became a Personal Assistant to multimillionaire and billionaire families. You may think, "Aha! Look how that worked out!" But, sadly, my negative experiences, ignorance, and assumptions blinded me.

I forgot my old questions—so answers floated past me day after day and year after year. Why? Maybe I wasn't ready. As the saying goes, "The teacher appears when the student is ready." And, I had too many bitterroot expectations keeping me confined to a narrow way of thinking. They helped me care less for enlightenment. Or, maybe I was in survival mode, "Just let me do my job and go home." Clock in, clock out.

Together, these issues cast a spell over me, sending me into a slumber, for over a decade. I am embarrassed to write I did not grasp my dichotomy for a very long time. I had one foot in a normal income world, and one in an affluent world.

Steve Jobs once said, "Sometimes life hits you in the head with a brick." I can relate to that because it wasn't until last year when life flung a brick at my head and my reality came into focus. It was polarizing and painful, but it woke me from my slumber.

HINDSIGHT SPURRED

Two bricks; two painful experiences spurred my 20/20 hindsight fourteen years later.

Brick #1: I began working with a new client who didn't have an M&B mindset. Chaos was her modus operandi. I didn't realize how much working with self-made M&Bs changed my subconscious behaviors until I worked with someone who didn't want a copacetic life.

Brick #2: A car accident caused blunt force trauma to my head and rendered me incapable of processing life as I did before. It wiped parts of my hard drive, my brain, without consent or backup. I couldn't find several programs, including one program filled with assumptions and assessments of myself and others.

This Judgments Program was on a secret, internal tape recorder I never knew existed until it disappeared. Thankfully, my subconscious no longer had access to this secret recorder. The loss enabled me to start over and write new software from my observations of what the wealthy do and why.

DOUBLE LIFE

But, to write a new program requires asking questions about what used to be and how it should be in the future. So, down the rabbit hole of self-interrogations I went. I asked myself about my career and motivations. Then I questioned myself: "Why am I here, in this lifestyle?"

The truth revealed itself and startled me. In my mind I saw unfold the double life I lived. Here am I, someone who loves truth but didn't see it for almost fourteen years. Bitterroot judgments are powerful, and they can blind.

What was my double life?

My mind recalled a magazine advertisement of a young couple on a yacht drinking martinis. I believed that was the everyday life of the wealthy. If I made loads of money, I would do that too.

Oh my, writing this is embarrassing.

I dreamed of what millionaires did (per the magazine get-rich-quick scheme)… while I worked with them in their private lives.

Sigh. Disillusionment unmasked. What was I thinking for so long? My fantasy (appraisal of what it means to be rich), didn't match reality.

I think that's called denial.

RICH MAN'S REALITY

Here I worked, in rich peoples' worlds. In each one, I witnessed a similarity with them all I found toughest to admit: None of them make money in hopes of escaping their lives. They are happy where they are.

This find made me ask myself another question: What was my fantasy *truly* about? What did the ad really say to me? I waited and listened, then the breakthrough came; that ad isn't *really* trying to sell the lifestyle of M&Bs… because their lifestyle is A LOT OF BUTT-BUSTING WORK. The truth is: These ads promote escape!

They promote, "*Easily escape to the lifestyle of the rich and famous on this yacht when you buy our product.*" What it doesn't tell you is: Self-made M&Bs are not on a yacht every day, because they're too busy working.

Even upon retirement, the M&Bs I know, are still working. One M&B has been trying to retire since 2007. He can't because his Passion keeps him from doing so.

ZOMBIE ZONE ESCAPE–THE 5 PS TAKE SHAPE

After this realization of escape, I asked myself why I fantasized: "If I just had all the money in the world, then I could ___." What was my "___?" I had no answer.

So, I pondered, "From what do I want to avoid?" I didn't have work or relationship conflicts. What was it? I waited for the answer…

Then, like an explosive sting of a bee, the truth erupted.

I wanted to escape because I rejected my Passion, a part of me, every day.

Doing this day-after-day turned me into a numb being, a zombie. And, a believer of lies.

REASONS ARE REALLY LIES

The truth led me to another discovery; I rejected my Passion with reasons.

I had three reasons:

#1: I thought my Passion had no practical application for business.

#2: My Passion was only my personality, a small fact about me, nothing more.

#3: I compared. I thought a Passion meant something spectacular. Since mine wasn't, I determined it wasn't a Passion.

Then a most unsettling epiphany came to me. My "reasoning away," was not reasoning: Those were lies, not reasons.

After considering these discoveries, I sat in a conflicted state. Do I stop dismissing, and accept this "factoid" as a Passion, or continue with an escape mentality?

The former seemed more promising than feeling robotic every day. So, I relented and agreed to acknowledge this little fact as my deepest desire, regardless of how deficient I thought it was.

PASSION AND PURPOSE

Passion is a zealous drive to accomplish a Purpose.

Without it, it's difficult to find meaning in living life.

I not only rejected my Passion, I buried it. Then when I realized Purpose doesn't stray far from Passion, I knew I had buried that as well. I felt discouraged. Living this way, without meaning, was a slow expiration of my Self.

Sadly, both my Passion and Purpose lay entombed beneath my "reasons."

But Passion is an old faithful compass, and it continued to point to my true north, fighting to realign me no matter what lies I believed.

WHAT'S MY THING?

After much deliberation, I realized: If I'm not driven by a "thing" to do, then I'm not working in my "Zealous Zone," or my bullseye. I was somewhere on the target, but not in the center. The center requires identification of Passion and Purpose. Outside the bullseye is The Zombie Zone: Mindlessly benefiting others but remaining unfulfilled.

I asked myself, "How do I distinguish what I believe in, that can help others?" Then I remembered a motivational speaker once recommended searching for clues in our jobs. So, I observed my work.

I didn't notice anything sensational, no "aha" moment came. That was a disappointment. But then, for the first time I looked at *who* I worked for in my job. I've been in their private lives for years, yet never once did I analyze them. And, never once did I compare myself to them because my skewed perceptions didn't allow it.

So at this moment, sitting by myself on a bench by the water's quiet edge, I chose to compare myself to my stowed observations of these self-made M&Bs.

Is it plenty of guts or nuts to measure myself against them when I'm at my lowest? Most likely not a good idea, but I did it because I needed the truth no matter how much it might hurt.

What I found pricked me.

Not one of the M&Bs I worked with buried their Passion and Purpose as I did. I saw how they went about their work, content in their Zealous Zones; energized by challenges and reaping rewards.

They weren't like me.

I went about work subconsciously thinking, "I'm just a working zombie; here to get a job done."

I sat stunned and broken.

Forever etched in my memory is the bench beside the water's edge where I understood our differences, and my shallow my existence.

MY THING

It troubles me to say, before this moment, I could tell you what each M&B's Passion and Purpose is, but I couldn't tell you mine.

I felt devoid of an identity, and sadness overwhelmed me.

But then... that old faithful compass directed me again. I knew my Passion, so I studied it. I evaluated where and when I expressed it. As I analyzed this sequence of expressions it revealed something.

It was my Purpose.

I found "my thing."

What's my thing? The little fact about me? I am passionate about truth. And, what does it drive me to do? Share it with others to empower them.

When I respected my Purpose, I traced how it weaved through my life, including my work environment. What I didn't see in myself, M&Bs valued: I found the truth in a circumstance and shared it, no matter if it was good or bad news. They appreciated this trait in me because they know truth empowers. They like empowerment.

M&Bs & Me, Our Vast Difference: Principles

I'm a reasonably smart person, but negative expectations have little to do with smarts. They're mostly based on hurts. They confined me to my dim perception, unable to acknowledge differences.

Until I honestly sought out our differences: habits and decisions, I couldn't pinpoint what kept me from living like an M&B. *A person need not earn like an M&B to live like one.* Turning chaos into copacetic is living like an M&B. This was possible, and what I wanted.

I ended my self-assessment with a question: Why are they in the zone but I'm not? I knew it wasn't the difference in bank account size. Making money can make some people miserable. These self-made M&Bs certainly weren't miserable.

I spent a significant amount of time pondering this question. Then, when it was ready to, my subconscious revealed a cache of memories with M&Bs. But they didn't answer my question. So, as I sought an answer, I relived each memory as it presented itself to me.

Then a small clue appeared.

These memories reverberated a theme.

One that was unpleasant to see.

Each one reared difference between M&Bs and me.

My subconscious mind bared specific memories, not to condemn me, but to help me. Each memory was like an oyster; inside, a pearl or principle to apply, to change my fruitless ways.

The principles I gleaned from the memories are:

M&Bs found their Passion and their Purpose, then mastered their talents and skills. They positioned themselves in an industry capable of paying them well. And, they prune their lives of distractions. Pruning is vital to building and maintaining prosperity.

Prosperous people practice these without thought, hence why I call it naturally subconscious behavior.

NATURALLY SUBCONSCIOUS

I liken subconscious self-made M&B behavior to software; it runs in stealth mode. How stealth is it? Not even M&Bs know it exists.

Many years ago, I created a mentorship program for young professionals. One self-made M&B I knew agreed to help start it but not stay in it.

I wanted him to change his mind and stay with the program, so I thought if he positioned himself in an enjoyable role, he may stay as a mentor. To help him get positioned, I asked him, "What are you good at in business?" A blank stare came over his face. It baffled me how he didn't answer in a few seconds.

(Much later I realized two things. First: his response confused me because I presumed M&Bs know everything. Second: he didn't speak because he couldn't define what he's good at, because he does it naturally; subconsciously.)

In those few moments he analyzed himself. He forced his conscious mind to evaluate his subconscious behavior for the first time, hence the blank stare. Seconds later, he looked back at me and in a confident tone blurted out, "I'm good at building teams!"

Building strong teams in his industry enabled him to create multiple multimillion-dollar companies. He later sold them and tried to retire but his Purpose and Passion wouldn't have it. He told me he left retirement because he found it boring, he had to keep building.

When competitors heard he was back in business, they purchased every empty building near their facilities so he couldn't develop a presence. They fear him. At least now he knows why they do; he builds great teams.

The next self-made multimillionaire I asked to become a mentor owns several nursing homes. I assumed business always starts with a business plan, so I asked him if he would help young entrepreneurs develop one. He chuckled at my question. I noticed he felt a little embarrassed because he leaned forward, tilted his head to look at the floor and then in a sheepish tone said, "I don't know how to do one, I've never done one before." I gasped. The financial heresy!

My presumptions about M&Bs clashed with reality.

FINDING THE FORMAT FOR YOU

Spending many years in the personal lives of self-made wealthy people elicited internal conflicts in me. When I analyzed those conflicts, I realized they stemmed from my unfounded expectations and my inability to identify their subconscious system.

Now that I recognize my judgments and understand their system, it has become my secret treasure trove. I share it with you now, in the 5 Ps: The success-building behaviors practiced by the self-made M&Bs.

CHAPTER TWO

From Chaos to Copacetic: the 5 Ps

"There is an immutable conflict at work, in life and in business, a constant battle between peace and chaos. Neither can be mastered, but both can be influenced. How you go about that is the key to success."
Phil Knight

"The reason I've been able to be so financially successful is my focus has never, ever for one minute been money."
Oprah Winfrey

"In the world of business, the people who are most successful are those who are doing what they love."
Warren Buffett

When I read Phil Knight's quote, I realized it summarizes the wealthy mindset. It's something like this: If you want to build a business, a marriage, a career or anything of value, chaos will counter your every effort. And peace doesn't come at a whim—you must fight for it too. We can't conquer, but we can influence.

Accept that nothing good comes easily. And, no guarantees exist to get what we want, because circumstances are fluid. Therefore, we must daily contend in the battle against chaos, for peace.

Knight's next sentence is pivotal. It's the secret to success. He said, "*How you go about that…*" The "How" is, *mindset* and "… go about that…" is *practicing the mindset.*

A mindset is beliefs.

Practicing is choices.

What are the tools these successful people use every day to influence their environment? The 5 Ps. They are the "How you go about that…"

IT'S A GROOVE THING

The 5 Ps can help etch a groove for success. This is a lifestyle, not a quick fix. We get out of problems with one healthy decision after another, just like the old donkey that fell into a pit.

When the owner realized he couldn't rescue the old donkey, he decided to bury it alive in the pit. It was an old beast of burden, and the hole needed filling anyway. So, the man used his shovel to move dirt into the pit. But the donkey brayed and shook with each mound of soil thrown on its back. After much time and much shoveled earth, the burrow stepped out of the hole and sauntered off.

While in the pit, the donkey stomped the dirt until he stepped up and out of the pit.

Whether or not the story is true, there is a message. When we fall into a pit, or bad circumstances, sometimes there isn't an easy way out. It requires making one beneficial decision after another.

This is what the rich practice. They don't have quick fixes, but they use strategies, and a mindset to make wise decisions to build themselves up, and out of a pit.

It's never too late to start a new approach. A new one can produce instant, positive results.

LET ME INTRODUCE YOU

The 5 Ps are tools the wealthy use to make life productive, and copacetic. They are the shared beliefs, behaviors, choices, and habits of the self-made. I didn't create these principles from contrived interviews with rich people, allowing them the opportunity to engineer responses. These are commonalities I observed during their private, sometimes painful, raw moments.

Not one millionaire or billionaire I worked with knows I watched him or her, or knows I documented The 5 Ps. Nor do they know of this book. Yet.

THE VAST DIFFERENCE: THE FIVE P'S

Sometimes the only difference between people is what's between their ears: knowledge, assumptions, and expectations. Regardless of income, we are all human. Affluent folks have struggles and difficult circumstances too, but they have unique habits to manage them.

We make our habits, and then our habits make or break us: How we live life, with a certain mindset and habits, can build or destroy our success.

THE 5 PS: WHAT IS SUCCESS TO AN M&B?

The word "success" can seem vague or intimidating. It doesn't offer "how to," nor does it give a definitive measurement. A word I hear M&Bs use in place of "success" is "productive."

PRODUCTIVE DEFINITION: Yielding favorable, or useful results.

If you yield useful results you are successful. Mastering the Five Ps leads to more opportunities to yield favorable results.

PASSION | PURPOSE | POSITION | PRACTICE | PRUNE

PASSION: Wants and needs are seasonal, but Passion isn't.

Affluent people recognize what "thing" gets them moving. Sometimes we can identify Passion when someone talks incessantly about a topic. For example, I have a friend, Erin who isn't verbose, until you get her talking about ballroom dancing. She was a ballroom dance instructor and competed professionally. She gave it up to get a "real job." I could see she missed teaching, so I suggested she start a dance class. She did. She packed the venue every week. It was rewarding to see her come alive again.

Passion provides the drive to accomplish tasks. It is our cheerleader.

> *You can do anything if you have enthusiasm. Enthusiasm is the yeast that makes your hope rise to the stars… the sparkle in your eye… the swing in your gait, the grip of your hand, the irresistible surge of your will and your energy to execute your ideas. Enthusiasts are fighters. They have fortitude. They have staying qualities. Enthusiasm is at the bottom of all progress: With it there is accomplishment. Without it there are only alibis.*
>
> Henry Ford.

Successful people, or producers, risk their position in life and work to follow their Passion. They don't live to retire after finding work they enjoy. Their profession isn't easy, but their Passion catapulted them past mundane requirements. It was stronger than the daily grind. And, they found more to love than to hate.

A multimillionaire I know said after he graduated from university, he joined a gym and got great results from lifting weights. He loved it so much he worked at the gym for five dollars an hour helping others improve their health. This irritated his father—he paid for a college education to give his son a better chance at a *real* job, not work as a gym rat.

But this gym rat became a fitness nut who developed a successful chain of gyms. He's now a multimillionaire.

In the beginning, Passion made him care about his Purpose, not how much money he made. He invested in his Purpose and now it pays him a nice return.

Disclaimer: Becoming wealthy may not be everyone's ideal lifestyle. People incorporate their Passion into their careers and reap rewards more valuable than money. And even though not every Passion creates affluence, our impassioned work can produce priceless results. Never once did I see a millionaire or billionaire get teary-eyed over the size of their bank account. but when a multi-millionaire shared how his new drug cured a terminal patient of cancer, he choked back tears.

"To try to make the world in some way better than you found it is to have a noble motive in life."
Andrew Carnegie

PURPOSE: The "why" behind the Passion.

Why did Erin like her dance instructor position? Because she loved helping people develop and trust their new skills. Dancing increased their self-esteem. She adored watching a room full of her amateur students dance with their partners without colliding.

Better yet, six individuals found their life-mates in her class. These happily married couples continued to attend lessons, one even at nine-months pregnant. The couple later brought their newborn baby for all of us to admire. My friend created a place for connection, a community we loved.

POSITION: Increasing your chances so luck will show up in your favor.

The right place at the right time matter. M&Bs practice their expertise in a field that can pay them handsomely for it. My friend didn't Position herself to make millions as a dance instructor. She didn't care to. And I only helped her return to her Passion and Purpose. She gained a following and began building a business because she followed her desire. But alas, she fell in love with one of her students. She is now a full-time mother of twins. When she is ready, she can position herself to build her business again.

PRACTICE: Becoming an expert in a field of Practice.

This is no ordinary feat. It requires time and commitment. When zealous people become experts, they become excellent. M&Bs are excellent. They practice their Passion and are passionate about their Practice.

PRUNING: Cutting out distractions.

Chaos is a killer. Productive people cut chaos out of their lives. Pruning is practicing the 13 Cs, or Chaos Cutters. They make every circumstance in life produce to its fullest potential. Pruning is the subconscious software daily running in the M&B's mind.

PRUNING AND THE FEAR OF SUCCESS

Successful people don't fear success because they don't think of it as a "thing" that happens to them. They know it naturally occurs from beneficial decisions. How do they do this? They focus on a Want, reduce distractions and make deals that bring their Want to fruition.

My friend Laurie feared success, so I asked her if I could share with her a strategy M&Bs use to succeed. She obliged. I suggested she treat every challenge like a deal, but not as though it's a final deal that determines life as a total success or failure.

I asked her to define what she wanted from each of her struggles. What arrangement could she make with herself to influence her circumstances? *We strike subconscious deals with ourselves all day long, so why not become conscious of them and learn to negotiate with ourselves?*

Each struggle is a deal. That deal will happen with or without your consent. So why not influence that transaction before it goes down? Ask: How can I turn this into a beneficial arrangement for myself?

For example, my friend Pam is an attorney. She told me she suffers from a messy home office and it hurts her business. She groaned, and said she plays online games and watches YouTube videos instead of doing paperwork.

We pinpointed why she does this. It's because she's afraid, she doesn't know what success is supposed to look like.

To reframe her expectation (fear) of success, I explained the concept of "making deals." We made it a game of good pacts she made with herself. She made her first pact; she could listen to a

YouTube channel while she worked on her paperwork, if it is drama-free.

We also talked about the game of rewarding herself for even a small accomplishment. This thrilled her. She didn't need to tackle her fear of success at that moment but only focus on little bargains that would benefit her. This plan helped her realize she can overcome her inhibitions. It is a Win-Win for her and will empower her to create better deals.

Ironically, I never heard an M&B use the word "success." They prefer "definites" or measurable results: productivity. I taught Laurie and Pam to do what M&Bs do: define productivity, prune life, and continually raise expectations on that productivity.

Now they have freedom to make pacts with themselves, and be their own best partner and cheerleader, just like M&Bs. They're on their way to "success."

THE 5 PS ARE A FRUIT-BEARING TREE

Fruit comes by pruning and caring for an entire tree, not just the blossoms because they turn into fruit. It's a process from the roots up that one must manage daily for the trees to produce ample fruit. Passion drives a gardener to care for the soil on up, not just the produce.

When M&Bs work The Five Ps they create a unique commodity desired by the marketplace. When people pay them for it, M&Bs regard this is a double reward. First, they are productive (successful) because they yield something they take pride in, and second, doubly productive (successful) because someone pays them well for it.

Moral of the analogy: find a tree (a passion & purpose) you enjoy cultivating (so you get your first reward from cultivating) that others will pay a premium for its fruit (the output of your cultivation, your productivity).

THE 5 PS, AN M&B'S LUXURY

Magazines, movies, and media tell us the wealthy live a lifestyle of overwhelming luxury. Some people use the words LUXURY and GLAMOROUS interchangeably. But I've found the affluent folks I work with have their own definition of luxury and it isn't synonymous with glamorous.

There are a few ways their psyches define luxury: A moment of controlled chaos, which allows them to relish in their accomplishments. A place where the 13 Cs happen to them, for them, not managed by them. It is momentary freedom from the drive to produce or fix a situation. Or it is when an experience unfolds perfectly without their intervention.

The Fifth P, Pruning is the 13 Cs. I equate them to an M&B's fine dining experience. Since self-made people prefer their environment to flow with accuracy, promptness and consistency, a nice dinner illustrates how they experience luxury.

They arrive at an upscale restaurant. Car attendants ensure they have a flawless transition from their vehicle to the maître d' and memorize each patron's vehicle for a smooth departure.

The maître d' seats them and becomes their manager for the evening. The waiter is prompt to the table and describes each menu item's preparation as if he prepared each one. After the staff takes food and drink orders, the countdown begins to a beautifully orchestrated dining experience.

Timing is precise at an elegant restaurant. While there, they can fully engage because no requirement exists for them to manage. They relax and let others do what they do all day long, The 13 Cs.

Luxury is the same feeling if you're a single parent busting your butt at work every day and go home to cook and clean for your kids when instead, someone steps in to do it for you. This is luxury because it gives you freedom.

Luxury isn't glamor, it's freedom. Freedom is rich. Give yourself some rich moments, and you will feel the same way a billionaire feels.

FREEDOM IS NOW

I saw a question recently, "You are free now, what will you do with your freedom?"

Some of us hold a belief we're not free because only great wealth can truly make us free. This isn't necessarily true because with more money can come fear of losing it, loss of time from managing it, keeping others from stealing it and the burden that you're not doing enough to grow it. Plenty of people want other people's money and are unashamed to put pressure on others to give it to them. Money can be a blessing or a curse depending on how you see it.

Some folks are content to have what they have. Contentment brings peace. If having more money means more stress, then it isn't worth losing your peace.

Find peace in all things.

CHAPTER THREE

Part I: Self-Confidence: Your Castle

Obviously everyone wants to be successful, but I want to be looked back on as being very innovative, very trusted and ethical, and ultimately making a big difference in the world.
Sergey Brin

"After I pass on to another life, I would like the people to think of David Koch and my brother Charles as people who did everything they could to make the world a better place to live."
David Koch

"To do meaningful work is to contribute–to create value in society."
Charles Koch

DEFINITION:	*having or showing great faith in oneself or one's abilities*
SYNONYMS:	*secure, assured, positive, convinced, capable*
ANTONYMS:	*destructive, negative, self-critical, wavering, doubtful*

ADRENALINE JUNKIES MAKING GAZILLIONS

After watching movies depicting M&Bs as crazed adrenaline junkies, I assumed they were. Then I learned they're not. Adrenaline junkies need a "hit" to feel confident. They assume if they start turmoil and control it, they have confidence. M&Bs don't operate this way.

I remember my first day working for an M&B. His wife sat in the living room watching a cooking show. I assumed billionaires are controlling people, so I held my breath, thinking, "Oh boy, as soon as he sees her, he will tell her to do something productive." He saw her—but did nothing. He focused on his work, and she went about her interests. When noon time arrived, he took a break to share lunch with her. When he finished, he went back to his office to complete his day's projects.

M&Bs contain themselves, they distinguish where they end, and another person begins. Their path is set, and they are set in that path. They don't leave their focus to cause disruptions. This taught me I could trust them to focus on their productivity and leave me to my own.

M&B SELF-CONFIDENCE

The strongest of traits, I believe, is Self-confidence and every M&B has it. It is the Commonality on which the other Cs thrive, without it, they wouldn't function well.

Foremost, M&Bs I've worked with don't develop habits that might erode their self-esteem. Instead, they seek interests that build up their faith in their abilities.

I used to imagine "confident" people were those with the latest designer clothes, a popular car, a great smile, possibly flirtatious, a great conversationalist, and somewhat forceful when expressing their opinions. While I watched people at an event, of whom I knew nothing, I assessed, "Wow, they're confident," based on outward appearance. Now I understand sometimes a grand presentation is only a charade for the self-conflicted, not-so-confident person. Having been in M&B private lives, I see confidence isn't always a gleaming smile with a dash of charm, but a low-key, steady persona.

I've observed M&Bs don't turn a conversation into a conquest to dominate. They enjoy charming others, not because they're insecure or need attention, but to engage people to talk. They don't care to change nor feel threatened by anyone's opinion. In conversation, they listen, ask questions, define what the person means and accept it. They keep it simple, and they don't create offense.

M&Bs feel secure in their own way of thinking and trust others do too. I notice they enjoy a good laugh, a light-hearted conversation devoid of conflict, and then move on to the next conversation, or out the door.

"I have always believed that the way you treat your employees is the way they will treat your customers, and that people flourish when they are praised."
Richard Branson

HOW DO THESE M&BS HAVE NATURAL SELF-CONFIDENCE?

Warren Buffett invested $100 in a Dale Carnegie course:

"... not to prevent my knees from knocking when public speaking but to do public speaking while my knees were knocking."
Warren Buffett

They know they don't have to know everything, just enough.

First, I observed M&Bs don't put themselves in unfamiliar or compromising situations. They don't get too deep into matters they're not acquainted with but stick to their field of expertise.

And when they don't know the answer to a question, they know how to find people who do have answers. M&Bs take pride in their aptitude to identify when they need an expert, and in their ability to find one.

M&Bs don't have unreasonable self-expectations. They don't shame themselves for not having advanced knowledge or skills. If they cannot read a foreign language they've never studied, they don't belittle themselves. Instead, they hire a professional linguist. They cut out the criticism, hire experts and learn.

"If somebody offers you an amazing opportunity but you are not sure you can do it, say yes – then learn how to do it later!"
Richard Branson

HOW DO THEY "GET" IT?

M&Bs build it through a consistent lifestyle of productive choices, one built upon another. I liken it to building a castle with a wide moat. The 5 Ps are how they "get" it.

YOUR CASTLE CALLED SELF-CONFIDENCE

"The most important investment you can make is in yourself."
Warren Buffett

With what you build your castle determines how it can weather chaos.

M&Bs start the foundation of their citadel with a pursuit, a Purpose. Upon this foundation they use their resources to build a wall. *Healthy productive habits build and reinforce the wall.*

Every castle needs a moat. M&Bs don't let many past theirs. Only trusted people, who do no harm but wish to enjoy the environment inside the castle wall get behind the wall. Otherwise, the bridge stays drawn.

KRYPTONITE: SELF-CONFIDENCE KILLER

Confidence to M&Bs isn't a presumption they win every challenge every time. They're selective and cautious. Like Superman, they easily pinpoint Kryptonite and willingly stay away from it. I call this "strategic avoidance."

For temporary Kryptonite, a circumstance they are unprepared to negotiate, they acknowledge their unpreparedness and withdraw until they develop the ability to manage it. This creates self-assurance, stability and security.

M&Bs don't measure their confidence by how capable they are at handling destructive people.

Permanent Kryptonite, such as destructive people; they avoid. M&Bs don't expose themselves to just anyone, they're protective of their being. They know their tolerance level and respect it.

What helps them stay cautious? They believe their plans are precious, valuable or worthy so they must protect them.

<u>Symptoms of Kryptonite:</u>

- Your body revolts with headaches, upset stomach or tension when around a destructive person.
- Someone continually lies to you.
- You second guess yourself when they're around.
- People who blame, gossip, don't move on from the past, and/or devise ways to get revenge.
- Activities that drain you, leave you feeling wasted.
- Foods that upset your body.
- People who want to do all the talking, don't listen and don't reciprocate good vibes.

Deactivate Kryptonite:

- Practice a Gut Check. Ask yourself how you feel with certain people, foods, activities and plans. As you practice listening to your gut, honor it, move away from Kryptonite. If your gut says "Kryptonite," but you ignore it, your gut will stop talking. This won't bode well.
- Get educated. Learn and practice healthy boundaries.
- Enlist accountability partners to help you navigate unhealthy people.
- Replace unhealthy people or environments with healthy ones.

Note: I've observed M&Bs "move away," by not responding directly to Kryptonite but waiting until it runs out of talk and goes away. During the deluge of unwholesome talk, they pick up a book or an item to "distract and redirect" themselves to a happy place. It's a great way to keep calm, until the Kryptonite goes away.

WHAT IS THE M&B'S SECRET TO SELF-CONFIDENCE?

How do they build it? Do they straightaway run for public office or jump into a sporting event with no preparation? Absolutely… not!

M&Bs build confidence by creating games they can win.

One game they play is a personal Honey-Do List. They choose what they will dominate and when. The list comprises small problems, projects, or items to organize or clean. It's a running list, so there isn't pressure to complete it in one day.

A little Honey-Do goes a long way!

Sometimes an M&Bs work environment is collaborative which may not allow immediate closure on projects. This can deter momentum and morale. Work can become boring. M&Bs counter this with a list of manufactured opportunities they control from start to finish to reinforce faith in their abilities.

Feeling powerless can inhibit self-confidence. We must recognize feelings sometimes catch us off guard and can assault our self-esteem. By controlling a task, from start to finish, it can melt away this emotion.

DO IT DAILY

Some M&Bs use a whiteboard, an app or a paper tablet to list their "to-dos." Slashing through a task on a list evokes a good feeling. It's a visual confirmation they made progress and created closure.

It's a small thing, and it may seem dull, but it works. I save a few lists so when that lie says I didn't accomplish much; I can review them and see I completed plenty. At the end of the year I read some of my slashed tasks. This inspires me for the new year.

PUZZLES AND RIDDLES

Another encouragement is working on a jigsaw puzzle. Finding the side and corner pieces to complete the puzzle's frame is an accomplishment. Fitting missing pieces in their assigned spots encourages us to work on a project piece by piece, little by little. We build upon the last work done and see it can come to completion—if no one lost a piece.

There are no time limits on puzzles. Spending five or ten minutes on one before work is a morale builder.

Some M&Bs consider a jigsaw puzzle as a respite for the brain. It allows them to recede from the mayhem of life. And, it is an opportunity to build deeper connections with friends and family. Puzzles provide confidence care; community, focus, closure and contentment.

KRYPTONITE AND HEALTHY BOUNDARIES

The affluent people I know maintain healthy boundaries. If too much conflict happens in a relationship and they can't resolve it, they become discouraged. Self-confidence is fragile. I think high performers know this because they don't spend time on unfruitful relationships.

M&Bs don't take on someone else's crisis. They will advise but not engage in the crisis. After advising they asses for progress. If there isn't any, they spend less time with this person until the relationship dissolves. There is no middle ground—either progress happens, or they move on to other relationships.

M&Bs also protect their Self by the company they keep. I never saw an M&B spend personal time with anyone who takes jabs at them, uses them for comedic routines, or criticizes them. This is abuse and only eats away at Self-confidence. M&Bs recognize this and remove it from their lives.

MY TURN

M&Bs don't carry other peoples' burdens.

An M&B I worked with informed me of a park slated for destruction in my city. She asked me if I knew of it and how I planned to fight it.

She kept simple boundaries, made suggestions of what she would do in my situation, and rejected complaining. "Get on it!" That's what matters, not my feelings, but what actions I planned to protect the park.

She didn't engage in my battle in my city. Reason being: M&Bs expect others to work out their own conflicts because they do. They think allowing others to struggle to find solutions is beneficial to them.

M&Bs Inspire Others

They encourage personal accountability and growth.

I observed people approach M&Bs with personal problems and expect them to solve the problem. These people didn't realize by doing this, they gave away their power to change their circumstances.

I watched M&Bs hand back their power by asking them what they could do to master their mayhem. This offended some, while others had a moment of clarity. Some people realized they have abilities that can change their environment.

These M&Bs never robbed anyone of an epiphany by fixing their problems for them. This is rescuing, and they don't rescue. They throw a life preserver and expect the person to swim to safety. The life preserver is wisdom in the form of questions and suggestions.

How the person answers the questions tells them if he wants resolve or rescuing. If he wants resolve and has a fighter spirit M&Bs will encourage him, which creates a synergy for both parties. It's a Win-Win. If he wants rescuing, the M&B will not engage.

M&Bs help people find what they need, they don't become the resource for those needs.

"What separates the winners from the losers is how a person reacts to each new twist of fate."
Donald Trump

K.I.S.S.

M&Bs like positive statements, so K.I.S.S. means: Keep It Simple Smarty. Even in relationships they keep it simple. Each relationship moves forward with trust, honesty, positivity, encouragement, fun and enlightenment, or it ends.

M&Bs prefer friends like them: those who tell the truth, and encourage others in their gifts, talents, and skills. They seek others who explore life and engage in new experiences and challenges. There is also accountability in their friendships. But relationships are not complicated, period. They do life with those who have the same mentality even if the income level may not be the same.

MONEY PROBLEMS

M&Bs don't believe money solves money problems.

Good money after bad decisions isn't a profitable strategy. That is why they don't give money to people who have nonstop financial problems. Instead, they help others pull themselves out of debt, with their own skills. They provide financial support to organizations designed to help others increase their net worth through education, counseling, networking, and other opportunities.

I used to judge, "Wow, this M&B could pay off so-and-so's debt so easily." But when I looked at so-and-so's lifestyle, I saw a lifestyle regularly in arrears. Now I don't criticize when a wealthy person doesn't pay off someone's revolving debt.

Money to the M&Bs I worked for represents hard work, dedication, and a prudent lifestyle. Therefore they don't have friends who live reckless lives, because sometimes these people blame others for not helping during repeated crises. M&Bs don't accept blame and they don't part with their cash for someone who doesn't live in kind.

OPINIONS OF OTHERS: O. O. O.

A little piece of wisdom I watch M&Bs follow is, "consider the source."

When others give opinions of M&Bs, M&Bs consider the character and experience of the person presenting the opinion. In general M&Bs don't give attention to what some people assume of them. Nor do they solicit opinions from those outside their inner circle.

Here is why: Long before they built their wealth, M&Bs created a mental list of qualifications they had to meet to be considered worthy. *They made the rules for their own acceptance.* In their mind, they met their expectations so they're acceptable.

So, they don't care what others think.

This reminds me of the analogy about barking dogs behind fences. Some people are like these trapped, ferocious dogs. They bark because they're jealous. They want to be where you are: free.

I thought it was an interesting analogy but had my doubts.

Many years later, I spent the weekend at my brother's house in a rural town. One night I took a walk along a gravel road. As I passed a chain-link fenced yard, a large dog bolted towards me, growling and barking. I was thankful for the fence as he slammed into it. This was an aggressive dog. It scared me, so I moved to the middle of the road.

It continued its aggression as I walked by the yard. After a few hundred feet away, the barking stopped. I breathed a sigh of relief and continued my peaceful walk.

Then I heard something behind me. I turned around and saw it was the dog running at me! I stood in shock. The ferocious dog was out and now after me! I couldn't move, I didn't know what to do.

Within seconds he was about five feet from me, then he bounded at me. My heart may have stopped at that moment. Before hitting me, he came to a sliding halt, wagged his tail and sidled up to me to say hello. I couldn't believe it.

Ferocious dog was now my best friend. He wasn't angry anymore because he was free, with me, going somewhere. We took a long walk together. On our way back, his tail wagging, I helped him back into his yard. It was a happy ending.

That analogy was true for me. Some people are the same, they stay behind their fences barking or badmouthing those who take risks to go somewhere. They want to be where others are but refuse to make efforts to get there. Just like the dog, they are jealous.

The dog's opinion of me didn't matter. My walk didn't end because of his barking. I didn't stop to soothe it or explain myself to it. Nor did I question if I did something wrong to cause the angry behavior. I kept walking.

M&Bs do what I did, they walk past barking dogs. They don't engage them. They don't stop at the barking dog to ask why it's angry with them. Nor do they respond to jealousy with explanations or arguments. They don't attempt to soothe jealousy; they leave it alone. Either those around them join them or they stay behind their fences. Whichever happens, the M&B keeps walking.

OPINIONS INFLUENCE

I remember when I witnessed a coworker turn into a millionaire. She stood with a group of us around a computer watching her stocks climb. Coworkers were excited and nervous, chattering that she should exit her positions at that moment. If she did, she could make a great profit, but if she waited, she might make her first million. I stood next to her listening to what others pressured her to do.

As she stared at the monitor, I whispered a question to her, "What does your gut say?" Her body jolted, she turned to me, looked straight in my eyes and said, "Stay in." Then she turned and walked through the pressing crowd. She later exited her positions when she deemed best and became a millionaire.

She didn't do as the peer pressure suggested. She was bold.

It took a great deal of education and experience to do what she did in the stock market. She steadied herself in her abilities, not in the Opinions Of Others. This empowered her to walk past them.

Most times O.O.O. are just a bunch of zeros anyway: Empty of any value.

RECAP

- Build your castle. With a moat. Safety first.
- Find and manage Kryptonite.
- Get your Honey-Do List going and crush projects. Pat yourself on the back when you do.
- K.I.S.S. Keep It Simple Smarty. Smart people keep it simple. Easy peasy.
- Move past jealous people. Keep moving forward on your planned path.
- O.O.O. Opinions Of Others are sometimes empty and worthless. Don't engage. Keep walking.

"Live the present intensely and fully, do not let the past be a burden, and let the future be an incentive. Each person forges his or her own destiny."

Carlos Slim Helu

Part II: Self-Confidence Components

"An entrepreneur is born with the mentality to take risks, though there are several important characteristics: courage, faith in yourself, and above all, even when you fail, to learn from failure and get up and try again."
Sheldon Adelson

SELF-CONFIDENCE COMPONENTS

From my observations, self-confidence is assurance in one's own capabilities to complete objectives. I discovered seven hidden elemental features in M&Bs that promote a robust self-confidence.

They are:

#1 **VALUES:** what they deem to be important

#2 **BELIEFS AND EMOTIONS**: how they think about themselves and react to those beliefs, judgments

#3 **RESPONSIBILITY & ACCOUNTABILITY:** how they manage their resources and themselves

#4 **SPIRITUALITY: THE GOLDEN RULE**

#5 **WORK ENVIRONMENT:** they love what they do and know what they're worth

#6 **PHYSICAL HEALTH:** they understand if a tree doesn't have life, it cannot produce fruit

#7 **RELATIONSHIPS:** support vs. approval and healthy boundaries

#1
VALUES: WHAT THEY DEEM TO BE IMPORTANT

Values are relative. They are personal decisions defining importance. They impact self-confidence.

If an individual doesn't have principles or ignores them, self-confidence cannot remain because it derives from adhering to healthy standards. Inappropriate ideals that don't abide by societal rules (laws) can cause conflict and unwanted results. Sitting in a jail cell isn't a self-confidence booster. Best to have clear morals, or others might create them for you.

Trade-Offs

When an M&B explained his industry to me, I bluntly asked him why he didn't pursue the opportunity to earn billions of dollars. With his patents, abilities, and network he surely would have become a multi-billionaire. Without reservation, or even contemplation he said, "*I want* to be a dad. *I want* to come home to my kids every night, other than an occasional work trip." That stunned me. His greatest worth was his identity as a father, not a businessman. I never saw him take pride in his work the way he did in his fatherhood.

He also retired early to become a stay-at-home dad for his children's pre-teen years. During his retirement he developed other streams of income that didn't interfere with his parenting plan. He asserted and honored his Values (fatherhood) which built up his self-confidence.

Another M&B belongs to a generationally wealthy family. I found him surprising too. He is married with two children. He works part time so he can stay home with the kids so his wife can pursue her career. They hired a part-time nanny for when they're both at work. I've never met a man more knowledgeable regarding every aspect of his newborn's life, including diaper activity.

It surprised me to find affluent people understand trade-offs are necessary if they want to hold to their principles. I assumed they didn't because they want what they want at once. (That is another poor assessment I had.) M&Bs don't believe they can have every desire at once, so they negotiate to get closest to each desire while honoring their Values.

Identify a Value

If we feel good when we honor something, it is of importance to us. Therefore, it is a Value.

Many people I know have a Passion to rescue dogs slated for euthanasia in kill shelters. They experience deep happiness when they give an abandoned dog a new home.

When an abused dog, once unresponsive to humans, now seeks their affection, they feel incredible. They share their rescue story with others because they're proud they helped an animal heal.

Their Value (save life) makes them valuable (to the life saved).

Find what good you create for others that feels good creating it. Shape choices and plans around that goodness. It's your Value.

#2

BELIEFS AND EMOTIONS: HOW THEY THINK ABOUT THEMSELVES AND REACT TO THOSE BELIEFS

Money is a resource to bring life and fulfillment, therefore it can impact emotions.

Before they made millions, M&Bs worked their Passion because they love what they do and abide by self-preservation.

A friend in the tech industry said three of his coworkers suffered a nervous breakdown, so they committed themselves to psychiatric care at a facility. Rumor has it, around these parts, a few psychiatric hospitals offer respites for techies. That's how they take a break, when they can't take it any longer.

Moral of the story? What we believe about ourselves drives our decisions. Passion doesn't cause burn out, but beliefs that drive us can.

Evaluate your beliefs about yourself, are they safe drivers?

You're different. Thank God.

View your difference as an asset. John Mason Brown once said, "You were born an original, don't die a copy." Believe that what makes you different is a strength. This is a foundational belief of M&Bs: their difference is a strength.

Safety First

M&Bs stay away from emotional conflicts they cannot resolve quickly. And since they don't engage in unsafe environments, it's much easier to stay away from pointless conflicts.

Sometimes we become victims of circumstance, but M&Bs will, to the best of their abilities, limit that opportunity. Once a bad experience occurs, they gain closure and refuse to subject themselves to someone or something that might reignite the issue.

From my observations, this is the only "item" these socially conscious people don't "recycle." They refuse to rehash, contend with or "recycle" the past.

M&Bs avoid conflict by choosing activities such as: reading industry related materials, non-fiction books, historical fiction, the arts, cooking, golf, gardening, tennis, running, skiing, or hiking. *These are interests where a positive, reasonable input results in a positive reasonable output.* It reinforces a mindset of: Expectation matched with practical efforts results in a healthy payout.

Emotions play an authoritative role in life. M&Bs understand this, so they quell feelings with productivity. That's safe. It has reasonable outputs. And it elicits feelings of fulfillment and advancement.

Note: Abusive or hostile environments do not embody stability or positivity, therefore cannot foster a reasonable cause and effect.

Picking Battles and Boundaries

One M&B purchased a home with an insurance claim against it. It may have been fraudulent, but rather than fight it, he paid for the claim. By doing so he released himself from future entanglements. He deemed freedom more valuable than fighting.

M&Bs don't practice self-defeating behaviors. They don't sacrifice themselves for the sake of others' expectations. They don't say, "Okay, just this one time," to make someone happy. M&Bs reject the shame and blame others want to bestow upon them when they don't comply to their expectations.

Even for the M&B, bad experiences can impact their wealth. So, when trouble comes, they get back into their happy place, their groove, as soon as possible. This is where they can compete on better terms and do well. They recognize chaos kills, but a good game brings life, so they get back to competing quickly.

The M&B who found himself sixty million dollars in debt overnight when his mortgage interest rates shot up to twenty-nine percent, rebuilt his fortune. A few years ago, many years after the experience, I asked him what it was like when he woke up to sixty million dollars in debt. I expected him to respond with a comment referring to how he felt then, but he blurted, "I'm still trying to get over it!" That surprised me. It happened over twenty years ago. Here he was, an M&B again, still resolving the shock.

My lesson learned; he didn't quit his groove because he experienced something traumatic. And he didn't wait until he resolved it to get back into his groove. He returned to his happy place to compete, to rebuild his self-confidence and recover financially. This strategy helped him overcome a dreadful experience.

M&Bs prize their future over their past pain.

For example, I have a friend who suffered two divorces. The second one cost him his possessions. I will tell the rest of his story in Chapter Twelve.

After his divorces and many dating experiences, he stopped to examine himself. He had a moment of clarity; he understood his unhealthy choices. He resolved why he made them and then chose healthier ones. After he rebuilt his life, he said in his Southern drawl, "I found a good woman." He's happily married now.

Perceptive People

Some people assume M&Bs don't have emotions. This assumption is incongruent with what I witness. They have emotions *and* a natural ability to influence their environment to suit their emotional needs.

I remember working as a waitress in an elegant restaurant while in college. The primary color for the restaurant was blood red: the carpet, the fabric chairs, the walls, tablecloths, napkins, art, and the wallpaper in the private dining room.

A Hollywood director wanted to host a dinner in the private room. When he saw the interior design, he left. It sounds silly, but he well understood which colors inspired his creativity and which ones impaired it.

Most people are not aware of their idiosyncrasies, so they suffer. This director didn't feel bad for leaving, he pursued what he needed at a different facility.

Like the director, M&Bs recognize and work with their sensitivities. They don't share them nor explain them to anyone for acceptance. They are responsible for them, meaning they move to a different environment if it doesn't suit their happy state of mind.

Also, M&Bs don't adhere to "suck it up to make others happy." Instead they're willing to take action, immediately, by negotiating or removing themselves from the setting as the director did. I am sure he procured a venue better suited for his party needs. He didn't settle with a place he found irritating. That wouldn't have been a fun party to serve.

Beliefs

M&Bs identify what they are, and what they are is what they refer to when critiquing themselves.

I never hear M&Bs compare themselves to others to determine what they're *not.* They may admire people who intrigue or inspire them, but they don't draw self-confidence from someone's recognition of them. Their self-worth comes from their self-assessment. And their self-assessment always finds value in them.

> *Take care of your body. Be as good to it as possible. Don't worry about incidents. Look at me – there's nothing of the Greek God about my physique. But I didn't waste any time crying about the unpleasant aspects of my person. And remember that things are only as ugly as you believe they are.*
>
> Aristotle Onassis

M&Bs don't become offended if someone dislikes them. They investigate the dislike, if a misunderstanding needs correction, they correct it. Otherwise if there is no resolution for the dislike, they advance to other relationships.

M&Bs don't ponder how to change themselves to be acceptable. They don't discount Self nor accept the lie they need to be someone else to "make it," in life. I find M&Bs are much like Aristotle's quote, they work with what they've got and believe the best about themselves.

M&Bs allow self-critique only to help productivity, not discourage or dismantle their ego. If they surmise they're weak in an area they don't complain, instead they read books, seek counseling or take classes. They don't let their lack turn into an Achilles heel.

They learn lessons and adjust immediately. If a health problem arises, they make lifestyle changes. They don't ignore their health, or medical findings. M&Bs have a strong sense of self-worth; they cherish what they've got.

Only As Ugly As You Believe

There is a doctor I know who long ago was a millionaire. In ten years' time he built his practice by saving or extending people's lives. He is a healer, not just a doctor. But, deep in his psyche he concludes businessmen are worth more than doctors.

After he built his wealth, a scam artist tapped into this belief and coerced him into a "big business deal." He backed it with all of his money and all of his money he lost.

Since falling prey to the scam, he gave up his practice and continues to chase after every supposed big deal he finds. He believes millionaires make big sexy deals all day long, without consultation, caution or calculation. His belief system tells him his gifts, abilities, and talents are not as valuable as the jet-setting businessman.

He's never recovered financially.

It's sad to see, since he once became a millionaire from doing amazing deals: saving lives. But until he recognizes his self-abasing beliefs, resolves them, and esteems the healing gift endowed to him, his "big deal addiction," will continue to lead him to unfulfillment.

#3

*RESPONSIBILITY/ACCOUNTABILITY: HOW THEY MANAGE THEIR RESOURCES, THEMSELVES AND THEIR ENVIRONMENT

I observed M&Bs pride themselves in responsibility. Responsible means "response-able," or able to respond, not react. When people understand they are response-able, it means they realize they have the ability to change outcomes.

M&Bs love knowing they are response-able so they thoughtfully consider their options.

I never heard M&Bs use the term "made a mistake." If a project doesn't produce the desired results, they don't blame or whine, instead, they simply "don't do that again," and then execute a different decision.

They make a new choice because they know the prior one wasn't a "final answer." The final answer is: when they obtain a desired result.

For the M&B the simplicity of the outcome is equal to the simplicity of deciding. Somewhere they learned it isn't a big deal if a choice they made results in an unwanted outcome. It wasn't a "mistake," it just didn't work out. M&Bs don't sink into despair over an outcome, they simply decide again.

An M&B couple owned matching hiking boots. One of the wife's shoelaces broke. They are unique shoelaces and sold only by the boot manufacturer. She ordered what she thought she had, but her husband knew they were not correct. So, he tried to convince her to get the correct ones, to no avail. When they arrived and I brought them to her she realized they were wrong. She said, "Oh, then let's get the other ones." No big deal. It didn't turn into an argument or explanation, she simply moved on to another decision.

She was "wrong." So what? There is no shame in trying.

Life Is An Experiment, Not Perfect

M&Bs are eager to learn. To them life is somewhat of an experiment and to be enjoyed. They're not perfectionists. They sometimes make a decision just to experience the outcome. It may be a small decision such as where to hang a bird feeder. We are familiar with what happens below bird feeders, but rather than focusing on that, the M&B says she wants to place it in a location to see how it sits, regardless.

It is an experiment. She anticipates a few results, but curiosity wins for now. M&Bs enjoy the sense of wonder and experimentation more than perfection.

By watching M&Bs I learned perfectionism is not success, nor does it guarantee it. I assumed all M&Bs were perfectionists in everything, until I worked with them. Maybe they're not perfectionists because perfectionism consumes time and says we're "never good enough." This can whittle away at anyone's self-confidence. That's why these M&Bs acknowledge it's "good enough."

One M&B had an ongoing outdoor project, sanding and staining antique teak furniture. Every day we spent time sanding the pieces. One day she asked me why I hadn't finished my section of the sanding job. I showed her my progress, I aimed for a perfect sanding job, a satiny smooth finish—which meant I was not far along. She burst into laughter and exclaimed, "I can always count on you to be detail-oriented!"

She wanted a light sanding job, so she completed her sections "good enough," while I continued to work on my first section because it wasn't "good enough." I aimed for perfection while she aimed for "good enough" and completion.

I am certain she felt better about her completion than I felt about still working toward perfection.

WARNING: Perfectionism can impede productivity.

Miriam Webster's medical definition of perfectionism states: "A disposition to regard anything short of perfection as unacceptable especially the setting of unrealistically demanding goals accompanied by a disposition to regard failure to achieve them as unacceptable and a sign of personal worthlessness."

After this and many more experiences with M&Bs, I realized one trait they *don't* have is perfectionism. They don't use the word "perfect" to describe themselves. Instead, they strive to do relationships, work, tasks or anything else, productively, not perfectly.

M&Bs believe "better" is best, because they can continually achieve "better."

This reminds of Microsoft Windows. Is it ever perfect? If Bill Gates were a perfectionist, we could still be waiting for Windows 2.0., but he's smarter than a perfectionist. He uses his customer base as software testers to "better" the software. There are over one billion people who pay to test Windows products all day long. Smart man.

In contrast a local software group continues to work on their software. It's been over nine years now. Not one release happened because it isn't perfect yet. They've lost money and investor interest because they refuse to release software until it's perfect.

"Better" trumps "perfect" is Gates' strategy. Better allows for updates. If he claimed his product is "perfect" then how could the next update be perfecter? Instead, it only gets better.

Fortune Means Flawless

I presumed all M&Bs think they're flawless because they found their way to fortune. But this isn't true. After listening to them critique their decisions and verbalize thankfulness around those decisions, I realized they don't think they're faultless. That's why they regard themselves as "lucky." They believe luck comes to the imperfect (those who don't get it right every time), while the perfect (those who get it right every time) don't need luck.

Sacred Bead And Stitch

Many years ago, I met old Chief Moses of the Blackfeet Indian Tribe, at a festival. I noticed a beautiful tribal blanket with him. He let me study its woven pattern of earth tone hand-dyed wool. It was handmade and perfect, until I spotted a small but blatant yellow stitch. I stared at the stitch. It irritated me.

Annoyed the weaver ruined a perfect blanket, I scoffed. So, I pointed out the imperfection to the Chief and asked why the weaver made a mistake and didn't correct it.

He said nothing but smiled. Then he held up his wrist to show me his tribal bracelet made of bone beads. Each one matched and aligned. It was another lovely handmade piece of art. It was perfect. Then he rolled his wrist over so I could see the rest of the design, and there to my mortification was a mismatched bead. I huffed, "ruined." Flustered, I wondered, "Why waste a perfect pattern?" I frowned and shook my head thinking "another mistake."

I looked at the Chief. His aged, soft face wrinkled with delight at my furrowed brow.

He motioned for me to come closer. When I drew near, Chief Moses spoke of perfection in a deep rhythmic tone. He whispered, "Only God is perfect."

He said the mismatched bead set by the designer, and the stray stitch intertwined by the weaver were purposed. Each piece of art bears a flaw to remind humanity of its imperfection. And imperfection is ok, because it was made that way. Just like we were. Therefore, we are acceptable.

Perfection; it is impossible to achieve, and detrimental to attempt.

Message In The Mistake

The mistake is a message: Your imperfection is accepted. So, accept it.

And the mistake is a warning: Avoid the pursuit of perfection. It steals peace.

The perfectionist in me focused on a single stitch in a large blanket, and one bead amongst one hundred others. But thankfully Chief Moses saw me and showed me compassion. When I stumbled upon a sacred teaching, he patiently shared his wisdom with me. I'm forever thankful.

Now when I study a piece of art and see imperfection, I don't think it's unacceptable, instead I think, "It's just like me!

Struggles and internal dialogue. Quick to quash the battle

I've watched M&Bs refuse to linger on negative emotions. Maybe because they know negativity can distract them from their desired result. To counter this effect, they first pause to acknowledge their frustration. Sometimes they pause by sitting still or taking a deep breath. Then they analyze the circumstance by asking questions: Why is this? What is happening that I cannot see? What pattern am I missing?

These M&Bs don't fear asking themselves tough questions. I know this because I hear them mumble the questions as they struggle through a problem. They talk to themselves *and* they answer back.

I don't see stress balls in their homes. Those are distractions. But they do make themselves relax when they're irritated. It surprised me to find they each created a version of a "pause and breathe" technique.

It's a powerful tool. It helps them self-regulate and quash the chaos. Sound silly? Well, several years ago I asked a retired Special Forces member how his team slept at night when they were out in the field. His eyebrows raised, he tilted his head and said, "You really don't."

I had no words, I couldn't imagine that every night, nor even one night.

I asked, "How do you relax or stay calm during a mission?"

He said, "Breathing."

"What?!" I bleated. Unbelievable. Special Forces teams work in hostile places, and when they're there, what do they do? They breathe.

I found this unrealistic, but I relented. I figured if it was good enough for him, it should be for me. So, I prodded him to tell me more.

He shared the technique. Inhale through the nose for a slow count of four, hold it for a slow count of four, then exhale through the mouth for a count of eight. Repeat as necessary.

We don't breathe properly when we're stressed, which constricts blood flow to the brain, decreasing our reasoning skills. Deep breathing opens lung constriction and brings more oxygen-rich blood back to the brain. Do M&B's subconsciously know how to gain control of their bodies and emotions by breathing? From what I observed, it seems so.

Never Quit

M&Bs don't quit because they don't believe projects or challenges are bigger than they are. They don't complain, "This isn't what I want," and stop working, but find a new way or better option.

Challenges are opportunities to invest in your skill set. So never quit.

Twofers And Morefers

When they get stuck, they devise the next solution: find help from a knowledgeable person to move forward. This isn't quitting because their Want is to fix a problem, if it means hiring someone to do it, it means they fixed it.

And they watch the person they hire so they can learn from him. That is a "Twofer" for the M&B. For the price of getting the project completed, they also received a free tutorial. They love Twofers and they love learning. It's a self-confidence boost for them because they hired the right person, learned something, and solved their problem.

Bud-Gets

Bud-Gets is how to keep wealth, not spend it. A simple way of looking at a budget is; "Every *BUDdy GETs* $___." M&Bs review their income and regulate who gets what.

Bud-Gets Strategies M&Bs use are borrowing, thrifting, hand-me-downs, outlet stores and waiting for sales. Items of little long-term benefit are low on the Bud-Gets list.

When A Need Isn't A Need

M&Bs review their Wants with a need-based approach. "Do I really need that?" Usually, the answer is, "No." Hence, why they don't leave shopping catalogs in the house which could tempt them to make an emotional purchase.

Time is more valuable to M&Bs than stuff, so they find special events to attend with their kids instead of buying them stuff. When their children ask them for a new toy, they usually meet the request with a meaningful conversation as to why the "Want" exists and a consideration to discuss it later. They wait to see if the request is a whim or a real interest.

I've learned M&B children aren't like the kids in the original Willie Wonka movie. M&Bs communicate "no" to their children, a lot. This teaches them to grow patience and practice delayed gratification. It also teaches them "no" isn't a personal rejection.

Splurges

The Splurge. For M&Bs I notice healthy food is their most consistent splurge. It isn't too expensive to buy a great piece of fresh salmon (value: Omega 3's for heart health). A bottle of red wine at the local grocery store with a score of ninety-six is good (value: red wine contains protective polyphenols). Shopping at a local bakery (value: supporting local owner-operated businesses). And, sometimes not cooking is a splurge.

Learning a new skill or art form is also a splurge (value: It keeps the brain sharp).

After they've completed a difficult project, or accomplished an objective, M&Bs splurge on a reward. One splurge might be a small piece of art to build an art collection (value: certain art retains or increases its worth when currencies weaken).

M&Bs don't create an art collection in one moment, but patiently build it. They Calculate and Control the splurge. But sometimes they have whatever they want. If they want to eat vegetables all the time, then they eat "whatever they want" all the time. They splurge on a "Want," but their "Want" is relative to the seven components of self-confidence.

Earning And Investing

Each M&B I worked with earned money in a niche and used a portion of that money to invest in other income opportunities such as startups companies, real estate investment, or consulting projects to build a diversified portfolio for long-term growth. They diversify, they don't abandon their field of expertise.

That's what the ex-M&B doctor did. (I use ex-M&B because he hasn't earned back his wealth.) He left his career to pursue "big business" without any business experience. But, I remind him of his love, his game, and encourage him to return to where he once made his wealth, as the M&Bs do, but he refuses. When I suggest he focus on working one opportunity the way he did medicine, he rejects that too. Instead, he abandons one random deal for another.

Investing: Always Run The Numbers

After working around the M&B mentality for a few years, I joined a real estate investment group. In the first meeting the founders explained they were hard-money lenders who originated the deals (foreclosed properties) for us and we could borrow from them to buy properties. Then once we purchased a property, we fixed it up, got a mortgage, paid off their loan and then quickly sold the home, or "flipped" it, for a profit.

Sounded simple enough, but then I used simple math. I didn't see how this would be profitable for me to flip properties with their interest rate. To make any money, I needed to buy and hold, not flip the property.

This meant my risk would be greater than they portrayed.

Because of my confusion, I met with one of the lenders. I asked him to review the math and show me how I would make money as they claimed. In a condescending tone he only explained how the deal worked from his perspective. He wasn't helpful.

Regardless, I took a risk.

After I purchased my first investment property, I met with a mortgage broker and explained my scenario. I told her I didn't understand why investors battled each other at the auction to buy properties under these conditions. She explained why: These "investors" refinanced the first property, took the equity and purchased another property, then financed another loan and continued this way with the next property. This was easy for them since some mortgage brokers provided shady loans.

After she explained the truth, I met again with one of the hard-money lenders to ask more questions. He wasn't pleasant. But I discovered the real strategy: they encouraged people to borrow from them, then mortgage a property at one hundred and ten percent of its market-price appraisal (before fix up, as if it were remodeled), use that cash (leaving the property with no equity and an over-priced mortgage payment) and buy another property, then repeat the process.

I didn't have a good gut feeling. I couldn't ignore the lesson of the sixty-million-dollar over-leveraged M&B. So, I told the hard-money lender I didn't earn enough money to back several mortgages if the rental market weakened. I conveyed I would only buy properties I could support monthly if I couldn't sell them, the market crashed, or I couldn't find renters.

He laughed, then said I didn't see the opportunity in front of me. He said I would miss out on making my first million dollars.

He used FOMO to taunt me.

FOMO was hard to ignore in a solid home rental market, but I invested within my financial limit, or what I could stomach if the market crashed. This decision made me the misfit, no longer part of the in-crowd in the group. I was too cautious.

But, determined to invest within my means, I held my own properties while partnering with someone on a larger property who had more cash available. Shortly after the purchase and remodel he wanted to implement the over-leverage strategy to suck out the (hyper-inflated) appraised value at one hundred and ten percent. I didn't.

He saw huge profits and I was in his way.

I consulted with two real estate M&Bs since this was my first real estate partnership. The first one said one word, "Sell." I will never forget the other M&B's surprised facial expression. He laughed and erupted, "If I could make that kind of profit that fast in real estate, I would sell!"

I grumbled, took their advice and sold my interest to my partner at a good profit. Soon after, a warning sounded of a housing market crash. Within the year, the real estate market ebbed. Many people suffered foreclosures and needed to rebuild their finances. They put their belongings in storage and moved in with family or rented tiny apartments. They didn't rent large, newly remodeled homes.

The apartment rental market went up, while the home rental market plummeted.

As for the over-leveraged investors, their newly remodeled mortgaged homes sat empty. Renters didn't want to pay five thousand dollars a month when they could rent a small apartment for one thousand dollars a month and save money for a new home.

It became a domino effect. Those who over-leveraged themselves couldn't find renters. Worse yet, if they didn't refinance out of the hard money loan, they faced twelve percent interest *a month* on each loan.

One investor agonized over five mortgages totaling upwards of twenty-six thousand dollars a month. He lost all five homes. Another investor lost fifteen homes. He said he was lucky—the judge let him keep one home for the sake of his wife and kids.

And the business partner I had who used the same poor strategy, he too lost his properties. But I was happy, I listened to my gut, the M&Bs, and ignored the peer pressure. I walked away from the market crash unscathed.

The moral of the story: Don't risk what you don't have. Get mentors, and respect O.P.E., Other Peoples' Experiences.

Their Most Valuable Valuables

I remember when an M&B handed me a large sum of money. She saw my surprise and said, "I trust you around my family, why wouldn't I trust you with my money?" That astonished me. I presumed M&Bs revered money above everything, including their children, but they don't. They understand they can replace lost income, but they can't replace their children.

Building Children

We naturally pass on habits to our children—it' subconscious for everyone. These M&Bs keep their kids organized, structured and productive. They challenge them to perceive, reflect, and communicate.

Their kids naturally learn the 13 Cs because their parents live by them and enforce them. Every day they work with their children to develop healthy habits and a mindful lifestyle.

If one child isn't tidy, the parent works with him until he learns to be so, even if it hurts his feelings. I remember one M&B told me she sneaked into her eight-year-old son's room one night to take his old tattered socks and underwear. He refused to let go of worn-out items. If he cried when they disappeared, she didn't offer coddling, but redirected him toward enjoying new, clean items.

After four years of work, he could part with his old underclothes.

M&Bs don't allow unhealthy behaviors to develop into habits. They are "nipped in the bud," cut off, as soon as possible.

One son didn't think he needed to study for a test (this is unacceptable in their homes—studies are ultra-important, overriding all extracurricular activities). He didn't earn an "A" but a "C" on the test. A "C" would be acceptable if he studied and did his best, but he didn't. The question posed to him was,

"Are you going to let that happen again by not studying?" The answer was a quick, "No." End of discussion. Nipped in the bud. He walked away and studied forever more.

M&B parents review their kids' homework with them. Some schools tell parents they're not allowed to do this, but these M&Bs spend hours teaching their kids how to do homework. They don't allow passivity in their own lives, so they don't leave it up to the schools to teach their children everything.

One M&B's son struggled with ADD. I remember when he entered eighth grade and homework became more demanding. He forgot his homework at school several times. He said he didn't bring it home because, "I have ADD, so I can't remember." His father told him people with the same struggles set alarms and use the calendar on their cellphones, so he could do the same. The son stood silent. He either realized he had no more excuses or realized he could overcome some of the shortcomings caused by the condition.

By giving him an opportunity to control ADD instead of it controlling him, his parents used accountability and responsibility to empower him. Even though ADD is a hardship, his parents never treated him as less capable. Instead they spent more time with him, teaching him how to push himself to complete a project. They explained he struggled now, but this would teach him how to conquer tough challenges later in life.

Years later when he and his brother both entered higher mathematics, the son with ADD easily managed his incorrect answers, he tried again without frustration. Meanwhile, his brother who never struggled with homework had emotional outbursts over his incorrect answers. Now the M&B dad spends far more time fighting through math and attitude problems with this son than he ever did with his son with ADD. Sometimes it's more difficult to teach a kid who never struggles with learning, how to press through a challenge.

Home Schooling With Dad

Kids can be cruel to other kids starting very early in life. M&Bs don't tolerate this behavior. I remember one M&B's two youngest kids teased each other incessantly. So, he resorted to the old-school method of assigning them sentences to write for each offense. I remember one offense was worth five-hundred sentences.

I watched the kids write their sentences. He only allowed them to take a break for dinner, use the bathroom or work on homework. These kids finally surmised hurting one another wasn't worth writing redundant statements.

It was a lesson on payout—is the offense worth the consequences? They realized their poor choices resulted in loss of freedom. This M&B taught them a Twofer, two great lessons, the value of their time and unhealthy behavior has penalties.

Frugal Teacher

I remember when an M&B's eldest son, who was in ninth grade, abused the family's three hundred texts-a-month family plan. He sent more than sixteen hundred texts in one month. He was a sweet and handsome fella, and the girls liked him a lot.

As I left the house, I noticed him on the couch pinned between his parents. They told me of his wrongdoing and how they were going to have a close conversation about it. I had to keep from smiling as he looked at me, hoping I might save him. But I gave him the, "You're on your own buddy" look and exited.

In five years of working with this M&B, that was his son's worst behavior. But it was serious to them because it expressed a lack of self-control. This doesn't fit the M&B's modus operandi of self-control and frugality, so it must be corrected.

Self-Confidence In Thought

"You have to act and act now."
Larry Ellison

When self-confidence gets pummeled, righteous anger kicks in and thinks, "Do something, triumph over the circumstance." And, it decides, "Start now."

It decides "start now" because it believes nothing is always stuck. M&Bs appreciate how the world is in a constant state of change. They love it because *change means more opportunities.* So, when bad things happen, they know they have an immediate chance to make good of it.

The self-confidence of the M&B who lost over a million dollars in one moment determined her experience was now the past, so she needed to "act now." And since confidence recognizes money isn't finite but a *representation* of smart, hard work, she concluded: If she generated it then, she can do it again, now.

Self-confidence is realistic, but it has far more faith in abilities, not the obstacle.

Self-Confidence In Word

Not "never," but "*when.*" M&B vernacular doesn't use dreamy words such as "someday," or "one day." Instead it uses, "*today.*" Today I can start making my someday, every day.

If an M&B says she will do something, it will happen. They follow through with their commitments. Living this way simplifies and stabilizes life. And, it fosters trust which promotes productivity.

Maybe I've worked with the best M&Bs, those who respect boundaries, don't make excuses for themselves, practice the Golden Rule, are professional, and clear. They don't practice vengeful or passive-aggressive behavior, they don't play mental games, nor have ulterior motives. Because of this candor, I never witnessed lying in these homes. With them, there is never a fear to tell the truth so there is never a need to lie.

Self-Confidence In Deed

Confidence contemplates, "What are my obstacles, and what resources do I have to overcome them?" Then I'll add my elbow grease, hard work, and see what transpires from my concerted efforts.

A sense of pride comes over them when they start a challenging project. They already have a stable sense of self-worth before the project begins, so the project is an expression of self-worth combined with skills and resources.

For example, when an M&B retired, he said the first thing he wanted to do is learn how to cook a multi-course meal. This may sound minimal to a chef or foodie, but to a scientist who looks through a microscope at one white blood cell responding to stimuli, all-day-long, cooking a multi-course meal is like conducting a hundred-piece orchestra. It intrigued him how several dishes with different cooking requirements end up on the table in perfect succession.

M&B in action: How to cook a multi-course meal.

Desire: He wanted to cook a multi-course meal.

Obstacle: He didn't know how to cook.

Resources: He theorized he could treat it as a science (his industry). He bought a book on the chemistry of cooking. It frames cooking as a chemical experiment, right up his scientific alley.

Elbow grease: He started his journey by first learning the grill. He learned how to grill salmon.

Support: Me. I gave him cedar wood planks. He thanked me, with a puzzled expression on his face. Then asked me why I brought him house shingles.

Result: Juicy, flaky, grilled cedar plank salmon.

#4
SPIRITUALITY: THE GOLDEN RULE

To Give Is Better Than To Receive

M&Bs don't project an attitude of, "If I only had ___, then everything would be better." They don't focus on what they don't have as much as they focus on what they do have and what they can do with it.

M&Bs build self-confidence by producing something to benefit others. They feel bigger when they can design and offer something of significance. This is the attitude of "contribution." They believe contribution is valuable while "taking" is not. Therefore, it is better to contribute than to take. M&Bs make focused efforts to teach their children the same practice. A contributor is acceptable and rewarded, while a taker is not.

Giving is empowering.

M&Bs believe they give more than they take, for example, they:

- Give their time and talent to develop new products to make other people's lives better
- Volunteer to help guide programs for those in need
- Give their coveted advice
- Make donations, give gifts
- Create Win-Win deals

The Golden Rule

I liken an M&B's spirituality to a concept of justice rather than an intangible term such as "spiritual."

Their concept of spirituality is: doing what is right and just, and treating others the way they prefer to be treated, otherwise known as The Golden Rule: Do unto others as you would want them to do unto you.

One billionaire with whom I spoke holds a deep conviction that wealth and an individual's spiritual health correlates. If people are not centered in the Golden Rule, they will not have steady progress in life. They will wrestle with guilt and negative consequences over questionable decisions. If they follow it, they've done their best, and have better results.

This same billionaire lives his conviction. He employs full-time workers at more than twice the federal minimum wage plus generous benefits. His employees don't work on Sundays so they can have time with their families. This Golden Rule way of doing business allows their business to attract the best managers in their industry who generate billions of dollars every year.

Benevolence

Giving is spiritual. M&Bs all practice philanthropic work or giving back to society. They join and give to organizations that provide educational programs to develop better social and employable skills for the needy. The M&Bs with whom I worked were not born into wealth. They experienced hardships and are thankful for what they have, and those who helped them. So, they pay it forward. This is their spiritual work, to create positive moments in the lives of others, to spur them on to greater achievements.

#5
WORK ENVIRONMENT: THEY LOVE WHAT THEY DO AND KNOW WHAT THEY'RE WORTH

Love What You Do

I found it surprising when I read an article about baby boomers, people born between 1946 and 1964. Upon retirement many of them reenter college to study what they really wanted to do for a career. This means they forsook their original love. Every M&B I know pursued a career relative to their passion so they have no regrets.

Know Their Worth

To love your work is to believe your product is the best and can compete with the rest for "The Best" title.

A college professor told our class to be cautious of where we worked. He said if you don't believe your company is excellent, you won't perform well. And, if you don't love it, you most likely won't compete well either.

He also advised us to keep a file of our own accomplishments so when confidence waned, we could refer to the list to encourage ourselves. This technique reminds us of our value to an organization. I didn't understand how powerful his counsel was until I needed it. And, years later, I learned M&Bs practice this technique too.

M&Bs do what they love, and love where they are; thus, they love to compete.

One self-made M&B works in the financial markets. She is proud of her work because she knows she's the best and has the best instruments to offer her clients. (*M&Bs acknowledge their "I'm good at ___," and see no shame in acknowledging it*).

One morning after reading the latest news, she mentioned how a few years prior, two separate prospects rejected her services. I asked her how she managed the meeting. She said she was honest with them about market volatility and how that can impact a portfolio. But both prospects bragged of a manager who guaranteed consistent annual gains and never a loss.

This M&B told them the guarantee was mathematically impossible and she wouldn't give them the same promise. So, they took the other manager's amazing offer. She said she didn't take it personally, wished them luck and continued working with suitable clients, those who were realistic.

Regardless of the comparison, she remained confident in her abilities and didn't succumb to feeling inferior.

Then she told me the rest of the story. To whom did she lose those prospects? To the most amazing manager; Bernie Madoff.

Because of her pride in her skills and work, she lost potential clients. But years later, those potential clients lost their fortunes.

Self-Confidence Performs

M&Bs don't find security in their money but in their knowledge and skills to produce it.

Going to work with a "What can I do better?" attitude creates self-confidence. It is empowering. But it also might bother bad managers who try to cut us down. I experienced this when I became a new hire at a large corporation.

After our corporate training, mangers assigned us our supervisors. When I had my first meeting with mine, she said, "I just want you to know, you already have two strikes against you."

I didn't realize we were playing baseball. I never met her, didn't know what she meant, so I didn't take it personal. And, I didn't ask why. That may have bothered her.

Instead, I shifted into performance mode and asked her for company performance expectations. I stayed focused on them at work and in my *many* meetings with her. I was golden as far as I thought because you need not like me, but you can like my work.

But, during our meetings she steered away from my performance. She told me, "You have to work harder at earning respect around here because of what you look like." She made it clear she didn't like me, my looks or my clothes.

I continued to stay focused on company expectations. When she told me I ranked at one hundred and seven percent of global company sales, I thought she would give me a good review. She didn't.

But numbers don't lie.

Later, after my new supervisor read my file he exclaimed, "You're at one hundred and seven percent, it's impossible to have a poor performance review!" All was well. My performance beat out her personal vendetta.

Personal vs. Performance

This too is a strategy of M&Bs. They don't take criticism or feedback personally (at least permanently) they just get better at performing. Like Steve Jobs. Apple fired him because he drove his employees too hard. He thought they loved work as much as he did.

When his own company fired him, Jobs used this "criticism" to give himself a review and begin again. He didn't discourage himself, he searched himself. M&Bs look at criticism as an opportunity for self-improvement. When you critique them, they think you're giving them the secret on how to prosper. Someone says to them "You're not ____," and they think *"Aha! Now I know what to do, get better at ___."* They turn criticism around to better their performance. Even though it may be a personal attack, they learn from it how to perform better.

In business and personal, the quality M&Bs give is what they expect. Hence why their expectations can seem high to others.

When I was in the corporate environment, in two different companies, each of the presidents came to me concerning customer perception. Low-level managers (in both companies) saw our president talking with me. Afterward, they cornered me, one with an index finger pointed at my nose demanding, "Why is the president coming to see you? What are you telling him?"

They didn't understand M&Bs focus on performance… not personal issues. It's nothing personal. These presidents didn't want information on "who did what," but only how customers perceived the company and how to perform better for them.

These low-level managers didn't understand the 13 Cs of M&Bs.

Knowing Worth Isn't Arrogance

Self-confidence is not arrogance. An arrogant person is one who thinks he knows everything regarding everything, therefore need not learn more. The M&Bs I work with recognize they're not all-around experts, so they continue to learn.

M&Bs respect their skill sets and refuse to let others underpay them. They study hard, work long hours, obtained the gray hair from countless late nights of consuming information and putting it to work. They earned it, they hit the mark. It wasn't a small feat. They respect their accomplishments.

I remember a high-end woodworker an M&B hired. He specializes in yacht woodwork, so travels around the country working on beautiful yachts. I asked him how he handles his bids for M&Bs. He told me he keeps the attitude of, "I'm not here to eat a hamburger so you can enjoy a steak" when he sets the price for his fine work. He will not underbid his skills for anyone; it must be an even trade so they both eat steak.

M&Bs don't show favoritism. They don't let some cheat them and others not. *They set their price based on their performance, not on someone's expectation.* This is a healthy boundary.

The ex-M&B doctor who made his million, and lost it, shows favoritism to those promising him big deals. He continues to give without reciprocation. I've seen healing and lives saved with his hands. I know one of his patients whose health was failing rapidly. The ex-M&B doctor determined he needed surgery to remove his infected gallbladder, but not one surgeon would operate on him because they alleged it was his liver instead. They left him for dead.

But, this ex-M&B doctor wouldn't accept this assessment, he found and flew his patient to a surgeon who understood. The surgeon removed the infected gallbladder and the man who was "destined" to die is alive and speedily recovering as I write this.

More than once I told the doctor my opinion, that giving a father back to his children or adding more years to a mother's life is priceless. Until he sees the power in his gifts and talents, others will continue to cheat him. When he honors his Purpose, knows what it's worth, and resolves the Seven Elements in his life, he will reestablish himself.

Negotiating: Ask For What They Want

M&Bs shamelessly negotiate contracts to get what they want. They have a strong faith in Self, it's nothing personal, everything is a deal.

In any relationship if they want something to change, they just ask for it. If it's met with a "yes," that's great. If not, then, "Why, and how do we fix it?" becomes the next conversation. It's that simple.

I've listened to M&B couples "argue." They are direct and converse on how to solve a problem. Negotiation is never a life or death, all-or-nothing moment. They work to find a Win-Win. They renegotiate until each gets steak.

6
PHYSICAL HEALTH

M&Bs understand the body is as valuable as the smarts, so they create a home environment to support their health, not degrade it.

Their keep a serene home, they don't fill up a quiet moment with a television. They get decent sleep, exercise, eat green vegetables, decrease high-fat foods, identify and control food allergies, and eat mostly organic.

Two separate M&Bs had a health crisis. Each managed the experience similarly. Foremost, they didn't feel sorry for themselves and continue to live life the way they did before the incident. They learned from the experience and didn't let it happen again. They changed what led to the health crisis and didn't regret doing so.

The incidents took a small toll on their self-confidence, but they re-built it by changing their lifestyles. They didn't "live with it," but managed it.

"Everything in moderation," as my one-hundred-year-old aunt says. When I visited her at age ninety-six, she cooked us dinner and offered me beer or wine. I declined while she had a little beer. It was a very small cup. The next evening when she cooked dinner, she had wine in a tall shot glass. At that age, she can have whatever she wants. But she chooses moderation.

This is what the M&Bs do. They practice healthy habits so they can have a body that can keep up with their mind. M&Bs aren't health nuts and they're not Martha Stewart who has time to grind her own grains to make flour while she's cooking a seven-course meal. They do what they can with what they've got.

#7
RELATIONSHIPS: SUPPORT VS. APPROVAL AND HEALTHY BOUNDARIES

Support vs. Approval

M&Bs don't confuse approval with support in their relationships. When they have a project idea, they look for support, not just approval.

Approval is an agreement someone thinks your idea is great, but when bringing the idea to fruition, you the idea holder, are on your own. Approval lacks help. It's nice, but sometimes you need more.

Support is a mechanism M&Bs use to fulfill a Want. It may be a software program, education, or a knowledgeable group of people to facilitate and complete a plan.

I never realized the difference between support and approval until working with M&Bs. In my past, certain people taught me networking was bad because it's only using people. But now I understand when I connect with others who may have the resources I need, and I may have the resources they need, it's a Win-Win deal. Nothing personal, it's just an opportunity for both parties to become more productive.

Sometimes when I want to start a project, I tell a friend. My friend agrees with my plan, is encouraging, but that is where it ends. I am on my own. M&Bs experience this too, but the difference is, they find the support structure to build their project.

For example, an M&B backyard farming couple wanted to expand their hen population.

Desire: M&B couple wanted more hens in their backyard farm inside city limits.

Approval: She told her family and friends she wanted more hens, they said, "Great idea." They agreed, gave Approval, a pat on the back and that was all.

Proper authority (when necessary): She checked the city ordinance to understand her rights concerning backyard farms. She found the ordinance would not allow her to have as many hens as she wanted.

Obstacle: Narrow ordinance. The only legal option was to make the city change the ordinance.

Support: She identified and networked with backyard farming organizations to find out what resources were available to change the ordinance.

Elbow Grease: She organized a community town hall meeting for those interested in backyard farming. The organizations advertised for the event, and it filled a venue. A group of people agreed to speak at the next city council meeting to ask for a broader ordinance for hens.

Result: A change in the regulations. More hens allowed.

RECAP:

- Know your trade-offs.
- Identify your values.
- Know and protect your emotions. Safety first.
- Are your beliefs safe drivers? If not, get new ones.
- When you get knocked down, go back to your happy place of best performance and start again.
- Remember Chief Moses: When you see imperfection, realize you belong.
- Breath. It keeps you alive. Practice the Special Forces Breathing Technique during stressful times.
- You are response-able, so build your self-confidence with productive responses.
- Practice the Golden Rule and benevolence. It will bring good fortune.
- Don't fish in the wrong pond. Know your worth and where it's worth the most.
- Get support, not just acceptance.
- Everything in moderation, you only have one you.

CHAPTER FOUR:

Control

"Successful people don't choose the right decisions, they make their decisions right."
Elliot Hulse

"One thing we can all control is effort."
Mark Cuban

People with good work habits have to-do lists that are reasonably prioritized, and they make themselves do what needs to be done. By contrast, people with poor work habits almost randomly react to the stuff that comes at them, or they can't bring themselves to do the things they need to do but don't like to do (or are unable to do).
Ray Dalio

DEFINITION:	*to exercise restraining or directing influence over, power or authority to guide or manage*
SYNONYMS:	*restrain, reserve, check, contain, bridle, direct, point, master, hold, call the shots*
ANTONYMS:	*lose, powerless, let go of the wheel, submissive, loose*

HERDING CATS

Control is a powerful tool used to create balance and produce profitable results.

I presumed M&Bs had excessive controlling behavior. But, after observing them, I learned there is a vast difference between controlling parameters and excessive controlling behavior. Those who use control to suppress rather than to create balance and profitability, have what I call E.C.D.: Excessive Control Disorder. They need to control essentials for reasons other than what a project or circumstance may need.

In my opinion, Excessive Control Disorder crushes productivity while control encourages it. One of my favorite examples of control is the Herding Cats advertisement created by EDS (with over six million YouTube views). A few of the actors are real-life cowboys who practice control all day long.

Cowboys know when to drive the herd and when to let them graze. Control is the ability to balance many factors at once. Cowboys discern when to "restrain, reserve, check, contain, bridle, direct, point, master, hold and call the shots," until they bring the herd home. As one cowboy said, "It ain't an easy job." "Ain't a feelin' like it in the world. I wouldn't do nothin' else."

M&Bs have years of experience herding ideas to fruition. To do so requires the tool control. It is the ability to identify, allocate and herd resources, for the best results possible.

CONTROL TIME

"You've gotta keep control of your time, and you can't unless you say no. You can't let people set your agenda in life."

Warren Buffett

M&Bs understand their most powerful assets are money and time. They also recognize time isn't a recyclable or renewable resource. Hence, they plan.

One evening while shopping I saw an M&B with whom I worked, so I said hello and started a conversation. She said two short sentences and then said, "Okay, I've got to go now." She didn't stop to have a coffee break just because our paths crossed. This seemed austere and impersonal to me at first, but I now understand their preference is to stay on schedule.

M&Bs don't wait to see what will happen to them. There is much to do and little time to do it. What is possible to control, they will. Hence why I am certain they never state they're bored because they make life happen, it doesn't happen to them.

FAMILY PLANNING

M&Bs use a family calendar to control the direction of their family. Their kids know where the calendar is and use it. This teaches them time management at an early age.

Planning is in writing, not just on a smart phone. A physical location creates a gathering place for the family. It creates unity, a sense of belonging and encourages contribution to the family.

CONTROLLING WORDS

Time disappears. Idle words are useless when there's a task to complete.

M&Bs dislike meaningless chatter. Small talk is for specific times, not when they're focused on a project because it can lead to questions, which become distractions. They like to keep conversation simple when they're engrossed.

M&Bs use words to elicit understanding and closure, not to escalate confrontations. A quarrel is of no value compared to a completed task.

CONTROLLING RISKS

Sometimes M&Bs dabble in "controlled risk." One M&B couple remodeled their house. The guest bathroom was off-limits to the family. But it had a great jetted tub. Upon retirement the M&B took a small risk by taking a hot bath in the guest tub without his wife's knowledge. M&Bs keep risk to a minimum.

CONTROLLING FINANCES

When M&Bs donate or lend money, it's to produce a desired result: productivity. They are skeptical people, so they research organizations and choose which will give them the best return on their investment. They also sit on the boards of these organizations to ensure they manage resources as wisely as they do.

Generating wealth affords M&Bs the opportunity to direct more projects. Finances are a tool to build something lasting. I know one M&B is planning his business for the next one thousand years. That may seem ridiculous, but when one family in Italy has owned a coffee house for three hundred years, and the Seguso family business, Murano Glass, is over six hundred years old, it isn't so unfathomable.

CONTROLLING INFLUENCE

M&Bs control their emotions and things that try to exploit them. They're quick to disengage. When I watched them do this, I used to think it was odd. But now I understand the science behind their behavior. They may not know it, but when they disconnect the access, they protect their brains from unnecessary turmoil.

We naturally experience other peoples' pain, so when we hear too many sad stories, we can become overwhelmed and fatigued. This wastes mental energy, increases stress, and drains the body of valuable nutrients necessary to support normal functions.

Instead, we can have compassion for others with no need to explore every painful detail of what they experienced. Compassion is awareness, understanding, and a desire to help relieve tragedy. When we're enmeshed with tragedy, it reduces our ability to do more for those suffering from it.

M&Bs experience compassion but don't expose their emotional state too often to painful stories. Instead, they get a synopsis so they can control their emotions and spare themselves depletion.

Every second of negativity can negatively impact our health.

CONTROLLING RELATIONSHIPS

M&Bs don't spend time with negative people. Who needs Eeyore all day long? It's counterproductive.

When I asked the M&B in the financial markets how she engages with clients who, with every market change, visibly panic and berate her, she said she fires them. I thought that was harsh. But M&Bs control their relationships. They control who and what will influence them, including over-reactive clients.

Jim Rohn said we are the average of the five people with whom we spend the most time. M&Bs must know this because they're careful with relationships. They look for patterns in people. If they see destructive ones they distance themselves or end the relationship.

They abide by the Italian proverb "When a man deceives me once, it is his fault; when twice, it is mine."

M&Bs don't engage in others' pain. At first I thought this was unkind, but then I learned they have their own pain, and worked through their own problems, so they believe others can do the same. They help others by addressing facts, giving suggestions and encouraging them to follow through on their advice. They don't rescue others by thinking for them or executing a plan for them.

I also noticed M&Bs don't sacrifice their wants, work or assets to take over someone else's struggle. But they help, like The Good Samaritan did.

While on his journey, he found a man robbed and beaten. The Good Samaritan brought him to the nearest shelter and paid for his stay and recovery. He didn't stay to mend the man. He gave what he could and went on with his business.

The additional parable I find in this story is about control. The Good Samaritan did what he could do and didn't stray from his intended task because of a crisis. He maintained control of his circumstances. To stay on task, he put the man with someone who could better help him.

Also, the man respected boundaries because he didn't expect the Good Samaritan to stop his life to care for him. The Samaritan didn't assume guilt for not sacrificing his control and didn't take over the man's crisis. The injured man didn't use shame to make him do so.

They both respected boundaries and managed what they each could.

I find this parable illustrates boundaries when a crisis occurs. I apply it to M&Bs because many times I witnessed people expecting M&Bs to manage their crisis because the M&B has money. When this didn't happen they were quite perturbed.

CONTROLLING KIDS

Raising kids can be like herding cats. Here is what I observe:

- Until their children learn self-control the M&B parent controls their environment.

- M&B's are engaged parents, they monitor their child's homework and activities.
- They know where their kids are at all times.
- They monitor their children's teachers.
- Limit TV and movies. They don't abide by an age-appropriate rating but stay well below it.
- Limit internet time, and monitor it with security settings and parent(s) near-by.
- They're specific. They correct you if you aren't.
- They're literal. Their kids turn out the same way.
- They don't lie to their children to manipulate them.
- The kids can't use words such as uh-huh or yeah. They must speak in full sentences.
- They enforce tough love and consequences.
- They don't use food as a substitute for attention.
- They give feedback and acknowledgment.
- They express continual positive reinforcement and displays of encouragement.
- They show their kids they are proud of them.
- They make a big deal about progress and less about mistakes.
- Instead of negative reinforcement, they distract and redirect their children to better choices.
- When they realize their kids cannot break through a barrier, they work them through it. Or they find an expert to help.
- They teach their kids to become better, not bitter, when painful events occur.
- They don't leave their children alone to their own understanding and devices.
- They encourage their kids to ask them questions anytime.

- They understand they are their child's primary resource for everything.
- They have age-appropriate expectations for their children.
- They teach their children their parents must manage them until they learn and earn independence.
- They create small opportunities for their children to develop independence and self-management.
- They teach their children their parents are teachers and will help them gain self-sufficiency, so they won't think their parents are vending machines.

ENCOURAGED IGNORANCE

M&Bs also control what information their kids have when they're younger. Their kids don't understand they have "successful" parents. M&B parents don't brag and don't brag to their children.

They want them to have parents, not titles. I tested this theory. I asked each child of an M&B what their mom or dad does for work. None knew. So, one time I said, "Let's google your dad!" When we did, he was on the first page, and it shocked them (and me) when they read of his accomplishments. As we read about him, he walked into the room. His son said, "Dad! We googled you—" but before he finished his sentence, the M&B's face flushed red with embarrassment and he walked away.

KIDS WILL BE KIDS

Kids are kids, regardless of their parents' portfolio.

My presumption used to be M&Bs had it made, so parenting was easy. Maybe that is why these stories stick out for me, because I was wrong. Becoming an M&B doesn't give them perfect children.

I find this a fun part of my work, observing how M&Bs practice parenting. One of my favorite observations was with the M&B PhD scientist. He sat at the table helping his twelve-year-old son with homework. The father perused the homework and said, "This information is wrong."

His son said, "Dad, no it's not, my teacher gave it to me."

Then the father said, "No, son, this is my research I did for eight years and they've got it wrong." He proceeded to explain the inaccuracy.

When he finished, his son rebuked him, "No, dad, it's in black and white and it's right."

The M&B didn't say another word. It was hilarious to hear this conversation. I had to keep from laughing. Here is a master researcher, worth millions of dollars and his sixth-grade son told him he is wrong concerning his own research.

IT'S NEVER ENOUGH

Even though an M&B child grows up in wealth, they too think they would be happier if they had different circumstances. One evening I babysat an M&B's five-year-old son. We went to a local pizza place. He brought a small Lego toy to work on while we waited for our dinner. The hostess seated us up against a half-wall with tables on either side of the wall. A young couple with a boy, about five years old, sat at the neighboring table on the other side of the half-wall. Both boys could see over the wall to each other's table.

The family finished their dinner while we waited for ours. Their server brought the boy a small bowl of ice cream. At that moment, each boy peered over the wall to look at what the other one had. The boy with the ice cream stared at the Lego toy while the boy with the Lego toy stared at the ice cream. At that moment I realized it doesn't matter how rich or poor, young or old we are, we all have the same tendency to compare.

Another M&B and his kids were on their way to spend the afternoon on a friend's yacht. Their boys played on the same sports team. When the M&B walked away his kids talked about the yacht. They compared how they don't have one (while they're standing in a million-dollar-plus home with a Porsche in the garage), but their friend does. I could tell what they were thinking, so, I asked the kids if their teammate's father attended any of their games. They said no. Then I mentioned they played in the state tournament. I asked if the yacht owner attended. They said no because he traveled for business. I asked them if *their* dad was at all of *their* games. They said yes. I then asked if their dad was at their state tournament. They said yes. And so, I left them with this, "That kid has a yacht and you have a dad."

I explained to them three things. First, their father chose them over advancing his career. Second, we're all equal, we each get twenty-four hours a day no matter how amazing we are. Third, they too will have the same responsibility with their twenty-four hours when they're older, and to consider how they will spend it then.

Wealth Redefined

These kids without a yacht perceived themselves as poor. I didn't realize until I witnessed this moment that even though they lived in a million-dollar-plus home and their parents are multimillionaires, they didn't understand what rich or poor means.

From this experience I learned if parents don't have excess discretionary income, they need not notify their kids. Instead, focusing on what they do have can make them feel wealthy. And feeling wealthy doesn't solely come from having money.

I remember when my family lived in a farming community. We had two distant neighbors and were several miles from a store. It was also lean times. We went outside for entertainment since the TV produced only two fuzzy channels.

I remember wandering through the woods and coming upon a small raised field. It was a ten-foot by twenty-foot area under a few trees. In it grew a large patch of one type of wildflower. I couldn't believe my eyes.

The stark contrast between the bright yellow flowers against a mostly brown world overwhelmed me. I remember I studied them and soaked in their sweet fragrance every day while they were in bloom. This was euphoria: their secret location, their beauty and intoxicating scent.

There will never be another place like it nor equal to it. Its greatness surpassed anything I had or wanted. I felt fulfilled, or rich, because of their rich beauty in my life.

I notice M&Bs teach their kids this same concept. They encourage them to find beauty in the forces of nature, in what they cannot control. They enjoy a spectacular sunset or outdoor activities with their kids. M&B parents want their children to find good things around them, to sense richness because of special moments, not because of money.

CONTROLLING SPACE

An M&B's home environment is uniform, quiet, and steady. They might play relaxing music infrequently, but generally, it's quiet. A TV isn't on all day. They strive to keep a calm atmosphere, and anything that comes along to distort it, they crush it. The home is for connection, not for distraction or chaos.

M&Bs encourage a stress-free home so their children can focus on their own enrichment. When M&Bs arrive home, they don't share their adult concerns with their children, but meet them where they are in their day. They give their children space to focus on themselves.

There is no allowance for yelling or aggression. They discourage their kids from destructive behavior, instead they teach them to talk through conflicts to find resolve.

They organize it. When the kids want to play, they have their bedrooms, playroom, and the outdoors is for rough housing. Fun has its place. The foosball table isn't in the kitchen.

This can work for any size family or income level. I remember while in college I regularly babysat for strangers. One couple had three preschool age girls and lived in a two-bedroom apartment. The girls had a play location in a corner of the living room.

Living in small quarters means noise can travel. As the parents left, the girls raised their voices during their game. The mother whispered, "Girls, you're raising your voices." They quickly lowered their volume to her level. It was impressive, these parents use a whisper to remind them to play quietly.

An interesting couple had a very interesting eight-year-old girl. They allowed her to watch a lot of TV, which was a surprise. But then they explained why. She wanted to be a surgeon, so they used TV to encourage her desire. The day I babysat I walked into the kitchen to greet her. She sat eating her breakfast in front of the TV, engrossed in an open-heart surgery. I stood in amazement as I watched her watch the surgery. The cutting of flesh, blood and goo didn't dissuade her from her yummy bowl of cereal.

Another couple had seven children under the age of ten. I babysat for them once. They too were orderly and kind. As I fed the newborn dinner, the other children excused themselves from the table. A few moments later I remember hesitating, "I can only see two of the seven kids, I have the youngest and the eldest with me, any of the rest can sneak out of the house and I'd never know." I panicked, looked at the ten-year-old and exclaimed, "Where are number two, three, four, five, and six?"

She calmly reported, "Number two and number three have number six in the playroom, number four and five are playing in their bedrooms."

The parents established a daily family routine. When they left, the children followed it. The routine provided stability for the children, and the babysitter.

CONTROLLING CIRCUMSTANCES

If M&Bs cannot control a negative experience, they create an experience elsewhere they can control with a rewarding outcome. They practice the "distract and redirect" method for themselves as they do for their children. This strategy builds self-confidence. They can't prevent every bad thing that happens, but they can make it turn out better than if they left it alone.

M&Bs never let a good bad thing pass by. A situation may be bad, but they can cause something good to come of it. If an awful event occurs, M&Bs become their own advocates. They accept reality that bad things happen to good people. So, they never consider themselves a victim. They also know if they stay a victim and look to someone to fix their problems, they relinquish their power in the situation.

M&Bs refuse to lose control of a circumstance. They take ownership of it by creating an opportunity to use their resources to influence it.

M&Bs practice damage control. They endeavor to mitigate additional negative effects from a negative scenario. For example, an M&B hired me after his divorce. He realized his car reminded him of the painful breakup. Since he couldn't change the past, he decided he could create a good outcome from it. I helped him sell the car below market value to benefit someone who couldn't afford it. He made a bad experience produce something good for himself and another.

CONTROL THEIR BEING: MIND, WILL AND EMOTIONS

This is probably the most important skill: self-control. M&Bs have plenty of it. They control themselves and make no apologies for it.

The first rule to developing self-control, is to say "No" a lot. This helps develop thick skin.

M&Bs don't care about consequences for saying no. And they don't care about FOMO, Fear Of Missing Out because they value their own experiences more than someone else's opinion. Running after FOMO makes someone common, or ordinary while self-control makes it possible to harness individuality to produce progress. And, for the M&B, progress is necessary, otherwise fulfillment doesn't happen.

SLOW AND STEADY

A wealthy private zoo owner wanted an unattainable African gazelle for his collection. The locals said he would never catch one. So, he identified his resources, developed and followed a method, and ignored the negativity.

For many weeks he provided sweet treats for the gazelles. While they grazed, at a distance, he set posts for a corral. The gazelles ignored him. As they came each night to graze on his treats, he continued to build parts of the corral, around them. Then one night he set the last slat of wood in place to complete the enclosure, capturing the gazelles.

M&Bs manage their emotions this same way to attain their desire, no matter how long it takes. M&Bs are "Steady Eddies," just like the private zoo owner, they patiently follow their methods until they accomplish their Want.

To stay steady, mental stamina is necessary. I noticed M&Bs have exceptional working memory and retention. They strengthen their mental stamina with memory games, such as Mensa puzzles. They also stay active in their industry and live a healthy lifestyle.

The M&Bs I worked with don't develop addictions. They manage their brains and bodies as they would any other asset. M&Bs harness it to make it produce, they don't compromise it. When under attack, they don't turn to alcohol or drugs, but look for opportunities to produce a beneficial result. An M&Bs type of addiction is "productivity and efficiency."

SELF-CONTROL AND SOCIAL INFLUENCE

M&Bs measure themselves in terms of productivity. Doing so helps them control their environment with ease. Either something is productive or isn't, if it isn't then they switch to something that is. When they do, they feel better. This too builds self-confidence.

Since M&Bs measure themselves this way, they don't aspire to look like the front of a trendy magazine. Instead, they look their best. They don't let a brand, social group or peers pressure them. Instead, they dampen these by controlling what information they receive from outlets. They are selective because they're independent thinkers.

M&Bs enjoy their life perspective and their ability to perform, so they're not bothered by opinions. Not once did I hear an M&B mention what someone said or thinks about them. Usually they don't know because they end negative or useless conversations. Maybe they do this because they follow the Golden Rule. They reason if they're not destructive toward others, then they won't accept it from others.

They receive constructive criticism but not destructive disapprobation.

FAMILY BUSINESS

One man designed a product and built a manufacturing business around it. The business is five generations old now. He structured it so not one family member could control it, consume it or mismanage it after he died. He bequeathed it as an interest-producing asset so no heir could treat it as an inheritance. Each family member is a shareholder with voting rights and annual dividends.

Four generations after his death, it still produces. Through strategic estate planning, this man controls the outcome of the family business from the grave.

CONTROL LIABILITY

"Not my circus. Not my monkeys."

M&Bs limit liability by not prying into others' problems and directing people to professionals who can help. Being nosey can create liability, so they don't search for private information that doesn't involve them. If someone acts inappropriately, they excuse themselves from the relationship.

An intuitive person once told me I rescued people. She said by doing so, I interfered with their own process of self-realization and personal growth. In a blunt tone she said I, "Rob others of experiencing their own epiphany of self-sufficiency and resilience."

After this confrontation, I compared myself to M&Bs. None of them tried to save people the way I did. Maybe they don't because they're fighters who rise from the ashes like a phoenix and assume others can do the same.

After watching them, I realized the best help is to allow others to struggle through their own problems. Otherwise they might not realize how capable they are at conquering challenges.

CONTROL APPLICATION

To culminate this concept of Control, below is a story of an accountant who became a CFO, but not without serious challenges. When her coworker tried to destroy her career, she used control to manage the circumstances.

CONTROL WORDS. She didn't talk with the coworker or her boss about the behavior. She kept conversations at work, about work.

CONTROL INFORMATION & INFLUENCE. She refused to listen to any gossip said by this coworker regarding her.

CONTROL RELATIONSHIP. She refused to have a personal relationship with this woman or try to change her mind. She formed a personal support group made of healthy people.

CONTROL PROJECTS. She worked to her best ability to do an excellent job at her work. She made "performance" her measurement against the circumstances.

CONTROL TIME. She spent her time on positive things, rewarding activities, her family and business acumen. She controlled it by sidestepping defending herself or arguing. Instead, she used her time to produce.

CONTROL SPACE. When this M&B left her office, she focused on her personal space. She shared it with emotionally stable people. She didn't let the malicious coworker into her personal space physically or mentally. And she didn't engage in unhealthy activities to cope but found healthy outlets to take her mind off of the attacks.

CONTROL FINANCES. She didn't spend money to manage the struggle. Some people self-sabotage by over-spending their finances. This is a distraction, keeping them from overcoming their real struggle. M&Bs don't do this.

CONTROL PERFORMANCE. She built a plan and her business skills to prepare her to perform at each level she attained. That plan comprised of staying away from conflict and performing to meet expectations and company needs. She realized she could produce good things in a negative situation rather than waiting for the environment to change.

CONTROL LIABILITY. She didn't engage other coworkers in the chaos. Discussions could lead to disputes, which could make her liable.

CONTROL SELF, MIND AND EMOTIONS. She focused on her desired results and channeled her resources toward them rather than fixating on what this coworker might say. If she performed well, she believed she was acceptable. Her feelings were in alignment with her plan, not the coworker's chaos.

"It is our choices… that show what we truly are, far more than our abilities."
JK Rowling

RECAP

Control is a method encompassing; pointing to, checking on, directing, restraining, forming, and goading to make something produce.

One can observe the DEFINITION and SYNONYMS of control in the EDS Herding Cats Commercial.

M&Bs control information, relationships, and circumstances because they impact productivity.

You can control what gets your time and attention.

Never let a good bad experience pass by—make something of it.

You can control a negative experience by defining a Want and directing action to get that Want.

Control the chatter, internal and external, with meaningful tasks.

Control the influence of media and people. Choose wisely.

Use TV, games, and resources to build up good qualities and habits.

Let others build their self-resilience; don't rescue. Help them find professional helpers.

CHAPTER FIVE:

Cautious

"If you don't design your own life plan, chances are you'll fall into someone else's plan. And guess what they have planned for you? Not much."
Jim Rohn

"Honesty is a very expensive gift. Don't expect it from cheap people."
Warren Buffett

"If I say anything, I know it (the low price he is interested in) will be gone. You can't telegraph your punches in a financial situation."
Warren Buffett

DEFINITION:	*having or showing a close attentiveness to avoiding danger or trouble*
SYNONYMS:	*watchful, conservative, conscientious, guarded, careful*
ANTONYMS:	*regardless, thoughtless, neglectful, indiscreet*

CAUTIOUS FOR A CAUSE

When first working with M&Bs, it bothered me how cautious they are. I was lax in cautiousness compared to them. M&Bs are cautious for a cause, to execute a plan for results. There is a beginning and an end to their caution. From them I learned caution is not paranoia or random accusations, it is proactive and not reactive.

CAUTION STRATEGIZES

An M&B wanted to bring in another partner to service her growing clientele. She wasn't interested in others knowing her plan because she wanted to select a partner on her own terms. She defined the terms, primarily competence but also similar traits. Her personality is swift and positive, so she sought a partner with equivalent strength.

First, she surveyed her industry and networks to find those who might meet her qualifications. She asked other professionals who they thought were high performers in their niche. She read the local business journal's Who's Who and attended industry focused events to scrutinize potential associates.

When she found someone she thought might be a good partner, she connected with this person for a philanthropic reason, something unrelated to their industry. The unsuspecting candidate accepted the invitation, and they developed an acquaintance.

Then she assigned me a task. It was to deliver philanthropic materials and offer my help on behalf of the M&B. But the real purpose was to detect the candidate's personality.

This was my first time meeting this person. When I arrived, I made a simple effort to drop off the materials and offer my support. Within the candidate's first words, a tirade erupted over how life is difficult. Negativity abounded and too many personal (unhealthy) things disclosed. It was abnormal information to share with someone when first meeting. No matter what encouraging words I offered, the candidate shooed them away with a raised hand and a flick of the wrist. After a few moments of this I felt exhausted. I realized this is someone happiest in a negative state of mind. I shudder at the memory.

When I returned, I didn't need to say much to the M&B since she appreciates concise conversations. I told her two sentences about my experience. Enough said. She moved on to another possibility, a much healthier one. It was a relief I didn't have to see the last candidate ever again.

Interestingly, the M&B didn't care to find out *why* the potential associate was so high strung. She didn't look for reasons, then try to resolve them so they could have a partnership. M&Bs realize if a person cannot solve their own problems (by getting support) they can't solve them either. So, they move on to a healthier prospect.

CAUTION CRITIQUES

The more money a person earns, the more vigilant they should become at protecting it. There are people who prize getting and spending other peoples' wealth. It seems like scammers can smell money.

One M&B I worked with invited me to attend a meeting he had with a businessman looking for funding. He asked me to pay attention to his behavior and critique the presentation. The businessman didn't appreciate me attending, he became defensive when I asked questions.

Usually my presence only irritated the scammers looking for money from this M&B. In time this became a game, for nearly ten years. If a presenter displayed animosity towards me, then the deal was off.

Caution is strategic and empowering. Fear keeps us from practicing Caution the right way. And practicing it makes those of us hyper-aware people a fraction more relaxed.

CAUTION ALERTS

Trading and investing in stocks are a great example of practicing caution. It requires strategic thinking and continual research. When you eat, sleep, and breathe something, it becomes second nature. So, after extended research and experience sometimes a decision comes down to a gut feeling.

Not long ago, I actively traded in the stock market. A coworker and I planned to work together on trades. I didn't have a good gut feel on most of the trades he presented, so he did them on his own. We reviewed his positions and more times than not I said, "I'd get out now." Each time I said this, he ignored me, and the stocks moved against him.

Based on the trading strategy we selected, I pointed out he had a terrible habit of listening to "old news." I consider that once news hit MSNBC, the trade was over. When I told him this, he was not fond of my insight so refused to work with me.

To whom do you listen? I learned not to listen to the latest "hot tip" from my broker who sold me a "hot stock." It was hot until I bought it. This became a joke amongst a few of us. If someone asked, "Got any hot stock tips?" We responded with, "Yes, never ask for a hot stock tip."

CAUTION PLANS

M&Bs are skeptical; they don't take hot tips. They don't get word-of-mouth information from someone and act upon it at once. Instead, they do the boring stuff: research to calculate any potential financial loss. It can seem somewhat of a killjoy at first until all the fun (money) gets sucked out of a project because of poor risk assessment.

M&Bs take calculated risks. This means they do due diligence before exposing their *ass*ets. None of the M&Bs I know find losing money "thrilling."

A group of new investors had thrilling experiences. A few of them funded business deals that surprised me. There was a startup company of three men looking for funding. Two new investors invested in the startup. I asked them why they did so since the same team (same guys, under a different name) failed two other times doing the same business. For any investment the past is a decent indicator of the future. These new investors didn't consider the past, nor were they skeptical. It baffled me. They said, "The numbers, the numbers tell us what will happen!" And a few months after the business opened, it closed. On the front door hung a sign, "Remodeling – Reopening soon." It never reopened.

Those new investors were more excited than cautious.

They were "newbies" to investing because they had "new money" or recently earned wealth from the tech industry. They earned a stable paycheck from a company for creating software codes. Their job offered them stock options which later turned them into millionaires. Because they were millionaires, the SEC considered them "qualified investors." Qualified because they had money, not because they had startup business experience.

Some of these new investors join angel investment groups where they investigate new ventures. I remember during one investment presentation, an M&B leaned over and asked me why the current presenter traveled across the country to "our little pond" to look for capital. He questioned the presenter, "What's wrong with money in your neck of the woods?" and, "Why did you have to come all the way over here?" They were great questions. The presenter couldn't answer, so he didn't receive funding.

CAUTION DISCRIMINATES RELATIONSHIPS

With caution brings discrimination. When used in the right manner discrimination is productive. M&Bs are cautious of who or what influences them. They don't immediately trust people. How do M&Bs discriminate? They naturally practice a formula I learned from a psychologist-friend:

Behavior + Time = Trust.

He said most people use the Talk = Trust Formula. We take others at face value, we believe everything they tell us. We assume they are forthright, so we trust too soon. By using Behavior + Time = Trust we use caution as the M&B does. If we meet a stranger or haven't spent ample time with someone, we remove Time from the equation. Behavior + ~~Time~~ = Trust. Now we have an incomplete equation, so we remove the solution. We remove Trust: Behavior + ~~Time = Trust~~. We find this leaves us with only Behavior. This is our starting point for every relationship. We do not lead with trust but watch for trustworthy actions.

When we realize Behavior is the only variable we have in the beginning of a relationship, we must first determine what behavior we desire to receive. Once determined, the next step is to observe the behavior displayed. If it doesn't meet the criteria, then we remove the variable Behavior. ~~Behavior~~ + ~~Time~~ = ~~Trust~~. Thus, no equation. No equation means no relationship. We no longer spend time around someone who displays unhealthy behavior.

But if the behavior meets the criteria with each successive encounter, then time spent together can increase. We now can insert the variable Time back into the equation. Behavior + Time. The result is a complete equation with a reasonable result: Trust. Behavior + Time = Trust. We should trust only after we see consistent, healthy behavior.

M&Bs aren't open to everyone and not quick to trust. They're not scared, insecure, nor disparage people—they simply consider their time, state of mind, and the tradeoff for spending time with someone. This is a healthy form of self-preservation.

CAUTION DETERMINES TIME-WORTHINESS

M&Bs understand time is a non-renewable resource. Therefore, they're cautious about who gets it. I find the most imaginative analogy of my analysis of the cautious M&Bs is a storyline from a Seinfeld TV Show episode.

In Episode 119 Elaine Benes, played by Julia Louis-Dreyfus, finds out a manufacturer discontinued her favorite contraceptive sponge. She first panicked, but then created a plan. Wherever she could find the sponge, she bought it, in bulk. Then she developed a detailed interview to screen which men she deemed to be sponge-worthy.

How serious Elaine was with her limited supply of sponges is how serious M&Bs are with time. Exchange the storyline object, "Sponge" for "Time." M&Bs do what Elaine did: they devise a screening system to decide who or what is "Time-worthy." They are cautious because they like to stay productive. In stark contrast, Elaine had no interest in being productive.

M&B SCREENING

M&Bs are cautious because they want a stable and enjoyable environment. That is why most M&Bs have relationships with experts or knowledgeable persons. From what I perceived, this preference is not because experts have a title, but because they were stable and disciplined to earn the title. This requires commitment and reasonably healthy patterns, and these individuals aren't usually aggressive or argumentative. They enjoy connecting with others on an intellectual level and tend to their own business. It is a stress-free engagement for M&Bs.

M&Bs are also partial towards knowledgeable people because they can learn something of value. That is why a title or letters behind someone's name can create instant interaction for an M&B. If they see designations, they can categorize people and know where to begin a relationship with them. When they meet a stranger without documentation (such as a business card), there isn't a foundation for the M&B. So, the M&B becomes cautious and the questioning begins, "Who are you and what are you after?" A business card with expertise listed helps them forego their initial level of caution.

An M&B's gift of trust is never for a lifetime. If someone breaks trust, they'll limit contact with that person or no longer have a relationship.

I soon became aware of M&Bs limited tolerance for "mishaps" in relationships. If someone disrespects boundaries, the M&B becomes more cautious. I know many people who make excuses for others' behaviors and end up in bad circumstances. Similar to me with the ex-friend who found it entertaining to spike people with an umbrella prong.

Her behavior shocked me, but I thought I should overlook it. Then I realized after reviewing our day together, the qualities I thought existed, didn't.

I remember an advisor once told me I had a problem: he said I wanted to ask "why" instead of "run." I laugh now because I was twenty-five years old at the time but didn't understand what he meant. He intended to say my weak point was I wanted to understand why a friend did something when I should run from the friendship. Now after being around M&Bs, I notice they practice "run" instead of "why." They leave the relationship; they don't analyze why someone did something.

Caution is good to practice because time is precious. There are millions of good people to have wonderful relationships with instead of engaging in stressful events with boundaryless people.

THE CAUTIOUS M&B PARENT

I mentioned in Chapter One an M&B didn't approve of his son's friend, so he didn't allow him to spend time with him. His friend had a painful past—his mother died, and his father wasn't present very often. I thought it hypercritical of this M&B to reject this poor boy. *But what I didn't know about myself until this experience is, I had a hidden prejudice that M&Bs were elitists who don't want to associate with people who have "shady" or painful pasts.*

I felt sorry for this boy, so I encouraged the M&B's kids to invite him to their house and show him kindness. I thought they could give him a healthy environment to help him manage his difficulties.

The M&B also spent time with him. What I didn't notice at first was the M&B cautiously considered this boy's choices and mindset. While I judged the M&B's motives, the M&B judged this kid's future by the choices he made.

I remember a college professor told our class, "It doesn't matter where you've come from, but where you're going." That stuck with me, but I never fully realized the depth of this meaning until this moment watching the M&B. He was wise. He weighed every variable evenly while I gave weight to only one, the boy's traumatic experiences. Here are the variables I didn't consider the M&B did:

Their community is keenly active in the lives of children. There are kids' clubs, Big Brother programs, mentorships, school sports, and counseling available. The police department takes an active role in educating kids and energetically engages with them around the neighborhoods. It hosts "have coffee with your neighborhood police officer" at the local coffee shop. This small city provides many resources for kids to choose relationships over drugs.

There were far more good variables available than bad for this pre-teen. Although there were several, he chose drugs instead of help and good relationships. He didn't want a healthy father figure with the M&B, instead, he headed in a dangerous direction. The M&B didn't want his kids encouraged to do the same.

I realized I was the judgmental one because I assumed all wealthy people judged on outward appearances. I was wrong. And I also realized I allowed unhealthy behavior from this boy because I blamed his actions on his home life. I made excuses for his decisions and inappropriate behavior.

CAUTION HELPS US CHOOSE WISELY

We sometimes don't get to choose what happens to us, but we ALWAYS get to choose how we respond.

Someone taught me a unique perception about clay and the sun. The same sun can soften some kinds of clay (making it resilient) while it can harden others (making it hard, or stubborn). It depends on the clay. Clay symbolizes the heart, and the sun symbolizes hardships. We can let hardships make us resilient or make us incapable of recovery and growth.

A wise M&B told me, "We always move towards what we really want." This M&B identified what this kid wanted and didn't want it for his kids. He was cautious and correct.

My lesson learned from the M&B: Don't make excuses for someone's current behavior because of painful things in their past. Help them make healthier choices, if they don't, boundaries are best.

RECAP

Caution is strategic, not fearful. It works from an end desire, not fear of an outcome.

Caution plans to prevent. A plan prepares for the worst and the best and how to handle them.

Caution is conscientious and observes.

Behavior + Time = Trust. Caution discriminates with time and watches behavior.

Caution is honest with Self and others about Wants yet guards them carefully.

CHAPTER SIX:

Calculated

I insist on a lot of time being spent, almost every day, to just sit and think. That is very uncommon in American business. I read and think. So I do more reading and thinking and make less impulse decisions than most people in business. I do it because I like this kind of life.

Warren Buffett

"From him I learned the value of the 'scuttlebutt' approach: Go out and talk to competitors, suppliers, customers to find out how an industry or a company really operates."
Warren Buffett

"Everything in life is luck."
Donald Trump

DEFINITION: *Engaged in, undertaken, or displayed after reckoning or estimating the statistical probability of achievement or failure. Done with full awareness of the likely consequences*

SYNONYMS: *measured, considered, weighed, reasoned*

ANTONYMS: *hit or miss, haphazard, half-cocked, cockamamy, random*

M&B CONSIDERATIONS

Before this job I had no involvement with people who have the ability or drive to calculate and anticipate like an M&B. Initially, it boggled my mind.

M&B's calculate because they want the most from every experience. Their ultra-proactive behaviors were intense for me at first because my family lived haphazardly. We called it "spontaneous," but it was beyond spontaneous. Since there were several kids in our family, the planets had to align for an event to go as planned.

If my dad looked outside and guessed the day called for a drive in the mountains, my parents packed the family into the suburban and off we went.

My family still practices spontaneity. At a more recent family get-together, an idea spawned. One of my brothers did what our dad used to do: he looked outside to see what the day called for. Today it was skiing. He looked for which mountain was closest, then we piled into our vehicles and headed in its direction. We are not a family of skiers. The attitude was, "We'll learn everything when we get there." That is how we rolled.

M&Bs are different. They plan and prepare extensively, even for non-work-related outings. I remember when one M&B couple wanted to learn a winter sport. They studied it to determine if they could master it. When they concluded they could, they purchased the recommended equipment and studied all the manuals long before they took a lesson.

This was not my reality. Who studies an activity before trying it? M&Bs. Who reads manuals? M&Bs read manuals. They dislike knowing there could be something else they didn't know.

M&Bs Have Arrived

Before working with M&Bs, I couldn't tell I discriminated against wealthy people. I didn't realize I had expectations of them until they didn't meet those expectations.

One of my prejudices was rich people have "arrived in life;" therefore, they are omniscient, they know everything about everything. It may sound odd, but I expected that once a person reached a CEO level or became a millionaire, he or she must fathom everything.

I likewise presumed they needed no one and nothing. Now I understand how ridiculously inaccurate this is.

The first conflict with my judgment occurred right after college, before I worked in the private lives of M&Bs. I was a sales representative for a global organization. One afternoon the company president walked through our department. I never met a company president before. (My hometown didn't have CEOs or big businesses, so this was a new experience for me.)

I felt awkward as I stood holding a product schematic. I didn't know what to say, so I made up a question about the product to ask him. He smiled at me and said it wasn't his expertise. Our conversation died because his response did not line up with my expectation. He was the president of the company, so why couldn't he answer my question? Answer: because I assumed individuals at the top know everything about business and life. I was wrong, he wasn't omniscient.

Luck Calculated

"Luck is what happens when preparation meets opportunity."
Richard Branson

M&Bs I worked with never fear conveying a direct message. Sometimes this appears offensive, but that isn't their intention.

Because they internally calculate how to resolve a problem, they formulate their decision privately. Then they have an open debate to test their conclusion. Rarely do they have an open discussion if they haven't built a conclusion yet.

In the beginning this calculated mode of operation startled me because it came across as blunt. But I eventually grasped it. Now I find it interesting to watch how others, who don't work in this environment, react to M&Bs. For instance, a local business college asked a billionaire I worked for to speak to their students at a private event. He is a humble man and willing to share what he can, so he attended and delivered his presentation.

His presentation is the same one he gave to his board of directors. It comprised the company history, successes, and plans for the business. The opportunity to view the private presentation for a company that generates more than one hundred million dollars a year is a rare experience for most anyone.

During his address, he said something shocking. I found it eye-opening and comical considering the shock waves it sent throughout the venue. If it is possible air can get sucked from a room, it did. Most of the students sat in silence, bewildered by what he said. The billionaire used the word "luck" in his presentation.

"Luck? What?" students whispered. Then one young man raised his hand to speak. He grinned, "You didn't mean luck, you meant…" This shocked me. He raised his hand to correct this billionaire for using the word luck. An unemployed student tried to correct a man who generated billions of dollars.

Without hesitation, the billionaire replied in a patient and kind manner. This was significant to me, first, because this student's criticism didn't ruffle him. Second, because the billionaire showed no disrespect towards this student and in simple terms explained "luck" to him.

The billionaire stated we cannot control every variable in business. We are sometimes at the mercy of chance, so we must be in the right place at the right time. We can only prepare for chance or influence it, but we cannot control it. And, he pointed out, no matter what happens, the result is always fifty-fifty, a desire happens, or it doesn't.

After hearing this, I realized he no longer spoke from a planned presentation. He spoke from his personal perception, from his subconscious. I'm not sure if anyone else grasped what he revealed in that moment. It was a hidden gem of insider information about his kind of people. The gem: An acknowledgement that there are uncontrollable variables in business, therefore "luck" is a real element. M&Bs know they cannot control everything, but they know they can control their attempts at influencing variables.

M&Bs calculate to create a synergy that will put them in an ideal place at an ideal time. They analyze what they can control to influence their chances. How they influence is through relationships, skills, financing, experience, and whatever else they consider an asset. Since M&Bs calculate this way, they have a genuine and positive concept about chance. They really have a "Why not me?" attitude. Why not? It's a fifty-fifty chance, regardless.

NO MAGIC FORMULA

M&Bs don't strive for perfection because they don't believe perfect exists. Not once did I hear the word "perfect" used in conversation, regarding expectations nor finished work. Nor did any M&B mentioned he or she was after perfection. They never use it as a guide. Instead, they calculate what they can do and what resources they have to do it with.

M&Bs don't have a magic formula to get them what they want. But they know they have capabilities they can apply to influence or create a new opportunity. When a product or service evolves from their efforts, they exploit it to the best of their ability, win or lose. As the billionaire said, it still ends up a fifty-fifty chance; either it happens, or it doesn't.

In 1996 Larry Ellison, founder of Oracle, developed the NC, a desktop computer. It failed to influence the market as intended. There were additional variables that affected its inability to create the desired market acceptance, but predominantly it's because Ellison was ahead of the internet's development.

His timing was off. He was not in the right place at the right time. It had a fifty-fifty chance to happen, and it didn't.

And so, as with every chance, timing matters. I believe M&Bs understand they can only work with (and are a catalyst for) the synergy from strategically arranged resources. They respect the fragility of chance and recognize business requires a network of competent people who correlate.

RISKY BUSINESS & LUCK

Perhaps risk is the variable in business which keeps these M&Bs humble. They realize business is a blend of science and art, thus it requires adaptive creativity to make deals happen. Business isn't composed of simple rules to success. It requires dedication to adaptation every day. None of the M&Bs I've worked with have a three, four, or five-day work week.

Work, or creating deals, is a lifestyle not a job. They love what they do, and because of this love they continually calculate variables.

Since high performers understand the world continually changes, they position themselves to provide and create products or services to help others manage change. In general, the creator makes the money, not the end-user.

To position oneself as a creator doesn't always afford a steady bi-monthly paycheck for redundant work performed day after day. Positioning is risky, which requires copious amounts of calculation to influence a chance at luck.

HOW DO M&BS CALCULATE BUSINESS VARIABLES TO INCREASE CHANCE AT "LUCK"?

They…

Get educated.

Dislike echo chambers.

Don't do group think.

Don't let others calculate for them.

Learn enough and then delegate to experts.

Estimate their best calculations then consult with experts.

Ignore the emotional hype and get down to basic calculations.

Calculate the payout.

Find the best support tools.

Network to find: the best people to hire, new leads, products, referrals, and additional assets.

Research their industry, the market and competition. Work from a S.W.O.T. analysis.

Manage life and work with the 5 Ps and live the 13 Cs.

AVOIDING GROUP THINK

I remember a true story about a hyped software company with plans to go public on a major stock exchange. This company raised over ninety million dollars. That colossal sum of money came together because of word-of-mouth hype and a "friends and family" program. This program allowed the company to sidestep producing proper investment information the S.E.C. requires qualified investors to receive. For reasons such as these the M&Bs I know let the hype pass them by and wait for the boring financial details to qualify the probability of success.

They skip the emotionalism. Not me, I invested.

It was a spectacular promotion, but the product was not spectacular because the product didn't exist. It was a fraud. The creator of the fraud is still serving a twenty-year prison sentence.

CALCULATE THE PAYOUT FROM THE TRADEOFF

M&Bs measure productivity, not feelings. They calculate if something will help them make progress, not how exciting it is. And M&Bs don't have a "herd mentality." They thoroughly investigate their options and stay clear of blindly following fads that have no merit.

I likewise notice M&Bs calculate what the payout is from every effort. We usually call this a "consequence," but M&Bs look at consequences as payouts. There is always a payout; sometimes it's good and sometimes it isn't.

HOW M&BS CONSIDER THEIR CHILDREN

M&Bs have a direct influence on the management and measurement of their children's development. I've seen M&Bs just as concerned about their kids' development as they are with their professional lives. They don't spawn offspring then let them go about life their own way.

I knew parents who said, "We let our son choose. We wait for him to ask for something," when he was only two years old. A child doesn't know how to navigate life on his own. If he doesn't know what a Lego is, how will he ask for it? This parenting style isn't how M&Bs operate. They recognize a child is like a sponge. They introduce to their children what they want them to absorb.

TV AND THE M&B CHILD

M&Bs believe some TV programs can diminish their influence over their children. They don't want television programming their children. It does the same to adults. That's why M&Bs do not indulge themselves, nor their family, in excessive use of TV programming.

To expose a child to non-stop TV doesn't teach a child to reason for himself. M&Bs prefer to let their kids become "bored" so they can develop the ability to change their own circumstances.

M&B CHILDREN AND ACTIVITIES

M&Bs have a well-thought-out reason for their decisions, it is never a random one. Each effort builds upon another. In particular they don't enroll their kids in casual activities that look fun. They measure what tools they will gain from the activities, such as fine motor skills, learning, and social skills.

M&Bs build their children into critical thinkers. An activity may have wrapped the child in a fun atmosphere, but the M&B calculated the skills "fun" made happen.

None of the M&Bs I worked with encouraged heavy contact sports like football. I didn't understand why. Then I heard from each one, at different times, their concern: head injuries. Their disregard for contact sports wasn't to withhold their kids from a fun sport, it was their concern for their health.

Instead of telling their boys "no" or using fear of a head injury to deter them, they used the "distract and redirect" method to engage them in a safer sport or activity.

M&Bs distract and redirect. They don't force. They reason how to create an interest in their kids to do something good for themselves. M&Bs inspire them to contemplate and negotiate within themselves. They teach their kids how to calculate.

M&BS CHILDREN'S SCHOOLING

One M&B couple live in a small neighborhood where most of the parents have an acquaintance with one another. It surprised me to discover they emailed each other regarding their kids' daily lives at school. If school stressed a child, parents communicated to see if other kids experienced the same problems. If they, as a group of parents, agreed it was necessary to discuss with the school, they sent emails to the school staff. I found it humorous. These poor teachers received scads of emails addressing progress and children's' daily affairs. The teachers understood these parents cared about the little things.

Then I wondered, how did the parents get information? Where did they glean details to build a case for these teachers? So, from that moment on, I paid more attention to what happened in these M&B families.

M&B COMMUNICATE WITH THEIR CHILDREN

I first watched the kids interact with their M&B parents. My observations revealed they encourage open communication. No topic is off limits. M&Bs ask their children questions about school and activities just as they ask adults questions. They respect their children as they respect adults.

When one M&B parent arrives home, his kids tackle him, they wrestle and share lots of hugs. He doesn't shoo them away, they come first. When the kids tire of him, they go back to their activity. That's when dad attends to his personal space.

The M&B re-enters their world after he's settled. He observes where their focus is, then engages in that moment with questions to stimulate a conversation. It allows him a subtle way to connect and to hear what his child feels. This creates an environment of trust.

I also noticed M&Bs treat them as though they can contribute at any age. They welcome their thoughts. M&Bs teach their kids early in life they are interested in them and their opinions; therefore, they can share whatever they wish to share.

And, criticism isn't awaiting them when they have a problem. Instead M&Bs show them how to explore their own issues by asking questions that guide them to draw a healthy conclusion.

M&Bs also expect their kids to give meaningful and deliberate reflection in conversation. They're not allowed to grunt or give a one-word answer to, "How was your day?" This sometimes annoyed the kids, they whined, but their parents didn't become upset over their whining, nor give in to it by disengaging. They continued with their expectation of a meaningful conversation. This directed the children to move through their feelings to something better—a great conversation.

After observing how the parents engaged with their kids, I became curious. I wanted to know how the kids perceived their parents' behavior. I asked one of them about his parents. After a sigh he said, "We call our parents helicopter parents." I had no comprehension of what that meant, so he explained. Then I realized they labeled their parents' awareness of them and their actions as hovering. I found it humorous. It wasn't overbearing behavior, but the kids perceived it as such when they wanted their own way.

After all the years of heart-felt communication from the M&B father to his son, the saddest thing I witnessed was when his son grew older and considered his dad "too old" to be around. He wasn't as cool as his friends. It broke this M&B's heart; his son was his world. But instead of burdening his son with his broken heart, he displayed happiness for him to have good buddies. Fifteen years later, this father and son are best of friends.

M&Bs And Their Pets

As I mentioned, M&Bs hate to waste time and influence those around them to not waste it either. They manage their pets with the same calculated rationale. One M&B who is childless has two pets; one has health issues, so he has an eight-page protocol for her. When I first saw it, I assumed there was a serious control issue going on in the home. My rational was, "Why in the world does a dog need an eight-page protocol?"

Then I realized I made another inaccurate assumption. The M&B created a procedure packet to reduce his stress while he was away and simplify the process for the caretaker. This made the dog sitter more confident while caring for this sweet retried service dog. It wasn't about excessive control but preventing problems.

The dog is a very happy dog, so he is a very happy dog parent.

M&B PROFESSIONAL AND FINANCIAL CALCULATIONS

M&Bs take calculated risks. A risk is an expectation they want to fulfill without a guarantee they can. They could lose their investment of time or money. So, they calculate the risk in relation to what they want.

After they develop their strategy, they manage disruptions until they reach their desired result. If an unforeseeable matter overwhelms their strategy, they may hire an expert to assist them in resolving it.

M&Bs prefer working with experts. Titles don't impress them, *but the performance it took to earn the title* does. So, they trust other experts because they too comprehend the sacrifice it takes to become one.

For instance, someone asked me to invite an M&B to an investment opportunity. It was a Ponzi scheme. For an unknown reason, I found his request funny. I laughed and mentioned that the last thing an M&B might do is listen to me concerning finances.

Since I blurted this out, I didn't realize at that moment this was another subconscious belief I had about wealthy people.

Then he asked me again, so I explain again: Long before I came into their lives, M&Bs set their groove for earning wealth. They don't need my help. I'm there to help manage what they have while they build more.

I further clarified: they don't jump out of a profitable groove for an overnight opportunity. He couldn't understand this because he had a mind-blowing deal that could make anyone rich.

After another explanation that M&Bs don't employ me as a financial consultant, and it would be foolish of me to depict myself as one, I realized an epiphany began to take form. This frustrating conversation stimulated my prejudice to reveal itself.

I felt exasperated. He refused to accept "no" for an answer. Finally, I told him I was not in that "category" for these M&Bs. As soon as I said those words, I felt a shift inside, and I understood the lie I believed.

I realized I judged M&Bs were snobs because they categorize people. This is partially true. Just like any lie, it has a little truth. The whole truth was, M&Bs do categorize people, but not in the way I assumed.

After several varied explanations, he still didn't grasp the meaning. He was bent on getting what he wanted, which had no connection with truth. And he refused to review any research I presented to him involving Ponzi schemes. He preferred to hold on to the "hope strategy" as in, "I hope it is what the promise says it is."

His hope strategy didn't work, the Ponzi scheme fell apart. He lost his money.

I always remind myself of what a State Court of Appeals Judge once told me. He said the judges he works with have a pithy expression: If it smells like poop, looks like poop, acts like poop, its poop. He explained no matter how they argue about what it could be or should be, it is what it is, as it is. So don't dress it up because it will still smell.

M&Bs Discriminate

As I mentioned earlier, M&Bs discriminate. Until this moment I didn't realize this was another bias I held: I thought M&Bs were "discriminatory," or they unfairly judged individuals based on how much wealth they had. I assumed they ranked others as lower or higher than themselves.

That was my reality until this Ponzi experience conflicted with my subconscious judgment. By explaining myself to Ponzi Guy, I verbalized my belief. When I heard it come out of my mouth, it was the first moment I heard what I believed. It wasn't truth.

The truth is M&Bs discriminate but they are not *discriminatory.* To discriminate means to classify, separate, distinguish, or differentiate.

M&Bs distinguish how they earn money. They choose to earn it the old-fashioned way, by providing a product or service someone else wants and pays to have. M&Bs classify who they listen to; who will advise them and who won't. Measuring and classifying are instinctive habits for them. A random person inviting them into an investment opportunity not regulated by a government agency, such as the SEC, doesn't get their attention.

Experts Manage Their Produce

M&Bs "eat-sleep-breathe" their industry. They discriminate they are best at doing what they've mastered: solving problems and generating income for solving problems. As they grow their wealth, they may hire a savvy financial advisor or planner to preserve their earnings.

When M&Bs generate their first million dollars, they don't stop working and leave making the next million up to the financial advisor. They don't believe a financial advisor will create millions for them. And, advisors don't turn clients into millionaires, it's proven they don't.

M&Bs know they're their best chance at building income, so they build and hire experts to manage what they build.

NON-M&B BEHAVIOR

A non-M&B hired me to oversee a remodeling project on his property. A situation required a unique tool. Since I have experience with this application, I bought the proper tool. Without telling me, the non-M&B purchased a incorrect tool. When I explained he selected the wrong one and what would happen if he used it, he exclaimed, "I researched for hours to get the proper tool for this application!"

He wasted his more valuable time researching rather than letting me do what he hired me to do. He doesn't practice the 13 Cs as an M&B does. M&Bs let their qualified staff do the job they hired them to do.

As one proverb says, "The eagle chasing two rabbits catches neither one." M&Bs know to stay focused in their groove.

M&BS RE-CALCULATE FOMO

M&Bs don't suffer from Fear Of Missing Out. I trust it's because they don't look to others to provide praise, stimulation or guidance. They have an independent way of thinking, so they never run dry of projects, curiosities, or desires. I call this the NMO (Never Missing Out) mentality. They're focused on their desires, so they're never missing out.

My realization of the calculated trait in M&Bs taught me to measure my objectives, expectations and potential outcomes and recognize my own NMO, like now, while my friends enjoy the beach, I'm writing this chapter.

RECAP

To calculate is to prevent chaos.

The art of calculating can save you from frustration years in advance.

Calculate means to discriminate, verify, and validate.

Calculate the trade-off for everything, it reduces waste and frustration.

Calculate passion and then calculate how to feed it so it can produce.

Forget F.O.M.O. Instead, calculate your N.M.O. Never Missing Out with your own values.

Calculate to increase luck, practice: How do M&Bs calculate business variables to increase chance at "luck"?

CHAPTER SEVEN:

Cost-Conscious

"One of the great responsibilities that I have is to manage my assets wisely so that they create value."
Alice Walton

"If you're short, take a loan. Never ask for a small amount. Ask for what you need, and always pay it back, the sooner the better."
Aristotle Onassis

"I think frugality drives innovation, just like other constraints do. One of the only ways to get out of a tight box is to invent your way out."
Jeff Bezos

DEFINITION:	*careful about spending, knowing how much different products and services cost, and not wanting to spend more money than is necessary. Implies absence of luxury and simplicity of lifestyle*
SYNONYMS:	*frugal, thrifty, and uses things to their best advantage*
ANTONYMS:	*squandering, wasteful, prodigal (the one who spent his inheritance, he didn't invest it)*

To have it isn't to spend it because to spend it isn't to have it.
~ Laine

FRUX IT!

I've heard people use the words "miser" or "frugal" interchangeably to describe the way other people manage their money. After working with M&Bs, I like to use the word "frugal" to describe their money management style.

The word frugal has an interesting history. From Merriam Webster:

> *Frugal Has Surprising Roots. Those who are frugal are unwilling to (lavishly) enjoy the fruits of their labors so it may surprise you to learn that frugal ultimately derives from the Latin frux, meaning 'fruit' or 'value,' and is even a distant cousin of the Latin word for 'enjoy' (frui).*

I assumed M&Bs spent money as soon as they earned it. But this isn't correct. M&Bs *"frui" their "frux."* They enjoy the value they produce. M&Bs sacrificed a lot to make a lot more money.

They love the fruit of their labor; they like to see it but not consume very much of it. Consuming it is not enjoyable. Instead, they enjoy its value by protecting it and only spending it on items of equal or greater value.

Frux it! means: *Value it.* M&Bs consider how many hours they worked for what they have. That one meal could cost as much as a day's labor. They consider if that's a good way to frui their frux.

MEASURE MONEY

Money isn't only money. Dave Ramsey made this clear in his Financial Peace University program. He advised students to assign money a task or identity; otherwise, it will be nothing more than money. We tend to "blow money," but we most likely won't blow "kids' shoes." Give money a purpose so it doesn't sit unprotected from a worthless identity such as "random emotional purchase."

I watched how M&Bs spend their money. They assign it a category, because the M&B has a purpose for it. If one category depletes, they don't take from another to supply it. They're quick to curb spending so it doesn't consume all their cash.

FRUGAL FINANCES

"I don't understand people like Warren Buffett who pride themselves on living in their first house and driving a used Chevy to work, despite being billionaires."
Sir James Goldsmith on Warren Buffett

A friend who is an M&B purchased a fourplex. He lives in one unit and rents the others. He works from home and drives a modest car.

Then he fell in love.

He married a woman who seemed fine with his work ethic and frugality. But once they married, she expected him to quit working so they could drink lots of wine in exotic places every day. "Got money—why work?" seemed to be her motto.

When he didn't slow down his productivity, she became angry. She couldn't live with his work ethic or frugality, so they divorced.

He's back in his groove, with friends who appreciate his principles, kindness, and generosity. This is a much better tradeoff, with a great payout.

FRUGAL PARTY

I judged M&Bs were big spenders, so when an M&B's wife asked me to buy party items for their St. Patrick's Day Party for twenty people, I thought I'd splurge. What better time to spend money than on other people for a party?

When I returned from my shopping, she asked me for the receipt. She looked at it and gasped because I spent one hundred dollars. Then she looked for a high-priced item to return to justify the splurge, but the most expensive one was two dollars. So, she gave up on the idea.

My attitude, as I looked around their million-dollar-plus home, was something a minion would say… "Whuh?"

Real-Life Frugal Practices Of M&Bs

The wealthy use credit cards with benefits. And they read their card benefit information so they can use every benefit.

They're never shy about asking to save money. They ask for seasonal discounts, age-related discounts, or damaged item discounts. They call their insurance agents to check for lower rates. They use U.P.S. instead of the post office because they get a discount at U.P.S. with their A.A.A. membership. Who knew?

As I do for my clients, I now ask for my dime back for bottles or bags, even in the face of snickering teenagers behind the register working for minimum wage. Nothing personal, it's a game.

Having money isn't, "Oh darn, I busted up my laptop, I'll go buy the latest model." M&Bs use their warranty or insurance to replace broken hardware. If that doesn't work, they'll find a model on sale and use it until it dies.

They don't indulge in a lavish lifestyle of the seven deadly sins. I knew a few people who enjoyed such a lifestyle and it quickly consumed their wealth via drugs, partying, extravagant travels, and clothing.

PURCHASES

Purchasing stuff makes some people feel good about themselves. So, to continue to feel good, they must purchase more stuff. M&Bs are practical; they don't purchase purely for the sake of the experience.

They like quality at a bargain price, so they'll look for a brand name at a secondhand store, a fashion outlet mall, or online. They work a deal to see how much they can decrease the dollar amount on a sales tag.

They don't feel good because they can afford the inflated price; adversely, they feel good because they know they don't have to pay it.

Once I overheard a guy in his thirties brag how he didn't need to shop at Target anymore. I found it humorous because a few weeks earlier, an M&B bragged to me how he bought his new cargo shorts at Target for fifteen dollars. The M&B boasted he spent less money while the non-M&B boasted he spent more.

LIMITING LIABILITY

M&Bs cut off anything that might become a financial liability, including relationships. I never thought people could be a financial liability until my umbrella incident occurred.

My new acquaintance and I had lunch. It began to rain, so we borrowed golf-sized umbrellas from the restaurant. Since we were walking down a city sidewalk, I walked behind her to allow others to pass by the enormous umbrellas. She giggled and said we needed to walk side-by-side to force people out of our way. That stunned me, but I ignored it and stayed behind her.

As I her questioned her suggestion in my mind, I stayed focused on the ground. When I looked up, I saw a man grimacing in pain as we passed each other. Then I looked at her. She was laughing. I asked her what happened, she giggled and said she hit him in the cheek with a prong of her umbrella. I stood in shock. She thought it was funny she hurt someone.

After that event, I never met with her again because someone who enjoys hurting others has serious problems. I don't live my life that way, so I don't associate with those who do.

A week later while conversing with a former college classmate, who generated a large amount of wealth, I mentioned the umbrella incident. It still bothered me. He emphatically demanded I never spend time with her. I didn't understand why. He then asked me, "What would happen if the man she hurt sued for damages?"

I didn't consider that.

Then he explained the police might consider me an accomplice to her "battery" since she thought it was funny to cause an injury. That seemed extreme, so I argued. But he had a point: when someone gets hurt and is angry, he may sue for damages for the sake of justice.

He also explained her maleficence could lead to litigation, which would require me to hire an attorney to prove my innocence. Attorneys aren't cheap. Screeching wheels moment—I hadn't thought of this. Here is a wealthy friend telling me that friends' behaviors can indirectly consume your wealth.

I was less than excellent at connecting the dots.

Then I remember an M&B discussing which kids his son spent time with because one friend had problems with the police. I realized that is another reason why M&Bs are selective with whom they and their kids work and play.

After I understood this concept of liability, a few years later an M&B mentioned someone invited her to a drug party. I think my eyebrows raised on their own. The M&Bs I work with don't use drugs. They want to be in full control of their entire being at all times. This makes life more predictable, productive, and safe.

Her sharing this piqued my curiosity. She associated with someone who throws drug parties? I asked how she knew this person. She said it was an acquaintance who decided she would inform everyone of her drug use by hosting a drug party.

Gasp. She waited for my response. Recalling my umbrella lesson, I said, "Well, there goes that relationship."

She said, "Yes," and walked away.

Now that I understood how to connect the dots, I get why M&Bs are careful. There is too much to lose. Every M&B I've worked with sticks to rules, not because they're scared, but because they're smart. They don't think the liability is worth the financial risk.

TIME AND MONEY

Foremost, for the M&B, time is just as valuable as money, or more so because it can generate more money if used properly. So, they don't waste it. They spend it to generate the most profit. *A profit is not just money, but also is a healthier relationship with others, networking, or taking care of important matters.*

M&Bs are mindful of time. As an M&B tended to her divorce, she calculated the cost and determined it was best to comply with the demands rather than attend time-wasting meetings with attorneys. Meetings minimized her opportunity to earn income. This M&B knew she could generate more money with that time and her talent than what she would lose if she complied with the negotiations. She chose her battles based on this: How much will an activity net?

WHERE THEY SKIMP AND SPLURGE

"... if you let yourself be undisciplined on the small things, you'd probably be undisciplined on the large things too."
Warren Buffett with a $10 bet.

M&Bs have a mix of second-hand, antique, and new furnishings. Antiques go up in value, so furniture becomes an asset. One M&B bragged about his antique bar cabinet he found on Craigslist. M&Bs rarely buy "market price" items, unless it is work-related, such as attire. Otherwise, they shop for trendy items at less expensive stores.

Long ago I read an article written by a fashion designer. His photo displayed him in jeans and a white long-sleeved collared shirt. He recommended people buy high-quality pieces such as blazers, slacks, shirts, pants, dresses, and skirts. Buy them in solid colors of tan, camel, white, black, blue, or navy. They are staples for a wardrobe because they last through every trend. He then recommended buying time-sensitive fashion at retail stores that bring in similar designs at a fraction of the cost.

After I read this, I observed what fashion designers wore at their fashion shows. Most of them wear what he recommended. Then I looked in the closets of M&Bs, and no surprise, they do this too.

A few years later, I spoke with a friend from my college days. I remembered he never cared about fashion while our other friend dressed like he walked off the cover of *G.Q. Magazine,* every day. It was an extreme visual contrast when the two stood side-by-side.

He called to tell me about his latest conference experience. While in a meeting, a man blurted out he couldn't bear the way Jeff dressed but then took pity on him. He pressured my friend to let him teach him how to dress. Jeff complied.

This fashion-passionate man recommended they visit the nearby outlet malls. He spent the day teaching Jeff how to suit his Scottish features of blue eyes, ginger hair color, and milky white skin.

He created a wardrobe for around three thousand dollars. This impressed frugal Jeff.

Who was this fashion-passionate man? I didn't believe my ears when he told me. He is a fashion consultant, acknowledged by the Queen of England, and qualified to dress the royal family. Imagine, a consultant identified by the Queen of England, suggested outlet malls.

Then Jeff said the most surprising thing happened to him when he returned to work. His coworkers took notice of him. He said the company president dressed nice every day, and this always intimidated him. Not once in the seven years he worked there did the president acknowledge him even though his office was a few doors down from Jeff's.

A few days into his fashion transformation, he sat working in his office when, to his surprise, the president strolled in and sat down across from him. He wanted to converse with Jeff about his new fashion sense. It impressed the president; he liked his style.

A change in attire changed the atmosphere. They have a great rapport now.

DAILY COST-CONSCIOUS LIVING

Here are a few M&Bs habits:

They:

- Fight with insurance until a claim gets resolved.
- Wait for what they want because they get a better deal with a sale.
- Categorize expenditures and monitor spending habits on their budget.
- Analyze their electricity and water bills every month.
- Turn down the heat in the house and wear sweaters to save on the electricity bill.
- Keep their receipts and I reconcile them to their credit card accounts. (I found waiters regularly stole from one M&B by

adding ten dollars to his tip after he signed the bill. If he didn't keep the receipts, I never would have identified the theft.)

- Package and freeze left-over food. They'll use a dehydrator before fruit and vegetables go bad.
- Return, recycle or repurpose items if they're not using them.
- Make donations to foundations and organizations that help others.
- They all don't drive ultra-fancy cars. Car collections sit in a safe location.
- Vacation at B&Bs or rentals instead of buying timeshares.
- Know the amount of their paycheck does not dictate their spending level. Increased income doesn't mean increased spending.
- Review their credit card statements and dispute inappropriate small charges, even if they're twenty cents. It's about principle and not tolerating abuse.
- Hate fines and fees, even library fines. They never think, "Oh it's only a ten-cent fine for the book."
- Get books for their book club at the library. If it is not available there, they borrow it, or purchase it from a secondhand bookstore.
- Love coupons, coupons, coupons! Rewards too. They register for any rewards options available. And they use them.
- Dislike shopping at high-priced grocery stores. One M&B said he just finished shopping at "Whole Paycheck." I didn't understand what he meant until he said Whole Foods just opened a store in the area.
- Use rechargeable batteries.
- Switch to LED lights. One bulb can now last twenty-five years.
- Keep revolving debt low. They don't have several credit cards. They use one for work and one for personal.

- Get a quick pass for the airport because time translates to money. They waste money standing in line.
- Save and re-gift gift bags, bows, and ribbons.
- Use paper bags from the grocery store as trash bags.
- Pay bills online and repurpose the envelopes that come with the bills to mail other items.
- Recycle paper for scratch paper.
- Bring leftovers for lunch.
- Don't keep money pits; items that need constant repair.
- Wash and reuse plastic zip baggies.

MICROMANAGING FINANCES

When I grew up, cash disappeared. I'm certain my parents' heads spun with so many kids. So, when I walked into the tightly reigned world of the M&B I didn't understand money could be managed so well. It was disappointing to find they are frugal people. I thought I would witness lots of spending with no regard for a budget.

Instead, I observed M&Bs become their own bank, and they are their first customer. They don't merely spend money; they borrow it from themselves and then pay themselves back. And they decrease expenditures until they pay off the loan.

If they buy a bottle of vitamins and drop one capsule on the floor, it may be a meaningless capsule, but if that bottle costs sixty-five dollars and there are only thirty capsules in the bottle, how much is that one meaningless capsule worth? It has a value, so when it hits the floor, it's not a capsule, it's money. Therefore, some M&Bs say the three-second rule applies; they believe it's not contaminated if they pick it up and brush it off in three seconds.

The three-second rule saves a lot of money.

FRUGAL VS. MISER

Where is the line between miserly and frugal? Miserly is *to be frugal to the point of stinginess or even give the appearance of poverty.* One M&B had an estate worth around four million dollars. He refused to make necessary repairs to his home, so it became dilapidated. At the time of his death, he drove a 1983 Toyota and lived off his pension of two thousand dollars a month. Before he died, he refused to bequeath his wealth to anyone, so it went to the government.

Another M&B I worked with grew up in a poor family. Cost-conscious is still a strong trait in him after generating a billion dollars. One day he was on his way to a bank meeting. He asked me how he looked as he brushed lint from his coat sleeves. He wore a sports coat over a shirt, vest and tie, with khaki pants and leather shoes. I complimented him on his attire; he was well-put together. When he turned to walk away, I noticed the tattered hem of his pants. The rest of the pants were good enough, so he will wear them until they give out completely.

One afternoon as I waited for an M&B to arrive home, I stood in the kitchen admiring their home. A three-story six thousand square foot home with beautiful hardwood floors, vaulted ceilings, and picture windows with stunning views.

His wife walked past me while he went to sit down on the couch. A few seconds later he put his feet up on the ottoman. Then he quickly put them down after he saw the look of surprise on my face. The bottom of his socks had big holes.

I learned that day even M&Bs have favorite socks, no matter how much of them are missing.

FRUGAL CONDO M&BS

I know three M&Bs who live in six hundred square foot condos. One an attorney, the other a couple investing in real estate. The attorney downsized to send his kids to two good colleges while the couple uses their income to build their portfolio.

I asked the attorney if he originally planned to become a millionaire. He didn't. He simply enjoyed his work, so he worked a lot. But, he also knows the value of his work and abides by customary fees for his expertise.

Earning money represents him: his dedication, hard work, and good name. So, spending money is spending him. He chooses to spend himself on his kids' futures.

The real estate couple spend their money (representation of themselves) on real estate and entertaining clients. Their mortgage payment is approximately one thousand dollars a month. They're happy with the smaller space since there's less to clean and more money available to invest in real estate.

Before she became a real estate agent, she was a Ph.D. physicist professor. When she became a U.S. citizen, a prestigious university offered her a position, but the pay was very low. Then she learned how much money she could earn as a real estate agent, so she repositioned herself. She moved into an industry that could pay her for exceptional performance.

English isn't her first language, she learned it when she immigrated. Now she speaks English with a thick accent. She struggled to learn real estate in a foreign country with limited language skills, but she turned her pain into profit. Her pain is now her niche. She provides real estate services for people who are just as she was: new to this country, limited English and limited understanding of real estate.

She works hard in her niche, sometimes working seven days a week. If it means cleaning a house on her own to list it sooner, she does. She's a millionaire scrubbing toilets.

She also isn't afraid to acknowledge her work. Sometimes she asks me in broken English, "Can I talk about myself?" I always respond, "Yes, please! After all your hard work, you deserve to."

She tells me how proud she is of her deals, not because of the money, but because of the challenges she overcame to close them. Then when she hits a robust six-figure quarter, she tells me how much she earned because of closing those difficult deals. She praises herself, just like we used to do when we were kids. When did that stop? It doesn't with M&Bs.

I share these stories of "Condo M&Bs" to point out they practiced the 13 Cs before they became M&Bs. The only difference between the two is, one found a career early on that could pay him well, while the other chose a field, teaching physics, that couldn't.

M&B PROBLEMS

I assumed, before working for M&Bs, their lives were like a TV show. A controlled set, everyone had a place, life was easy and perfect. Then I learned the truth. M&Bs experience problems just like me:

Their:

- Cars have bizarre problems I never knew could happen.
- Toilet chain breaks.
- Fan goes out.
- Power goes out.
- Kids lose their retainers in the school lunchroom trash.
- Kids get sick.
- Pets get sick and die.
- House needs repair from water damage.
- Credit cards get stolen.
- Identity gets stolen.
- Insurance doesn't cover services as it should.
- Family members die.

They:

- Suffer divorce.
- Lose friends and family over their decisions.
- Receive annoying solicitations.
- Face health problems.
- Get confused, lost, and irritated.
- Get over-charged and double charged.
- Have software download problems.
- Burglars attempt to rob them, and more.

WE ALL SUFFER LOSS AND PAIN, JOY AND GAIN

I used to presume life was easier for them because they had money; therefore, they don't experience problems. I was wrong again. Having assets doesn't make them impervious to frustration, disappointment, or anger. Many issues irritate an M&B all day long too, but they use the 5 Ps to buffer and reduce the impact of those issues.

RECAP

FRUX IT ALL! Enjoy your money don't consume it.

Name your dollars, give them a purpose.

The frugal lifestyle is similar to creating a fine piece of art: it requires commitment to create one.

Being frugal doesn't have to be miserly.

Preserve wealth by choosing no-risk relationships.

Problems can consume money and emotions, use personal loan agreements and boundaries to preserve wealth.

Save dollars on your fashion passion by shopping at discount stores and second-use shops.

You're never too old to change careers or learn.

CHAPTER EIGHT:

Consistent and Committed

"You can never quit. Winners never quit, and quitters never win."
Ted Turner

"One day or day one, the choice is yours."
Paulo Coelho

"I like rich people. I like the way they live. I like the way I live when I'm with them."
Max Detweiler, The Sound of Music

CONSISTENT DEFINITION: *marked by harmony, regularity, or steady continuity: free from variation or contradiction, showing steady conformity to character, profession, belief, or custom, devoted*

SYNONYMS: *bring about effect, effectuate, implement constant, faithful, firm, nonconflicting, unchanging, steady*

ANTONYMS: *conflicted, variable, disobedient, falsity*

COMMITMENT DEFINITION: *an engagement or obligation that restricts freedom of action*

SYNONYMS: *promise, pledge, guarantee*

ANTONYMS: *breach, broken promise, irresponsibility*

"Sweat equity is the most valuable equity there is. Know your business and industry better than anyone else in the world. Love what you do or don't do it."
Mark Cuban

DISCIPLINED AND COMMITTED

In fourteen years of work, I only saw two M&B's call in sick, and for each, it was only once. And they worked from home while they were sick. None of them "played hooky" just to use their sick days.

ROUTINE, ROUTINE, ROUTINE

"You know… you keep doing the same things and you keep getting the same result over and over again."
Warren Buffett

M&B's start each day with a routine. I considered a routine as stodgy, boring, and narrow, but I now realize it provides freedom. Following a routine trains our brains to develop habits. Habits require less analysis which allows the brain's frontal cortex to contemplate more important issues.

Morning isn't a rush; they like to begin their day in a relaxed state of mind. Each morning has the same routine and starts early. Routines help M&Bs focus on their workday before it begins.

In contrast some people believe a chaotic morning is energizing. Negative energy gives them a buzz. This is counterproductive. Stress reduces deep breathing which constricts blood and oxygen flow to the brain. A morning of chaos can deplete us before our workday begins.

Routines help us experience stability. M&Bs know the value of routines so they're not easily derailed from them.

A consistent routine provides organization for the brain and establishes calm. M&Bs live by systems and patterns. They're not "free-spirited" hippies from the sixties, blown like a leaf in the wind, letting it carry them wherever it may. Instead, they will fold that leaf into a sail, use the stem as a rudder and ride the wind to where they want and the way they want, as best they can.

STAY STEADY

During difficult times, M&Bs refuse to panic. This is the opposite of how I reacted during my first scuba diving experience.

I took a crash course in diving while on vacation. I'm sure some of you reading this shook your head. You understand how dangerous it is to put people in scuba gear and drop them forty feet deep into the ocean without formal training.

It was a bumpy boat ride to the drop site. While we put on our dive gear, one guy struggled with sea sickness. He vomited in his respirator. Awful to listen to, and where can you go on a small boat to avoid that heaving sound? It encouraged the rest of us to jump from the topsy-turvy boat.

As we proceeded down toward the ocean floor, the water pressure increased, compressing my eyes and ears. I didn't find it sublime but tolerated it because I wanted to see the plethora of beautiful tropical fish the guides promised us. At about twenty feet below the surface, I began to question what I was doing. I realized I had a limited source of oxygen, only accessible through a *very* narrow hose.

Deeper we went, and I suffered more pain in my ears. When we floated a few feet above the ocean floor, the underwater world around me glowed blue, including a turtle and four tropical fish. I thought, "Well, now, where are all the fish? Everything is blue, what's the point of diving? Why am I here if everything is blue?" This irritated me.

Water pressure, ear pain, blue turtle, blue fish, blue sand, blue water, and a skinny hose overwhelmed my senses. So, what did I do?

I breathed harder, just like they told me not to do.

With my fast, shallow breathing I worried I might use up my air. Then the water squeezed me tighter. The air hose became a narrow straw upon which my life depended. Air didn't come fast enough. My emotions escalated.

I wanted out *right then*. Maybe if I took a big breath, ripped out the mouthpiece and swam to the surface, I might make it. But I might drown or get the bends. I needed an escape, but my only options might kill me. I wanted out, but not that way.

After this fast analysis of options, I caught myself professing, "Oh God, I can't even panic right now." This statement stunned me, it held me motionless, suspended between the water's surface and the ocean floor.

I had to *choose* my fate.

Realizing panicking could kill me, I made myself considered my choices again: death, the bends, or a calm and slow ascent. I didn't want any of these, but I settled for the least traumatic, the latter.

Because I listened to and followed instructions instead of panicking, I'm here today to say I made it to the surface, back to billions of liters of free floating non-compressed air. I ripped the mouthpiece out of my face and gulped in air through my skin, nose AND mouth.

I'm thankful I survived the most panic-stricken moment of my life.

For me this was a life-or-death circumstance. The most surreal feeling in that state of panic wasn't the panic. It was realizing by thinking, I overruled the panic. I learned I can separate the circumstances from my feelings and make a mindful decision during a distressing moment. For the first time in my life, I understood the truth: I'm not controlled by panic, that even in fearful times I can still find a moment to reason and then choose.

After this enlightenment, I realized I panic sometimes because I don't want a circumstance to develop a certain way. My panic button is really an ejection seat, it gets me out of it at once. Panicking was my easy way out instead of working through an uncomfortable circumstance.

The deep blue turned into a deep moment of deep self-reflection. That epiphany must have been the deeper reason I tried scuba diving, so I need not do it again. I choose to snorkel. Way bigger straw and closer to more air.

M&B SCUBA FACE

What does this experience have to do with M&Bs? I call it the M&B Scuba Face, and I see it often. It used to bother me until I remembered my diving experience. I probably looked poker face to the other divers forty feet deep, but I was in survival mode, contemplating my death.

Even though my experience was horrific, I managed to gain control of my emotions long enough to ask myself what options were available.

This is what M&Bs do. When something unexpected happens, they first "freeze" to have an internal conversation. They look as though they're poker face or in Scuba Face (the way I looked when I was underwater contemplating my death) because they're consulting with themselves first. When they finish their conversation, they make a decision.

What I had to learn in a life-threatening experience, M&Bs do naturally.

SQUEEZING PENNIES SQUEEZES YOU

Self-made M&Bs say "no" to expenditures often. This can put a squeeze on emotions and social life, but the desire to grow wealth is more important. And they impress upon others, including their employees, to have the same desire.

One M&B gave me a bonus, but on one condition: I invest it in my future. I cringed. But I agreed to the terms and made the painful pledge. It hurt each time I got a bonus. But Jim Rohn was right when he said, "He will either feel the pain from discipline or the pain of regret."

This M&B wanted to build me up financially by expecting me to preserve income. Because of her, I bought Facebook when it became publicly traded. Others mocked me when I bought it "too high" at forty-one dollars a share. They're not laughing at me now.

M&Bs practice delayed gratification and encourage others to do the same. Several profitable investments wouldn't have happened had I not made the decision to save and not spend.

COMMITMENT COSTS

Remember the self-made M&B accountant turned CFO? Her story is likewise a great example of Commitment.

When I first met her, she was a CFO of a NASDAQ-traded company. She is sassy, smart, energetic, funny, attractive, drives a Porche, and wears high heels and professional length leather skirts.

I knew she had to have a great story. So, I asked how she became a CFO.

She began her story, noting, when her company first hired her for an accounting position, a female coworker targeted her. She worked ten years building her career while a coworker maligned her.

I asked her if she was insane, staying in that environment. Her response surprised me. She claimed she wanted to pursue a long-term career there and chose to endure the battle with this coworker because she believed in the company and the president.

Three important elements I gleaned from her statement:

- She recognized she couldn't become the CFO without good synergy with others at the top.
- She recognized where her control ended and where someone else's began.
- Her performance wasn't the decision-maker; the president was.

I heard her identify her advantage over adversity: it was the president's integrity. She saw his wisdom and potential to grow the company. And she believed he would value her performance.

Essentially, she positioned herself. She rooted her expectation not only in her performance but also in a great leader and the potential of the company. *When M&Bs calculate their Position, they analyze leadership.* She "hitched her wagon to a star," a business and a boss with a promising future.

"Ok, I get why she stayed," I reasoned. But how did she keep herself from engaging with the coworker? Wouldn't she try to find out what the coworker said so she could counter it? From where did she draw strength to work hard every day? I wondered how she stayed consistent.

I asked her how she handled the negative coworker E-V-E-R-Y day.

She stated four things helped her. First, she joined an exercise class with a group of women who consistently attended. They dedicated to each other their support; it wasn't just an exercise class. She vented to her husband, as much as he could handle, but surrounded by women she resonated with was a big boost.

I heard her sigh in relief as she spoke of them. She said their support helped save her career.

M&B men practice this too. They give time to a group sport such as golf or tennis. Relationships and their competitive nature keep them engaged for decades. In these tight circles they build their moral.

The saying "it's lonely at the top" is somewhat true. It's lonely because few people vow to reach their pinnacle of performance. The ones who do must search for others who share similar convictions. When they find them, they keep them. Everyone needs camaraderie.

Second, and she said this was the most difficult to do, she had to trust that her boss, the president, inclined himself to see through the lies and look at her performance instead of the personal attacks. She didn't want him distracted from her work, so she never presented her coworker's slander to him.

She specified she wanted her commitment to her work to speak louder than the gossip he heard.

Third, she chose to "keep moving forward" by focusing on her performance and leaving alone what she couldn't control: the president's thoughts and decisions, and the coworker's behavior. She understood the only variables she could control were her attitude, commitment, and performance.

Fourth, she said, she processed her feelings. When she did, she saw an image of a cyclone instead of her coworker. She then understood this woman created chaos each time she went to the president's office. She tried to spin in his space, to suck him into her cyclone.

This vision helped the M&B desensitize the situation. She practiced visualizing a cyclone instead of a coworker which helped her disengage from the chaos. This M&B practiced this for a decade, earned promotions, and became CFO.

Storms run out of wind and dissipate. The cyclone (coworker) quit her job because they never promoted her.

ON TO NASDAQ

After her promotion to CFO, the company became a NASDAQ-traded company. It isn't easy dealing with scrutiny from the NASDAQ or investors. She said she faces constant pressure to please the board instead of customers. She compared it to, "Walking a tight rope most of the time."

She also mentioned people from both the board and the exchange visit her company. Sometimes these visitors don't know who she is. During one visit, her attire visibly irritated a man. He looked at her blonde hair, her high heels and condescendingly asked her who she was. She tilted her head and said she was a hairdresser. He rolled his eyes and gave her a "well that explains it" look, while she walked past him. Later he learned who she was.

After that experience, she made this her policy: if someone doesn't approve of how she looks, she doesn't care to correct their devaluation of her. If they want to make a nasty judgment; they can have it. She leaves them with it as she moves along her groove.

She's developed a thick skin. Now she makes a game of the sexism.

A second detail she happily shared was younger women at work tell her they appreciate how comfortable she is with her femininity in the workplace. They say the way she dresses encourages them to value their individuality. This is a "natural-born leader" in my opinion; someone who inspires others without knowing or trying to do so.

THE WRONG WAGON

As I wrote this chapter, a mini-crisis occurred with a non-M&B's home while the non-M&B vacationed in Asia. I needed a plumber, fast. So I called one that was highly recommended. He arrived posthaste, evaluated the problem, and scheduled sub-contractors for the next day. Great job.

The next day I waited for the sub-contractors. No one arrived. More damage ensued. I called customer service to ask for clarity and help. As I asked how to resolve the problem, the girl snapped, "I'm done talking about this," and hung up on me. This is an emergency plumbing company that just hung up on a client with an emergency, worth several thousands of dollars to them.

I called the plumber. He said he would fix the customer service problem. Several hours later this same service representative called me. Her tone was that of a person who didn't care and didn't want to amend the situation. This wasted my time.

I fired that plumbing company and hired a new one. Great results happened with the new plumber, and all the chaos disappeared.

Later that day the no-show sub-contractor called to tell me he lost his phone the night before so he couldn't make it to the job in the morning. I asked him why he couldn't call the office to get the address, since they're an on-call emergency service company. He didn't respond.

What does a plumber have to do with a CFO?

The CFO recognized where her amazing abilities ended—on the president's desk. This plumber didn't recognize what the CFO did.

The accountant realized her desire to become CFO depended not only on her performance but also on the president's leadership. This plumber didn't realize his future is reliant on no-show sub-contractors and unprofessional customer service. His excellence skills cannot make up for poor management.

This most amazing plumber can't control his coworkers' unprofessionalism. He lost the next two jobs: plumbing a new addition and plumbing a new home. And the company lost all future recommendations from two referral companies.

He hooked his wagon to a falling star, a poor Position.

ROUTINES AND ROLES REQUIRE BREAKS

Routines help M&Bs fulfill their life roles. This reduces minutiae and confusion. Each role keeps them present to experience a moment. Be the boss. Be the host. Be Dad. Be Mom. Roles are smooth grooves they slide into easily.

But roles can be never-ending. That's why they frequently use a break switch.

I worked for an M&B on the executive floor of the building he owned. He took naps on the couch in his office. Besides me, only his secretary knew what it meant when he closed his office door.

Why take naps or breaks? Taking them is a powerful strategy to maintain consistent performance.

I remember a motivational speaker shared a story of a researcher who wanted to understand why the top tennis players' performance was at a level no other players could match (no pun intended).

After many hours of studying their matches, he concluded their wins were not only because of great technique but also relative to mastering fatigue. These top performers far outlasted their competition. After a while, he concluded they must use illegal drugs because their performance seemed enhanced.

But then he saw it, something only the top performers did, and the others didn't.

He observed top performers take mental breaks during their matches. What does this mean? How do they take a break during a match? Watch Nadal or Federer play a match or two and see if you can catch the mental breaks they take.

These elite performers go to their happy place for a few seconds. They may play with the strings on their rackets or follow a quick setup routine before a serve. They do this to relax their bodies, to breathe deeper. Deeper breathing increases oxygen flow and decreases heart rate.

I believe the speaker said this practice can lower their heart rates by twenty points per minute. Twenty beats lower means they can last longer against an opponent whose body becomes constricted with each set.

The researcher noted the secret to their winning is their ability to rest in the sets.

A break, even a short one, to ground oneself is powerful for the mind and body. M&Bs take breaks to recharge so they can get back to what they love.

And noted by WebMD, "... researchers concluded that people who took naps at least three times a week for an average of at least 30 minutes were 37% less likely to die of heart disease than people who did not take regular naps."

COMMITMENT TO SOLVING PROBLEMS

M&Bs enjoy playing the Whack-a-Mole Game with problems. When one comes up, they knock it down. If it comes back up, they get angry and knock it down harder each time. After watching this behavior, I found it interesting how their self-perception doesn't change if a problem doesn't resolve as soon as they wanted.

They:

- Don't rationalize if a problem resurfaces, then something must be wrong with them as a person.
- Don't negotiate with guilt or self-criticism, instead they find another solution.
- Are relentless, they accept the reality that problems will never quit, so neither will they.
- Perceive quitting is failure, but having problems is not.

THE PAIN OF SHAME

Sometimes we unknowingly spend more time with shame rather than with our Passion. M&Bs spend most of their time with their Passion. They forgive and give themselves permission to pursue happiness. They snub shame; otherwise it can become a constant force working against them.

In my many years of experience, I can say none of the M&Bs I know feels guilty, but they all feel grateful. They consider it's a miracle they made it this far. Because luck is finicky, they're humbled it happened to them.

Gratefulness is another M&B tool. It isn't a weak gratefulness but a, "Whew, look how bad it could have been," or, "Made it by the skin of my teeth," perspective. They use gratefulness to keep a positive spin on their struggles, it prevents the negative downward spiral shame likes to inflict.

FIGHT SHAME

One way M&Bs fight shame is with a promise to do good for others. They exploit opportunities to help more people. This builds their self-esteem and encourages them to disregard shame.

M&Bs made peace with their pasts by choosing to build their self-esteem on their future, what will be, not what has been and gone.

Their concept of their future regards only what they can create. That potential added to their dedication to their passion, skills, gratefulness and a little luck is where they rest their esteem, not on a limited past. It has no potential.

M&Bs don't rehash their past. They settle it with forgiveness and treat it as a lesson learned. They have a conversation with Self and, if they can find something they learned from a poor decision, they gained value. That is most important. Value means productive. Productive means valuable. *They're productive therefore they're valuable.*

In all my years of my working with M&Bs, I never heard one use the word "failure." A decision either works out or doesn't. Even if it's a divorce or an unhealthy relationship, they label it with the phrase, "Did not work out." By doing so, they limit the opportunity for shame to inhabit the atmosphere.

If you can glean value from a negative experience, then it isn't a failure. It just didn't work out.

M&Bs Have Little Whine

"If you really want to do something, you'll find a way. If you don't, you'll find an excuse."
-Jim Rohn

I never heard an M&B whine. It's impressive. They too face serious problems money cannot fix. But they believe they can find a solution to work with, so that's why they don't whine.

One M&B reminded me of a butterfly more than any person I've known. When an undesirable circumstance encloses her like a cocoon, she bursts out of it with new wings. She always morphs into something better after each negative experience.

She is a true change-around artist because she devotes herself to her future, not her past disappointments.

COMMITTED TO THEIR CHILDREN

One late afternoon I watched an M&B couple debate over what to feed their kids for dinner. The wife is a self-made M&B; she mastered her industry and now manages a global company.

They picked an organic pre-packaged microwavable dinner from the freezer. Together they put the package in the microwave for the specified time. When it was finished, they each carried one end of the dinner to the counter to measure the temperature. It hadn't made it to the required 165 degrees, so they microwaved it again. They watched the microwave to track the time and when done, together carried it to the counter as if it was a ticking bomb.

They huddled over it again. It still hadn't reached 165 degrees. So they carried it together to microwave it again. And again. This happened four times. The process ended because the thermometer could no longer pierce the dehydrated meat. They threw it away.

They never bought that product again because it didn't abide by the rules. It didn't produce the promised results. There is no tolerance for things that don't follow the rules. *The rules are; follow the rules, because rules produce.*

M&Bs agree to follow rules and expect their children to do the same.

For children, when parents stay committed and consistent, it produces stability and security. An M&B couple promised their children one of them would always be home by six p.m. every workday. One day one child sat quietly doing his homework. He looked around for me and commented, "I know either my mom or dad will always be home at six p.m.," and then went back to his homework.

That was random and stunning. I didn't realize how important consistency is to children until that moment. I saw comfort in a child as a direct result of his parents' devotion. In the five years I worked with them, one parent was always home by six p.m.

OVERNIGHT MILLIONAIRE

I see sales pitches promoting how to become an overnight millionaire. They say to become one requires a person quit what he knows and pursue something he doesn't know, under the tutelage of the person selling the training.

The expert trainer promises shy people their personality will morph into the greatest salesman on earth. And within a few months, they'll be managing a multimillion-dollar business. This can happen, but rarely. From what I observed, it happened to those who hid their gifts to make a paycheck but came out of hiding to do what they do naturally—promote.

Self-made M&Bs I know didn't earn their wealth overnight or even in a few years. They kept their focus on one industry and worked it for decades. M&Bs understood generating and preserving wealth is a long-term strategy.

In addition to hard work, they made career adjustments. If they wanted to spin off into a subset of their industry, they investigated their interest while working their current position. They didn't jump from a ship that wasn't sinking into an unknown one just to become an overnight millionaire. Instead, they continued to work in a stable job until they developed suitable experience to modify their career. Fast money wasn't their aim, so they didn't follow the road sign that read, "Fast Money Ahead."

The ability of M&Bs to perform is their safety net, it's not in having money.

RECAP

ROUTINE, ROUTINE, ROUTINE. Create grooves to reduce brain fatigue and increase mental endurance.

AVOID MAX DETWEILER. He prefers to enjoy your commitment and consistency, so he doesn't need to produce his own.

ENJOY PLAYING WHACK-A-MOLE. Expect problems to happen so you can enjoy crushing them.

BRIGHT STAR. Stick with a position in a company with great leadership.

CRUSH CHAOS. Avoid cyclones, it's good for your health and performance.

LEARN TO SCUBA FACE. Step away from a stressful moment to think. Breathe. Then respond.

TAKE A BREAK OR A NAP. Lower your risk for heart disease while you boost performance.

USE LABELS FOR THE PAST. Simplify to "Did not work out," to avoid rehashing the past.

BUILD YOUR ESTEEM ON YOUR FUTURE NOT YOUR PAST. What you are becoming has more potential.

BE GRATEFUL, IT TAMES SHAME. Feel good about what good you will do for others in the future.

CHAPTER NINE:

Closure

"Part of being a winner is knowing when enough is enough. Sometimes you have to give up the fight and walk away and move on to something that's more productive."
Donald Trump

"The most important thing to do if you find yourself in a hole is to stop digging."
Warren Buffett

"Should you find yourself in a chronically leaking boat, energy devoted to changing vessels is likely to be more productive than energy devoted to patching leaks."
—1996 letter from Buffett to shareholders.

DEFINITION: *A sense of finality, resolution or conclusion*

SYNONYMS: *Cease, discontinue, shut off, stop*

ANTONYMS: *Continue, go on and on, remember*

CLOSURE IS MOVEMENT

I used to think Closure was the end of something, so if I made a decision, it was final. This meant my decisions had to be perfect. I regularly sat paralyzed in analysis, afraid that if I didn't make the right decision, there wouldn't be more choices.

Then I had a brief conversation with a retired soldier. He had the same problem when he first started as a second lieutenant. One day he shared with his colonel he was too nervous to make a decision. The colonel responded, "Just lead." This startled him, so the colonel explained "leading" means making decisions.

The colonel extrapolated, telling him a decision produces both positive and negative results, so don't worry about the results, but look for opportunities the decision produced. The results from each decision can be harnessed to produce his desired end-result, or close to it.

The colonel taught him that closure doesn't mean "finished," but, "make another decision." Closure helps us move closer to a desired result.

Thomas Edison continued to experiment until his hope to create incandescent light came to fruition. What others claim to be failures; Edison considered otherwise. After testing more than six thousand materials, he said he "... constructed three thousand different theories in connection with electric light." To Edison, decisions didn't produce failures, they produced more opportunities for more decisions.

A patent attorney echoed the same concept to me. He said the only way to handle a passion for a patentable idea that's been rejected is to challenge the examiner's rationale until it gets allowed or can't go any further.

Either kill it or bring it to life with your efforts.

CLOSURE IS GOLDEN

Closure is also the commitment to stop rehearsing an uncomfortable memory or poor decision. Otherwise, rehearsing can lead us to believe the experience isn't over. If it isn't over, there is possibly more embarrassment or pain to suffer. So, M&Bs make a decision about an experience, label it, store it, and move on.

Never do they go back for a swim in the muck they escaped.

Closure is a win for M&Bs, no matter what. They never consider closure defeat, but perceive it gives them control over the final impact of a circumstance. They decide its influence. Closure is their choice. Therefore, they don't fear it because it's empowering.

CLOSURE CUTS DEEP

One evening, before bed, I read a short article on high performers' habits. It mentioned they "move on." That irritated me. In my frustration I grumbled, "Whatever that means," tossed the article to the floor and went to sleep.

The next morning, I arrived at work at 4:45 a.m. The M&B calmly greeted me and said we were starting in her office that morning. As we stepped inside, she mentioned she wanted to shred paperwork. I shrugged my shoulders, still a little groggy that early in the morning.

I watched as she pulled from her desk two two-inch thick manila file folders. I didn't know what they were; I was simply there to help shred them. Then she faced me, held them up in her left hand, to the height of her head, and announced, "This is over one million dollars of assets that I no longer have. I want to shred the memory of it, get rid of anything related to it, and never discuss it again. [illegible]t to forget about it."

I stood frozen, now wide awake with shock, staring at the files. My chin dropped. I couldn't believe it. More than one million dollars, gone, that fast. Years of dedicated work, security and peace now gone.

Then I remembered the article. It clicked! I understood "moving on" and the grit it takes to do so. In my excitement of understanding, I blurted (to my own embarrassment), "Wow! You're just like the article I read about high performers. You move on and don't look back." I stared at her in amazement.

Right before my eyes, what I read the night before, I now witnessed on a grand scale. She no longer had this enormous amount of money, yet she chose to move past the memory of it.

Then I remembered how I scrutinized the article, "Yeah right, these people never face difficult things, they're on such a roll, nothing touches them, they have it easy." But there I stood, in the presence of an M&B, slammed by a huge financial loss, yet handling it *exactly* how the article said these people do. They shut it down, get closure. And—they plan for a comeback.

We shredded in silence, and my narrow-minded judgments surfaced. I felt sheepish. I couldn't look at the numbers I shredded. I questioned if I could experience what she did and then do what she did. Or would I crumble? I cringed thinking of it.

She did what the article said these people do: she rid herself of the memories of the loss and focused her attention back to doing what made her millions before. She redirected her anger to work her methods better this next time, on her comeback plan.

In the following years she earned greater income than before, and for the first time, earned national recognition for her performance. Ten years later, true to her commitment, never once was this experience mentioned. Closure helped her move forward.

Few times I am left in awe and humbled. This will always be one of those times because I've never seen a human do what a butterfly can do: emerge from a dark place, bigger and bolder than when it entered.

Useless decisions are those made today, for yesterday.
~ Laine

Every day after this event I watched this M&B move forward. She refused to nurse judgements such as, "I should have or shouldn't have..." It was over, and no going back. There isn't a memory jar of past losses on her desk.

M&Bs don't believe a bad experience defines their future. Every day they beat a bad experience into a good future. This is how they handle their present time.

M&Bs live in the present. They may dabble in a few memories and plan for the future, but mostly live in the now. They make decisions today: getting resolution on ideas, projects, or next steps. Making decisions today keeps them engaged in the now, where they are most powerful.

We all are most powerful in our now.

CLOSURE WITHOUT SHAME

Closure likewise means practicing honesty without any shame or guilt. This M&B didn't inflict herself with guilt or shame over the loss. Instead she moved on by clarifying what she wanted and the strategy to achieve it.

Time and energy spent on guilt and shame is time wasted.

HEROES AT HEART

Heroes bear similar character traits: courage, tenacity, dedication, compassion, loyalty, accountability, wisdom, honesty, sacrifice and more. Overall, heroes have a bent in life such that "the glass is half full." There always is an opportunity to seize somewhere; they only need to find it. This isn't a simple positive mental attitude or mantra but rather a healthy dose of heroism: specific characteristics applied consistently.

Consistent application brings about a hero's reward: "to the victor belongs the spoils." In our business-oriented world, a financial gain is the usual measure of a hero's triumph. Heroes know their traits are measured by their reward; therefore, they feel no shame in great gain.

M&Bs exemplify these same traits and exercise them daily to produce gainful results. Because they generate profitable outcomes for themselves and others, they sincerely believe their work brings good to the world. That's what heroes do; they conquer adversity to benefit themselves and others.

FAITH IS: WHERE YOU PUT YOUR TRUST

M&Bs have faith in their abilities, not in negative experiences. They don't converse with prior shortcomings, instead, they talk with their abilities. They discuss how to outperform and outlast the negative with plans of good objectives.

They trust in their abilities to produce. They contemplate and conclude, "I earned it this way before, so I can earn it this way again." Only next time they increase their productivity because the first time they had to cut the path—now every subsequent time, they follow it.

PAST IS SUPPORT

When M&Bs recall their history, it is to analyze prior experiences that helped them make beneficial decisions, not to seek shame or blame. They look back for the path that led them to productivity.

When the M&B lost her million, she didn't reason, "I lost all of that money, now I have to find a different way of earning money, because this loss means I must have failed at my earning strategy I used to grow it." They don't fall for that lie, they simply tweak their strategy, like Edison did, three thousand times.

The ex-M&B doctor certainly is in the mindset, "It won't work this time." He produced his first million providing specialized treatments for those suffering from degenerative diseases. It was a powerful practice.

When he reaches into his past he doesn't find support to rebuild, he only finds shame and blame. The underlying shame still has its grip on him. It tells him doctors are not as important as businessmen.

So he rehashes his loss, decades later. Sadly, he doesn't recognize his belief system helped him lose his money and continues to keep him from rebuilding it. He believes his profession is the problem, not his valuation of it. He cannot create closure due to his continued relationship with shame and blame. They're jealous, unhealthy lovers.

CLOSURE OVER CONTENTION AND COMPLAINING

M&Bs don't stray far from their happy place. Why waste good vibes on a useless argument? Conflict isn't their connection style. If conflict occurs, it is used to find resolve. They don't engage in a heated conversation to cause strife because that's unproductive.

M&Bs don't start frivolous debates or arguments to prove others wrong. They listen to others' opinions, politely disagree, and do not engage with those who cannot have a civil conversation. They don't believe they have to tolerate contention.

Instead they prefer to stay focused on positive events that remind them of progress made, what worked and what didn't. What they will do again or not. Negative memories are brief, labeled as a decision made, and then filed.

Closure is simple to them. How do I know? Because I notice when an M&B is lost in thought then suddenly says, "Remember when we did ___, and it fixed ______? That was great wasn't it?" They're always thinking about positive results and on to the next opportunity.

CLOSURE MEANS BANISHED

If M&Bs purchase an item but something goes awry, they don't keep the item and complain relentlessly. They acknowledge their frustration then take action to remedy it. A term they practice is "cut bait." That means they stop having a relationship with it; exchange or donate it, which brings closure to complaining and contention. They don't keep a "fix-it" pile. I used to judge this was wrong, they should fix things, but I soon realized how much time and space these piles consume.

Once an M&B creates closure with a problem, that newly resolved problem no longer gets attention. They extinguish it from their conscious memory. I never hear a complaint regarding something that happened a decade ago or last week.

They banish negative statements. I never hear them say, "you always," or "you never" in conversations. They work in the present only. They also understand complaining isn't a request. Instead, they state in a positive manner what they prefer to experience with someone.

ANTITHESIS OF CLOSURE

C[illegible]unday afterr[illegible] I heard my neighbor complaining about c[illegible]e caused by[illegible]e leak. Visibly upset and becoming more upset as she complained, I asked if the pipe and damages were repaired. I hoped she would find closure and comfort by remembering her insurance repaired the damage. In a fast breath she said it was repaired but hurried back to her complaints.

Her response surprised me. Why would she complain if it was over and repaired? Out of curiosity, I asked her when it occurred. She said it happened over fifteen years ago. I didn't know what to say. Sadly, it's as though it just happened to her.

Many years later, I overheard her telling a new neighbor the same story. As I walked by, I mentioned when it happened and the new neighbor sighed, "Oh, okay it wasn't recent." She felt released from the dramafest.

The insurance paid for a remodel, so why not be happy for the remodel and call it a day? It could be that some people prefer to stay in the battle instead of gaining a victory.

Sometimes closure is the best victory.

ELEVATOR PITCH

An elevator pitch is a brief description of a concept or idea used to help others gain quick understanding. M&Bs use these in business but also in their personal lives. They sum up a negative experience with a small caption or phrase, then use the phrase as a label. They use the label to quickly frame the experience and disregard sharing the offending details. M&Bs either recognize, consciously or not, that rehashing the past is stress inducing to the brain. Nor does it build confidence.

It isn't fear of the past for why they use these captions—it's so they can move on to something more productive. A label on a box can quickly shut down questions about its contents. By classifying a negative experience, M&Bs remind themselves they made peace with it already. They found answers, hence the label, so no need to dig around in the box for answers again.

M&Bs don't ignore the past, they process it, judge it, and label it. Labels save time and energy.

LINE IN THE SAND

M&Bs aren't perfect people, but they certainly move on the best way they know how. This means they're no longer in a relationship with what happened years ago, right now. They separate today from yesterday. They respect boundaries with themselves, their hurts, their memories, and others, and they don't cross those lines.

While in conversation with a U.S. Marine one day, he taught me something I still use to this day. He said while serving overseas, his project frustrated him, so he complained to his sergeant. The sergeant stopped him mid-tirade and asked him if he was working on a solution. He said, "No." Then the sergeant told him he was allowed to complain if he was working on a solution.

This Marine stood gaping. It first messed with his mind. He could complain? Then it inspired him because he could grumble all the way to a solution. This led to him making progress on his problem.

This sergeant prevented a Marine from heading into a downward spiral of chaos by interrupting him with a paradigm shift. It made this now old Marine, years later, choose to look for solutions when he wants to complain.

I watch M&Bs problem solve this same way when they're frustrated. They attack a problem; they don't stop to complain or fester over it. M&Bs are M&Bs because they're problem solvers, not complainers.

The M&Bs I worked with made their money by solving problems for those in need of a solution. They're happy to have a problem to solve, it's their job security.

COMPLAINING CREATES CONFLICT

I've not heard M&Bs complain incessantly about work. For an M&B, if they see a problem, they either fix it or they fix the person producing the problem.

Only once did I hear an M&B say something negative about a coworker. It surprised me since they don't like complaining. This M&B recently retired, then decided to build a new company. While he raised capital, he built his star team.

His prior employees and coworkers liked him so much they wanted to move with him to his new venture. Interestingly, he refused to take one former coworker with him. I asked why.

He said the coworker claimed he was a victim and refused to resolve his self-inflicted problems. He made ridiculous demands about what he deserved (even though similarly skilled employees didn't have what he deemed he deserved). In addition, he caused conflict with others inside the company.

The M&B captioned his experience with this coworker in a simple phrase, labeled it and never dealt with the person again. He called him a "whiner." M&Bs even keep their labels concise.

DIAL DOWN THE DRAMA

None of the M&Bs I've worked with are into histrionics, scary movies, or events that might cause fear. They stay in a mental bandwidth bereft of unnecessary emotional intensity.

For the M&B it wastes time to let a fiction story strew their emotions in negative directions for no good reason. It may only produce nothing more than a sleepless night. It is unproductive. I wonder if they do this because they subconsciously discern that stressful feelings can decrease I.Q. points in milliseconds?

Research documented in the book *Your Brain and Business: The Neuroscience of Great Leaders,* Pillay elaborates on new neuroscientific findings of the brain's fight or flight response.

Scientists discovered when chaos occurs, blood in the frontal cortex (decision-making area) of the brain shifts to the amygdala (the portion of the brain responsible for fight-or-flight response). This causes a momentary brain freeze which decreases intellect.

Additionally, internal conflicts, arguments or stressful information can over-stimulate the anterior cingulate cortex. This activity keeps the amygdala fired up, again robbing the frontal cortex of blood flow, leaving a person momentarily bereft of decision-making skills.

Maybe M&Bs consciously understand this or simply have a natural, strong sense of self-preservation. When they experience an overwhelmingly negative feeling, they move away from it.

Your Brain on Business also recommends shutting off T.V.s, radios, and social media when working. Even though the brain is focused on a task, it scans its environment. If it perceives background negative activity, it adjusts to it with fear, and fires up the amygdala. This decreases I.Q., limiting one's ability to stay focused and perform well.

I watch M&Bs cut out the negativity. Thus, they not only increase their I.Q., they practice a lifestyle that protects it.

FIGHT THE FREEZE

Imagine you're at a social event, in a casual conversation and suddenly someone snaps at you. You might feel stunned and say nothing. Why? Because you just experienced a drop in IQ. The little shock from that experience triggers your once calm amygdala into action, draining the blood flow from your frontal cortex. Thus, you feel at a loss for words.

Only when you leave the scene and regain your calm are you able to analyze what transpired. You think, "Wait a minute! What was wrong with me, and why didn't I say something?" Why couldn't you shut that person down when you had the opportunity? Because you were literally, not figuratively, in no state of mind to do so. You were in your amygdala, or flight, fight, or freeze mode, and not your frontal cortex.

That is what happens to your brain on drama. It's best to get Closure with people who create it. M&B's dislike catastrophizing and aggressive personalities, so they relegate them to the nether regions of their world. I wonder if M&Bs consciously practice this to protect their IQ?

Perhaps they can sense a drop in IQ when others cannot, so that's why they practice Concise, Clear, Consistent, and the other Commonalities. No matter their reason, this works. So, practicing what they do could save your IQ. *Results may vary.*

MINI CASE STUDY

Perfect timing. As I write these sentences regarding fear and its impact on the brain, my phone rings. It's my dear friend Marcia calling to catch me up on her fun adventures. She is fifty-six years old and has been traveling for several years since she retirement. Recently she and her husband returned from a sailing trip in the Greek Isles.

It was a lovely conversation, me imagining the islands as she spoke of their beauty. As she listed off her monthly plan for the year, she stopped and boasted, "In July, I'm running with the bulls in Spain." I froze. I didn't hear another word. My heart rate shot up what felt like a hundred points. I couldn't speak. I sat frozen as she elaborated.

She doesn't run—she doesn't even walk fast. My imagination overwhelmed me with a vision of her gingerly trotting down a narrow street as maniacal bulls speed from behind to crush her.

My face is flushed. I can feel it. I can't say a word. Clearly, my IQ dropped.

Our call ended. I regained my ability to reason, did a little research, and sent it to her in a text. I begged her to use a drone instead. She responded with, "Ha, ha. It's no different from jumping out of an airplane which I have done also."

I retorted, "But bulls didn't jump out of the plane right behind you to crush you."

I have heartburn now. Neuroscience must be right because I just experienced a "frozen stupid" moment.

MEET THE ROBINSONS MEETS ROCKY IV

A lifestyle that protects our state of being requires a positive perspective and tenacity.

In the animation movie *Meet the Robinsons,* the main character, Lewis, is an orphaned boy who wants to be an inventor, but his inventions don't function properly. So, he resolves to quit.

In the American sports drama film *Rocky IV,* Rocky experiences a pounding in the ring from the notorious Drago.

Both movies center on one phrase. One version palatable for a child to grasp hold of, and the other is gritty, for those familiar with challenges.

When Lewis's invention explodes, he hears cheers of approval. Those around him shout, "Keep Moving Forward!" Their stunning encouragement taught him it's acceptable to experiment.

When Rocky's son confronts him about his next fight, he responds with a direct message:

> *Let me tell you something you already know. The world ain't all sunshine and rainbows. It's a very mean and nasty place, and I*

don't care how tough you are, it will beat you to your knees and keep you there permanently if you let it. You, me, or nobody is gonna hit as hard as life. But it ain't about how hard you hit. It's about how hard you can get hit and keep moving forward; how much you can take and keep moving forward. That's how winning is done! Now, if you know what you're worth, then go out and get what you're worth. But you gotta be willing to take the hits, and not pointing fingers saying you ain't where you wanna be because of him, or her, or anybody. Cowards do that and that ain't you. You're better than that! I'm always gonna love you, no matter what. No matter what happens. You're my son and you're my blood. You're the best thing in my life. But until you start believing in yourself, you ain't gonna have a life.

Powerful words written by Sylvester Stallone. Moving forward is getting up after each knockout and fighting again. Doing so helps put closure to lost bouts.

LIQUID METAL T1000 MODEL

Sometimes my imagination runs amok. When I think of an M&B's desire for closure after a negative experience, I see Liquid Metal T1000 from the movie *Terminator 2.* Many times T1000 gets shot down to its foundational programming (liquid metal)… for a short while. Then it resets and rebuilds to its human form and goes back to what it intended to accomplish before the hits. M&Bs are much like the T1000, only a nicer version. They get hit, revert to their original programming, reboot and start where they left off before the offense occurred. No matter what, they continue to regenerate after every attack.

In my opinion their core belief about themselves (foundational programming) is what they rely upon in times of distress. The core belief? A healthy dose of heroism. It's simple faith in themselves. They may not be strong soldiers, fight fires or fight crime, but somewhere deep inside they consider themselves a hero in their own right because of the good they produce for society.

When hit hard, they do Scuba Face and have some dialogue with Self about what they've accomplished. They know themselves best and acknowledge their own sincere desire to do good.

M&Bs are their own best cheerleaders. They are relentless because of the truth; they provide benefits for others that must be shared. And, they feel great about that truth. They conclude they have no other choice than to be themselves, the hero within. The best closure to a bad experience is to recognize the hero within.

CLOSURE AND FEAR

M&Bs quickly shut down fear. They go on the offense to find a means to control it. Even if it is a small concern. For example, an M&B planned a weekend party for forty out-of-town guests. She imagined they may get lost if they try to navigate the events on their own. That wouldn't be enjoyable.

To escape this imagination, she asked herself a question: "What can I do to prevent losing guests?" Questions are scientifically proven to hijack the brain. So, she hijacked her brain from fear and directed it to solve the problem. She then answers her question: hire a shuttle service to manage the group's transportation and provide a packet of pertinent information.

Fear can shut down the frontal cortex. But M&Bs seem to know how to re-activate theirs quickly. Their secret? They ask themselves questions. Maybe this is subconscious for them, but they all do it. It is a simple and brilliant way to recover from a frontal cortex hijacked by alarming thoughts.

CREATIVE CLOSURE TO RELATIONSHIPS

M&Bs terminate boundaryless relationships. They fix the problem or move on. Ending unhealthy connections is the best gift to give people who don't respect boundaries; it no longer empowers their destructive behavior.

Sometimes it takes creativity to create boundaries.

One afternoon I spent the day wakesurfing with a few Caltech grads. While we took a break, I asked them to share their best college stories. They talked between themselves and then agreed these next two stories were the most memorable experiences they had at Caltech.

While in college, these guys all shared the same professor as their advisor. They mentioned their annoyance with the fact he lived at the university. Literally. In his office. They said he slept in his office because he didn't have a home. This denied him his right to vote because the university office was not a valid home address. To gain back his right, he rented an apartment. But he continued to live in his office.

This same professor preached all technology should be open source, while he lived off taxpayers' dollars produced by closed source technology. Maybe this is why he wasn't a favorite of other professors.

Their second story was about his office. They found it odd how the hallway to it was "like a jungle" because other professors had multitudes of plants in their offices. The professors positioned the plants to stick out of their doors or across their thresholds.

More peculiar, their advisor was the only professor who didn't have plants in his "home" office. Not one. Then they burst out laughing. They later discovered the open-source professor had Botanophobia, fear of plants. The other professors kept plants in their offices to keep him out.

RECAP

Closure is a good thing. It can preserve your I.Q.

Use phrases to describe past pain, so you don't have to dig it up and relive it.

The past is only good for support. If you can't find it (support), forget it (the past).

Complain only if you're working on a solution.

Keep moving forward, just lead. Make decisions so you have more options.

Disengage from hysteria, catastrophizers and negative news sources to save your I.Q.

Reboot from a core belief of goodness and respond like the Liquid Metal T1000 model.

Find the hero within by identifying what you provide that benefits others.

All closure doesn't have to be dramatic, get creative like the Caltech professors.

CHAPTER TEN:

Compete

"I enjoy the hunt much more than the 'good life' after the victory."
Carl Icahn

"I'd rather wrestle grizzlies than compete with Mrs. B. and her progeny."
Warren Buffett

"Loyalty is not won by being first. It is won by being best."
Stefan Persson

DEFINITION:	*to strive consciously or unconsciously for an objective (such as a position, a profit or a prize). Measure oneself. to strive for something (as a prize or a reward) for which another is also striving*
SYNONYMS:	*emulate, battle, spar, challenge, engage, maneuver*
ANTONYMS:	*refrain, disclaim, give up, retreat*

FRIENDLY COMPETITION

I was one of the youngest in a brood of highly competitive brothers, so there was no such thing as friendly competition in my house. It was survival of the fittest.

You never wanted to lose because there was great humiliation to suffer. My teenage brothers could really make my seven-year-old mind experience the depths of despair over losing at a game of Clue or Monopoly. Sometimes the loser (always one of us younger ones) experienced mean-spirited penalties for losing. My brothers made sure to enforce those penalties when Mom wasn't home, like the time I had to jump off the roof of our house.

I thank God today it was a low hanging roof. I don't remember how I faired; I still have a mental block. So, competition in my world was: crush or be crushed, which could mean emotions or bones. Therefore, I never cared for the drama of competition because it usually ended poorly for me.

BAD BILLIONAIRES AND MEAN MILLIONAIRES

Since my only knowledge of the wealthy came from Hollywood movies, I assumed the wealthy were malevolent moguls. So, when I first worked with them, I expected mean, conniving behavior. I assumed they would be like my brothers. How else did they get all that money if it wasn't from crushing people like my brothers did to me?

Yet again, that was another lie I believed. I started my job thinking I would be in a boxing ring, facing Ivan Drago from *Rocky IV*. Instead, I walked onto the set of *The Big Bang Theory* with characters who are cerebral, friendly, driven, and competitive.

COMPETITION: AN M&B GROWTH STRATEGY

"Competition makes you better, always, always makes you better, even if the competitor wins."
Carlos Slim

M&Bs I work with enjoy competing. But their version of it isn't a battle to the death or crushing humiliation like I thought. To them competing is friendly, which means no cheating or jumping from rooftops. They have no desire to kill the competition; otherwise they won't have anyone to play with later.

For M&Bs, competition is rewarding, no matter if they lose, because it's an outlet to demonstrate and hone skills. They're not seeking victims like my brothers who used my sister and me as football tackling dummies. With an M&B progress and productivity are the reward, not crushing bones.

One of the most important things for an M&B is productivity. They must produce, or they become madly bored. Competition drives them to produce.

I think one societal norm M&Bs find frustrating is the participation trophy for kids' sports. Everyone gets the same trophy, regardless of performance. This discredits hard work and doesn't teach kids how to be a good sport at winning and losing.

The M&Bs who worked diligently, suffered numerous personal attacks, sabotages, sexism, and losses, recognize how dangerous this teaching is for children. They know the world doesn't play nice or fair. They didn't generate mass amounts of wealth because others played fair with them, so they deem teaching children at an early age that life is fair, doesn't prepare them for reality.

M&Bs prepare their children by teaching them how to struggle through challenges. As they gain skills, their parents introduce them to competing with others to grow their abilities.

When the M&B's child hears, "No one wins, and no one loses," it thwarts their parents' efforts. I watched this happen with the M&B who became a coach for his kids' sports teams. Few of the coaches cared for this concept.

One M&B teaches his grandson entrepreneurialism because that is how he became a billionaire. He starts him with little businesses, such as importing a product they can build together and sell online. When their product doesn't sell, he teaches him how to compete. This helps him understand not everyone wins all the time, and competition can help him .

SPORTS MATTER TO M&BS

"I love to compete. To me, business is the ultimate sport. It's always on. There is always someone trying to beat me."
Mark Cuban

The world is full of variables and sports are a great way to teach kids how to work with them. M&Bs enroll their kids in sports so they learn how to compete, work with a team, and cope with losing and winning. Above all, they want their children to learn how to recover after disappointment. If adults don't allow kids to experience defeat, and don't teach them how to recover, they may never learn resilience.

M&Bs understand playing sports helps train resilience in their children. I've watched some non-M&B parents disallow their kids to participate in competitive sports. The kids attend a "special" private school without a grading system, where everyone plays nice, and trained to sing happy songs.

Now, one child fears competition. He is afraid to play baseball. But he knows how to build a Lego toy and play his computer game. He knows how to be alone, and sadly, he believes he can control his environment one hundred percent.

THE NEED TO COMPETE

"I'm addicted to winning. The more you win, the more you want to win."
Larry Ellison

M&Bs use competition or games as a healthy way to get a burst of energy. It brings a thrill to life even if it's a simple competition. And it has health benefits too.

Research conducted on carnivorous animals in captivity, zoos specifically, found carnivores need to hunt otherwise they become anxious and stressed. To reduce the stress of captivity, zookeepers provide games for the predators that simulate the thrill and reward of a hunt. These games also improve their mental and physical health.

We humans are similar. We need to feel alive. Competition provides a thrill and can reduce the stress of captivity, whether it be a job or difficult circumstance.

M&B CHAOS-FREE COMPETITION

Frenzy caused by good competition is the only drama M&Bs find tolerable. A robust challenge has a beginning and an end. When the competition ends, everyone goes home. Healthy competition is controlled drama, and it elicits positive intensity.

One M&B hosted a family and friends Christmas party. She wanted a friendly competition, so she planned a White Elephant Gift Exchange Game. Everyone drew a number and in numeric order selected a gift, either an unopened one, or by stealing another person's gift. Each gift can only be stolen three times.

It was a cheery competition for the holidays. And, better yet, it thrilled her to recycle an item she felt guilty for not wanting. I'm certain the whole game was solely to rid herself of this one item.

The item? It was a sad little blue flower vase. She rejected it, so I kept it on the back corner of my desk for a few years. I felt sorry for the rejected blue vase.

But this year she strategized to free herself of it at the game. She packaged it nicely and couldn't be happier. Every time she passed by the wrapped sad little blue vase, she perked up and smiled. Only a few more days until it would disappear.

Let the game begin! The night of the party, she wore a big smile simply because the vase soon would leave the house. As the game progressed, she frequently looked over at the sad little blue vase gift bag, nervously waiting for someone to take it.

Then it happened! A sweet old man picked up the gift bag, and the M&B beamed! She looked over at me, smiled, and nodded in excitement. The sweet old man opened it and fell madly in love with the little vase! It was a happy ending.

She looked over at me with another big smile as if to say, "I did it!" Her plan unfolded *exactly* as she wanted, and all was well. She sighed in relief and leaned back into her cozy sofa, no longer nervous about her plan. She enjoyed watching the rest of the game and a few times looked over at the sad little blue vase.

Happy little old man, happy M&B.

But alas. I looked down to see the number I drew. It read "#1."

I smiled at her and showed her my number. She was happy, seeing I got the best number to draw.

As my turn began, she watched me. I walked up to the nice little old man with the sad blue vase and as I reached for the vase she jumped out of her cozy sofa and shouted "Noooo!"

The guests sat stunned; she never yelled. No one understood why.

I took the rejected little blue vase from the once happy little old man and walked it back to my desk.

Laughter ensued after she told everyone the story.

Without competition, the evening would not have been as much fun. That game was the best part of the evening.

Six years later... sad little vase: still on my desk. She let me keep it. It was a good game.

COMPETITION: CHOOSE IT WISELY

"I don't try to jump over 7-foot bars: I look around for 1-foot bars that I can step over."
Warren Buffett

I never saw M&B couples prey on each other's weaknesses. They don't practice negativity toward one another. They work from a "complete" not "compete" motto. If competition doesn't bring them together as a couple, they stop the activity.

Instead, they find aspects to respect. I've heard the men brag about how capable and smart their wives are, while the wives respect achievements and encourage their husbands' dedication. It's always equal.

And, I see and hear them say these things to each other's faces. One billionaire told me he retired early so he could give the rest of his life to his wife. That was my favorite thing I experienced in their homes, their camaraderie. They truly like each other.

COMPETE AGAINST THYSELF

I bought one M&B Mensa puzzle and math quiz books after his retirement. He worked those books daily.

M&Bs play games against themselves to build their esteem too. It's interesting to watch them do puzzles. They gear up on high alert as if they're getting ready to run a race. It's as though they just had a double shot of Arabic coffee.

They compete in a private race against themselves in their own little world. Nothing can disturb their steely concentration. They're jogging their memory, calculating, anticipating, and then the answer comes. Victory! They relish in the win as if running a victory lap. And a victory lap includes sharing it with others.

They never minimize even a small victory by saying it wasn't a big deal, or it was easy. Every competition won is valuable and deserves praise. Even fixing little things around the house deserves praise.

Competition is used to keep the environment positive. It's an opportunity to feel good about oneself. They say, "Don't mind if I do," and pat themselves on the back for a job well done.

Do we praise ourselves this way? Is there anything wrong with it? I'm convinced competition is another secret M&Bs know that most others don't. I don't see my non-M&B friends celebrate little victories as M&Bs do. It must be a subconscious strategy they each developed.

I think M&Bs build upon little victories to build their self-esteem to prepare for bigger challenges. They estimate if they're always winning, then they're positioned for more and greater wins.

COMPETITION IS PREPARATION FOR PROBLEMS

M&Bs create lots of competition in their lives. We know it provides excitement. Notably, both fear and excitement are stimulants. Both cause increased heart rate and alertness. M&Bs prefer a positive stimulant rather than a negative one.

Practicing positive stimulants—competition, prepares them to fight fearful experiences.

When an unwanted circumstance occurs, M&Bs may be fearful at first, but they know what to do: they turn the circumstance into an opportunity. They don't simply defend against it; they make something they Want happen. That's turning lemons into lemonade.

Now, instead of worrying, they have something to achieve. This helps them trust they have some control in adversity. Regardless of the outcome, they acknowledge they manipulated an unwelcome situation to gain some control. That is rewarding.

Note: Their conversation with Self (Scuba Face) during adversity addresses how they achieved positive results in their past. They harness those stimulating memories to build an offensive strategy against fear and doubt.

COMPETE WITH TRAUMA

"The art of competing, I'd learned from track, was the art of forgetting, and I now reminded myself of that fact. You must forget your limits. You must forget your doubts, your pain, your past."
Phil Knight

When one M&B claimed he only had heartburn, his wife pushed him to go to the doctor. Result: he suffered a mild heart attack and had a blockage on its way to his heart. She saved his life.

After his stay in the hospital, his doctors prescribed blood thinners. He bled easily and sometimes didn't notice bloody cuts. This traumatized the kids who thought their dad might bleed to death.

Instead of feeding fear, their dad explained to them the blood thinner's job, and how it was a good thing. He showed them the meaningless cuts and simple scrapes that caused him to bleed and compared if they had the same cuts if they would bleed the same way. They understood it was the drug and not him.

Once they understood, he turned their reactions of alertness (from fear) into a game by first telling them he wanted (created a Want) help with his thin skin and asked* if they could point out things that might cause him to bleed. He responded with praise when they did.

He empowered his kids when he distracted and redirected their reactions from fear toward controlling the circumstance. The kids then prodded their dad over little things he did that made him bleed. They teased him if he had blood dripping down his leg and didn't know it.

Inadvertently, when we encourage others, we encourage ourselves. After he helped his kids, he helped himself to be more aware of his surroundings to prevent injuries.

**This is the same technique I mentioned in Chapter Seven: how to get the frontal cortex thinking again by asking it a question. He asked his kids questions such as what might cause him to get a bruise or scrape. It resolved the intensity and helped the kids control fear and worry.*

I categorized this experience under Compete because we must compete against trauma and negative circumstances to maintain our focus and peace. Practicing competition creates resilience, a technique transferable to life's harsh challenges.

NO CHEATING!

M&Bs don't strategize to cheat when they compete, not even on a Mensa puzzle, even if they take days to solve one.

I know a few M&Bs who are members of a tennis club. They're their own referees; they call the ball out on one another. One guy in their group, who is not an M&B, cheats. They recognize he calls the balls in his favor, so they gave him a nickname for his relentless fraudulence. He knows the nickname but doesn't care and continues to hoodwink to get ahead, even though he is a Psychologist with a Ph.D.

CHEATING: CONSIDER THE COST

I remember one day I arrived at work and an M&B told me what happened the night before in their neighborhood. Apparently, at five p.m. while his neighbor enjoyed dinner with his family, the F.B.I. knocked on his door, invited themselves in, and arrested him.

What we later learned was he had two sets of accounting books. One of the sets he used to distort company financials to investors. This paid for his Lamborghini.

His duality earned him a long prison sentence. He lost the car, the house and time with his family. More distressing, his children lost their father.

The M&Bs I know don't like that feeling of uncertainty that comes with cheating. They'd rather be at peace with the results from an honest try.

"I don't like paying taxes, but I like sleeping at night."
Leonardo Del Vecchio

ECHO CHAMBERS

To practice illegal activity means few only a few people can know. Criminals don't want to be discovered, so their world shrinks. They end up creating an echo chamber, a closed system that reinforces their negative beliefs. A chamber can become a prison.

M&Bs like competition because it keeps them out of echo chambers and out of prison. Competition allows for other's perspectives that can inspire. It also gives an M&B an opportunity to see what their competition does differently.

If a runner doesn't believe the human body can run a seven-minute mile, but then sees another runner achieve it, that can bolster his confidence to perform better.

Competition helps us get past our own self-limiting thoughts and helps build the "Why not me?" mentality. It helps us question talents in a good way, such as "Where did he learn to do that?" This stimulates a learning opportunity and undeniable growth. Competition also stimulates us to remember our passion.

M&Bs compete for their own self-development, enlightenment, or enjoyment. It also encourages M&Bs to be a Doer. M&Bs do, do, do, all day long.

COMPETITION INSPIRES

"Life's a journey. It's a journey about discovering limits."
Larry Ellison

An M&B hired a high-end contractor to build an addition on to their million-dollar home. The last phase required me to use blue tape to identify problems with workmanship. This builder did a great job, and I noticed only one minor issue: the wall with gorgeous floor-to-ceiling drawers and cabinets had a few drawers a sixteenth of an inch higher than the adjacent drawers.

When I kindly pointed this out to the project manager, he sighed and said all the cabinetry had to come out. That shocked me. When I asked him if there was another way, he said, "No, we do our job right, so we start from the beginning, again." They ripped out the entire wall of cabinets and drawers and reset all of them.

This is why M&Bs hire this builder.

Another M&B I worked with in a nearby city hired this same builder to remodel his kitchen in his one-hundred-year-old, four-story, gorgeous, Federal-style home. When the team ripped out the walls down to the studs, they found problems with the foundation. This caused a problem up to the fourth story. They stopped the remodel and informed the M&B that if they do the job, they do it right. The M&B moved out so they could resolve the problems from the foundation up. It's an outstanding and beautiful job.

Contrasted with a non-M&B who hired a contractor who didn't have a portfolio or reputation to show for his work. He hired him to repair minor exterior and interior water damage to their home. I watched his work. He didn't know my background, so he didn't realize I knew he took detrimental shortcuts. I think my chin dropped once.

After he completed his work, I pointed out a problem. He raised his voice at me, denying the obvious. He did nothing to correct it. Instead of fixing it then, he had to come back two more times to repair his repair work. This consumed most of his profit.

If he had competed against himself to do the best job the first time rather than cheat the process, he would have made more money. But he preferred his shortcuts. I don't call him for my M&B clients. Instead, I call him Mr. Mediocre.

MR. MEDIOCRE

My job is to make an M&B's time more productive, not a contractor's. A contractor and I should be on the same team. We are there to compete against ourselves to produce an excellent product. The game is: I'm hired to prevent problems, or at least attempt to solve them so an M&B doesn't have to get involved. Arguing to defend a poor job isn't good. That's being a poor sport.

The competitive contractors appreciate my feedback because I point out problems before the M&B sees their finished work. I can make a contractor look good. Mr. Mediocre didn't like my feedback because he didn't care to compete against himself to provide a great product. So, who will an M&B hire for multimillion-dollar jobs? Not Mr. Mediocre.

Those who compete against themselves to be the best are worth the additional cost. I used to want "as cheap as possible." Now I know better. I see M&Bs pay extra for quality because they know great customer service is behind it.

In most cases, we buy customer service, not a product. Excellence-driven companies understand this, so customer service is where they compete. They know it can establish them above their competition.

GENERIC GUTTER GUY

A non-M&B needed new gutters on her house. She wanted the cheapest deal possible. She found the two cheapest bids. The second cheapest offer was only two-hundred dollars more. She questioned the contractor why his bid was so much higher. He said because he wouldn't need to come back for repairs; he does it right the first time. That didn't matter to the non-M&B; she wanted the cheapest.

When she called to set up an appointment for an estimate with the cheapest gutter guy, he didn't respond for a few months. He eventually called and booked an appointment. When the appointment arrived, he forgot and didn't show. This happened twice.

I explained to the non-M&B that the past is a good indicator of the future. If he can't show for a quote and a job, then it most likely won't turn out well if there is a problem after he's paid. Needless to say, she ignored me.

The gutter job finally happened. A few days later I noticed a downspout too close to a window. The window couldn't open. To fix the problem requires him to remove and redirect two stories of gutter.

Now, what do you think transpired since notifying the gutter guy that his work impinged upon a window? He doesn't return phone calls.

This I have learned: we don't buy cheap because we buy quality; customer service.

HOW M&BS BUILD A COMPETITIVE SPIRIT

M&Bs make life a game. Rather than do life mindlessly, they turn little things into a game, so they have more opportunities to be a winner. Here are ways they set up winning opportunities that you can too:

- Did you wake up before your alarm? You win.
- Did you miss that pothole in the road this time? You win.
- Did you find a better-quality deal on a purchase? You win.
- Did you ask for a discount? You win.
- Did you challenge yourself to learn a new word today? You win.
- Did you make a little effort at cleaning? You win.
- Did you catch your child's falling bowl of cereal? You win.
- Did you stop at the stop sign when a police officer was watching? You win.
- Most important; did you praise yourself for your wins? Then you win!

We are competitive by nature. When you win at little challenges, you'll desire bigger ones.

RECAP

Compete against thyself and make it a good game.

Don't cheat yourself or others of your best. No Mr. Mediocre!

Compete to:

- Grow.
- Feel alive and reduce the stress of captivity.
- Find inspiration.
- Build healthy relationships.
- Avoid an echo chamber (prison).
- Get better, it's better than Perfect.

Build resilience. A great tool to learn how to create resilience in children (and adults) is the book: *Trauma-Proofing Your Kids: A Parents' Guide for Instilling Confidence, Joy and Resilience.* By Dr. Peter Levin and Maggie Kline.

CHAPTER ELEVEN:

Create Win-Win

"Our success has really been based on partnerships from the very beginning."
Bill Gates

"No man will make a great leader who wants to do it all himself or get all the credit for doing it."
Andrew Carnegie

"In business it's about people. It's about relationships."
Kathy Ireland

What's the sense of becoming rich if you're going to have a pattern of operation where you continually discard associations with people you like, admire, and find interesting in order to earn a slightly bigger figure? We like big figures, but not to the exclusion of everything else.
Warren Buffett

DEFINITION:	*A solution having a benefit for everyone that is involved or a benefit for one person or group no matter what the result is.* USEFUL OR ADVANTAGEOUS FOR EVERYONE INVOLVED. *The belief there is only Win-Win or lose-lose*
SYNONYMS:	*productive for everyone involved, favorable*
ANTONYMS:	*lose-lose, one side isn't benefiting, lopsided, infective*

AN EYE ON OPPORTUNITY

M&Bs know Win-Win opportunities don't magically appear, they happen because someone creates them.

To an M&B every need met is a deal made. It isn't uncommon for them to believe a Want is inseparable from a Win-Win opportunity. They understand deals are an exchange of Wants so they identify specific people who can profit from helping them obtain a Want or meet a need.

A simple illustration is when an M&B needs to rent his rental home. It isn't only about his Want, "I need a renter," but also, "Who can benefit from my need for a renter?"

The M&B creates an ad presenting how his property will benefit someone. A person sees his needs met by the ad and responds. Then both parties make an amicable agreement. The payout for the homeowner is income and someone to care for his property, while the renter has a nice place in a great location. Favorable for both, needs met, therefore a Win-Win.

MEET A NEED FIRST

This M&B offered to first meet someone's need by creating an ad. He didn't idly wait for someone to meet his need or wish to the universe for a renter. He created a Win-Win scenario.

M&Bs look for opportunities to create business. In my opinion this is why they do so much business. They find and put together deals for everyone to win.

This was surprising for me to learn about M&Bs. Before working for them I assumed they prospered because they demanded from people what they wanted, and those people had to comply. I have since learned this is not true. They prosper because they're unafraid to help others get what they want, *so they too can get what they want.*

NEVER GO IT ALONE

I used to believe M&Bs achieved everything on their own, so they were loners. I learned this was wrong when I observed the M&B who wanted a backyard farm, she attained her desire with the help of a community.

She didn't try to change the city code on her own. She joined organizations that supported backyard farming and networked to find others who might profit from her Want. Then she organized a town hall style meeting to garner enough signatures to push for the city to create more freedom in backyard farming. The group she organized attended a city council meeting and pushed for change. More chickens live in their community now because of this M&B who wanted to help herself and others.

The change didn't happen because she is an M&B; it happened because she knows to never go it alone.

She also didn't go it alone by raising illegal chickens. A neighbor might report her. The fear of the unknown from cheating isn't worth it to an M&B. They won't risk engaging in hard work and financial expenditure only to see it condemned or fined. Instead, they attempt to build a community, big or small, around their cause or desire to create change. Inviting people into an opportunity creates a better chance for everyone.

M&Bs understand they can't achieve some desires without help. Whether it is an app to use, or a person to hire, they get whatever helps them achieve.

One M&B pays his neighbor's son a few dollars to bring his trash bins up from the curb. This encourages the boy to understand entrepreneurialism and service while it helps the M&B when he's out of town.

Even the Lone Ranger has Tonto.

WARREN BUFFETT'S WIN-WIN MENTALITY

I remember a story a speaker told. He said his friend owned one share of Berkshire Hathaway stock when the price was six thousand dollars per share. His friend decided it might be fun to attend the shareholder's meeting with his one share of stock.

When he arrived for the shareholder dinner, they seated him at a table. To his surprise and embarrassment, someone seated Warren Buffett across from him. He fretted. Now he faced The Oracle of Omaha.

He fidgeted in his seat. He didn't know what to say. The moment was awkward for him because he only owned one share of stock, and they seated him across from The Man.

He contemplated for a moment and then confessed his shareholder position to Mr. Buffett. He leaned forward and exhaled, "I am one of your shareholders." Then he held up his index finger and in a deflated tone said, "I have one share of stock."

Without hesitation, Warren Buffett leaned forward and replied, "Well then, between you and me we can control this company."

I marveled when I heard this story. I first supposed Warren only tried to make this investor feel better. That may be true, but in addition, I realized he does what every M&B does: create Win-Win scenarios. In his response was a Win-Win. He turned a one-share owner into a partner.

It was a funny story, but it is an excellent display of the Win-Win mentality of M&Bs. They recognize they cannot grow a business without partnerships, so they always encourage them.

WIN-WIN IN THE GARAGE

This next story is my favorite example of a Win-Win. I saw an M&B take a sensitive circumstance and turn it into a big Win-Win. Possibly it was the most powerful lesson for me.

This M&B's husband has what I call a massive "tool garden." It's a large workspace, an area the size of a three-car garage. Tools on the walls, the floor the counters and every space available. Sawdust is everywhere. Random sizes of wood scraps lay on the floor, the counter, and lean up against equipment and walls, blocking storage racks and walking space.

It's a big mess. As it should be. It's what work in progress looks like, tools are right where you left them.

But the M&B wife doesn't agree with mess. Even though she doesn't see the mess every day, she knows it's there. To her a mess means less productivity and helping someone attain greater productivity makes her happy.

One morning when I arrived for work, she and her husband were eating breakfast. When he finished, she waited until he left the room. Then she asked me to sit across the table from her. She placed her hands on the table, fingers laced together, and with a big smile on her face whispered while nodding, "I need you to help me clean the work garage. It's a mess. Help me clean it while he's gone."

I froze.

I flashed back to my childhood, picking up after my dad's messes by putting his tools where they belonged. That never turned out well.

I returned to her request and said, "No." This is the only time I ever told an M&B "no." My experience taught me: Never clean a man's toolshed or workspace. Rich or poor. His tool shed is his brain laid out into many pieces. Mess with his tools and you mess with his head. It was a cardinal rule she was about to break.

I explained to her the idea was a mistake, so she decided not to clean it behind his back. I'd like to think I saved their marriage that day. I only jest. Although, tool gardens are quite serious for some men.

After my explanation, I assumed she abandoned her desire because M&Bs don't instigate chaos. Her Want was over.

So I thought.

Instead, she didn't take "no" personally, but looked for a Win-Win opportunity. She found one.

First, she prepped him by explaining how he might get his woodwork projects done faster if his work area is better organized. This was a fair argument. He agreed and purchased containers and tool hanging racks.

Phase one for the M&B completed. Phase two: the sawdust.

Even though he organized himself, this didn't resolve the sawdust produced by his activities. He didn't mind the layers of dust and shavings everywhere, but she did. So, she negotiated she could sweep a small path through the workspace to prevent tracking sawdust into the house. He obliged and let her sweep a narrow path, and only the path.

This was progress, leading up to the big Win-Win.

The big Win-Win? She encouraged him to build his own sawdust collection system. *This was a huge deal.* He loves to build things (he is a Ph.D. research scientist), and this project included researching how to design a system for hookup to large and small tools. It was a mechanical challenge for him.

He quickly went to work on his new project.

He designed and built an impressive system. It is moveable from overhead with hook ups for large equipment and small tools at different locations. His workmanship pleased himself, and he enjoyed showing off his system to everyone who visited.

Phase two completed.

His workspace is cleaner and better organized. He no longer misplaces tools and his projects come along much faster, while his collection system collects the sawdust. Win-Win accomplished.

And she still gets to sweep the path.

Now, outside the tool garden was fair game: printing and photography equipment, his man cave, and office area. He is a Ph.D. scientist, obviously very smart, but we all have blind spots. His wife noticed he became frustrated and wasted precious time (M&Bs hate wasting time) when he misplaced items.

The M&B didn't antagonize him over his struggle. She chose to help him without him knowing. If he complained he lost something, she gave me a signal which meant I went to his office and secretly rummaged through files, equipment, or his computer to find what he lost. Then I put it in an easy-to-find place. This decreased his frustration, and she was content he was less frustrated. Another happy ending from a Win-Win scenario she created.

NEVER REJECTED, SIMPLY FIND A BETTER OFFER

Another valuable lesson I learned while working with M&Bs is they don't take 'no' as a personal rejection. When they make a request, if someone doesn't accept it, they create a better offer, or work with a different party. They Keep It Simple Smarty.

The tool garden M&B eventually created an acceptable Win-Win deal for her husband. She didn't take it personally when he told her she couldn't vacuum or dust his workshop. Instead, she kept moving forward. She looked for a better offer.

As for me, I said "no" and did nothing. My loss. But I learned from this and similar scenarios.

M&Bs create Win-Win opportunities by studying how to work with other peoples' mindset. They work with them, not against them. His mindset? He loves to invent. This is much more important to him than the sawdust. He traded sawdust to create and use his unique collection system.

When creating a Win-Win opportunity, M&Bs don't play victim nor do they look to create them. They don't believe that one person should suffer for the advancement of another. That is a one-sided deal. M&Bs I've worked with don't practice one-sided deals. Agreements aren't a battle to the death or who can crush who.

M&Bs believe if the other person is satisfied with the arrangement, it only benefits them more because they not only created a good deal, but they built a relationship.

LIMITED HAND OUTS

Sometimes helping someone isn't giving them a handout, but a hand up. It's giving someone a chance to work hard so he can see what he can make of an opportunity. Then he can realize his own capabilities and reap a reward. Therefore, every opportunity has a greater purpose, a chance for self-realization. M&Bs understand this, so they prefer to give opportunities, or a "hand up," not a handout.

M&Bs also don't look to provide handouts because they desire an exchange. Even their donations are exchanges. They donate to places that help others transform their lives. M&Bs enjoy inspiring others to believe in themselves and grow. This is a hand up.

I notice some people around M&Bs don't want an opportunity, they want a handout.

Once, an M&B used her resources to give a young man an opportunity. After he returned home from his first year of college, he couldn't find a local summer job. This M&B created a job for him. It was generous of her. She didn't need him, but she devised a Win-Win scenario for each of them. She let him stain one of her wood decks. Since she did it herself a few years prior, and I did it the prior summer, she reasoned he could do it this time. A great Win-Win. He agreed.

It was a beautiful summer day, perfect for staining a deck. The college student arrived with his father, who came to oversee his work. I monitored intermittently from inside. As they walked along the deck, getting ready to prep it, the college student whined about how much time it would take. After what I heard and saw, I supposed his parents never introduced him to manual labor in his lifetime.

He moaned to his dad it was too hot and too much work for him. Then he grabbed onto a large ceramic pot, with a four-foot tall tree planted in it. He screamed, then said he hurt his back.

It was an odd thing to do.

When I saw this happen, I walked outside to assess. The father yelled at me that the expectations were too high for one person to stain the deck. He complained it was too big a job for one person, even though he was there to help.

He then accused the M&B of *forcing* his son to lift ginormous potted trees.

Here an M&B learned of a kid's plight, created a job for him, and this is what she gets for creating a Win-Win opportunity? I dislike when someone makes accusations against an M&B without her present. So, I gently reminded him the agreement was to stain the deck, not move pots. And I asked, "Did you call her or ask me to clarify the job scope?"

Silence.

Then he pelted me with more accusations. I tried to reason with him, I explained I stained it myself. He didn't like that. More screaming. So, I left them outside, and they left the job, never to return.

Based on what I observed, this college kid didn't want to do the job. He thought his dad wouldn't let him quit, so he pulled on a heavy pot and screamed he hurt his back. Job over. The easiest way out of the job was to claim victimization.

He was a victim, and it was the M&B's fault.

Hopefully, he will recover from his victimhood, as I am sure he has already recovered from a strained back.

None of the M&Bs I've met or worked with have a victim mentality. They may have been a victim of circumstances, but they didn't make it a lifestyle.

In my opinion this is why M&Bs give to organizations that help people recover and get back into a productive lifestyle. Handouts rarely turn victims into proud producers.

WIN-WIN IS A LONG-TERM STRATEGY

Self-made M&Bs are long-term planners. They earned their wealth that way, and they plan to keep it that way. So, if someone comes into their sphere asking for support, he should expect this mindset.

M&Bs don't adapt because an asker has his own agenda. A relative of an M&B had a financial need. He wanted his daughter to attend a good college but couldn't afford the loans. Moreover, he didn't want her to face unsurmountable debt after college, so he hatched a plan to ask his M&B relative for a loan. I don't know if he could pay off such a loan, but his M&B relative was willingly to help.

He and the M&B settled on an agreement, which was the M&B reviews his finances and he follows through on what she instructs him to do. If he didn't follow precisely, then the loan payments would end.

When he arrived with his financial information, they sat across the kitchen table from one another. As she reviewed his income, he squirmed.

She made her first assessment: too much outflow and not enough inflow. He cringed.

She next analyzed his expenditures. There were too many. She commented he needed to shut off his cable TV because he can easily watch movies and get news updates online. He balked.

Next, she convinced him to downsize. His home mortgage was his biggest expenditure, and now that one child left the house, they should move to a smaller home. He groaned.

Then she pointed out how he didn't work during the summers. He retorted he didn't have to because he worked for a school. He had summers off; therefore, it wasn't necessary to work during the summer.

Maybe he expected if he borrowed money from a rich relative, his lifestyle would remain the same. She pays for his daughter's school while he has his summers to himself.

But he soon found out part of the deal was he had to create another stream of income during the summers. His new business would include providing manual labor to complete projects around her estate.

As I watched this meeting, I first judged it was extreme how she expected to control the money after she gave it to him. Not only that, she told him how he would spend his money during the loan period. That was even more unreal.

I always thought we should give money away and expect nothing in return. When someone asked for it, they get it without strings attached. But I learned from this experience sometimes strings are beneficial.

This M&B attached strings to create a safety net to help him transition into his upcoming retirement.

I found this Win-Win scenario interesting to observe as it unfolded. At first, I could tell the relative was only in the deal for the money while the M&B was in the deal for his long-term benefit. This incongruence caused a snafu. But she didn't mind because she wanted her money to change how her relative managed his finances.

Additionally, I realized as with any investment or donation, it is reasonable to review financial statements to see where an organization spends money. The past is a good indicator of the future, so it is a fair assumption that if she gave him money, he might continue to live a lifestyle of over-extending his finances. That wouldn't help him overall, and it would waste her money.

Money is to change lives, not encourage the same limiting behavior. Touché M&B! I lost another argument.

I also presumed she wanted to control her money, as if it will always be hers, but I was wrong. This was an investment she could enjoy, and he and his daughter would surely enjoy too. She felt good helping him move towards a stable retirement and could help his daughter have a debt-free start after college.

It was a noble gift. I call this a gift because when a wealthy relative loans a large sum of money, expecting no collateral, she may never get it back.

BUSINESS START

The plan was set, the deal was done. He received the funds and planned his return in the summer to start his new business.

When summer arrived, so did the relative for his first day of his new job. When I saw him working outside, I went to say hello. He's a pleasant conversationalist.

When I approached him in the garden, he looked up, squinted at me through the sweat dripping down his face and growled that it was too hot outside to work. He ranted how he couldn't believe his relative asked him to weed the garden, wash the windows and plant new flowers.

I politely listened until... he accused her of controlling him with her money. He too blamed the M&B for his current position! When an M&B helps someone, and that someone accuses her while she isn't around, it doesn't make me happy.

I watched the transaction take place; they didn't know it. I heard everything, but he accused her regardless. So, I calmly responded, "Well, from what you just explained to me, it sounds as though freedom from your relative is your objective. So, let your daughter get loans and pay them off as other students do then you will have your freedom again."

He said nothing.

OPPOSITE REFLECTION

I remember watching the deal happen, each of them on either side of the table with differing perspectives. She enjoyed creating a path to freedom while he considered it a path of destruction; extinguishing the comfortable life he once lived.

He came asking for a loan. Instead, he got that *plus* a plan for financial freedom. I don't know one lender who helps a borrower avoid defaulting on a loan by overseeing his finances and helping him start a business.

And this deal was lop-sided, it was more of a win for him than for her. She gave him what he thought he needed (a quick fix, "just give me the money lady!") but she gave him what he genuinely needed; a long-term plan for financial stability in his retirement.

She used her wealth to create a way for him to avoid debt, build his finances and get his daughter into a good college. Some people will never appreciate a great opportunity.

NASTY BUSINESS

One time I provided relocation help for a non-M&B who recently moved into town. He demanded the cheapest dry cleaner. I found a sweet little old couple who owns a dry-cleaning business. They're well into their seventies, stand about four-and-a-half-feet tall, and wear big smiles. Very kind people. I thought I found this non-M&B a great Win-Win; a nice dry cleaner happy to do it cheap as long as he gets enough time to work with his old equipment.

Many months later, I stopped by their shop to say hello. After a short conversation, the little old man wilted before my eyes. He said he realized who it was I set up an account for months earlier, then begged me, "Please never let that person come back in my shop ever again."

The store owner said the man was awful and fought with him to lower his prices, even though his prices are the cheapest in town. It is horrible when a nice little old man feels abused and never wants someone's business again.

The non-M&B had to find another drycleaner, losing out on the best dry-cleaning Win-Win in town.

TWO PRIMARY WIN-WIN REQUIREMENTS

Payout

M&Bs don't help people without requiring a payout. They qualify the deal; it must have an equal or beneficial advantage for each party involved. Sounds simple, but some people can't see through deceptive practices.

The ex-M&B doctor asked an overseas supplier for an exclusive distribution agreement on their product. They agreed he could have rights to sell in the U.S. as long as he helped their facility gain FDA compliance.

The doctor asked me to manage the compliance process. But… since working with M&Bs I explained to him it's a waste of our time helping this manufacturer when he's not following through on the agreement. It isn't a Win-Win scenario because he would only use the FDA approval to avoid the agreement.

Thankfully the doctor committed to no more favors until the manufacturer signs the contract. A year later, there still isn't a signed contract.

Respect

Win-Win requires mutual respect; neither side takes abuse. Deals build relationships, it isn't solely a financial transaction. It's an effort to make both sides content and enjoy doing so.

M&B's don't throw tantrums at people they want to work with on an opportunity. I mention tantrums because I worked with a non-M&B who makes selfish offers and then throws childish fits when the other party confronts her. She doesn't disclose her full intentions but expects others to do what they're told since they're already in the deal. It's deceptive.

She wanted a job done which violated city code. She decided if she paid enough money, the electricians and plumbers would do the illegal work. She didn't recognize that giving them the job wasn't a win for them because it created a problem: if the city learned of the illegal work, they could issue an expensive fine or strip them of their business license. A Win-Win solves problems. It doesn't create new ones.

Now that this non-M&B has thrown her selfish and "rich" attitude around, no contractor who knows her wants to work with her. She has several unfinished projects.

RECAP

Win-Win is finding someone who can benefit from meeting your need.

Don't go it alone, become more productive with a Win-Win strategy. Look for partnerships.

If someone rejects your offer, create a better one. It's nothing personal.

Limit the handouts and create a hand up; it's a long-term win.

Win-Win requires payout, trust, and respect for everyone involved.

Win-Win solves problems. It doesn't create more of them.

CHAPTER TWELVE:

Correct

"He is constantly examining all that he hears: 'Is it consistent and plausible? Is it wrong?' He has a model in his head of the whole world."

Lally Weymouth on Warren Buffett

"The single best piece of advice: Constantly think about how you could be doing things better and questioning yourself."

Elon Musk

DEFINITION:	*to make or set right, to alter or adjust to bring to some standard or required condition, to point out usually for amendment the errors or faults of*
SYNONYMS:	*debug, precise, true*
ANTONYMS:	*obscurity, soften, inaccurate*

M&Bs Seek Accuracy

When I think of correct, Sheldon the character from the T.V. series *Big Bang Theory* portrays it best. He consistently seeks and spews accuracy. Nothing slips by Sheldon.

M&Bs are similar, but one difference between Sheldon and M&Bs I work with is they're open to correction. They recognize they have limitations, so they prefer the camaraderie of people who help them conduct business properly.

Memory Matters

Another difference I see between these M&Bs and others (such as myself) is their extreme memory retention. It's impressive. They can recall complicated grammar rules as if they were in an English class yesterday. The biochemist M&B can remember scientific information from many decades ago. They may not get the top grades in school, but they can recall and apply what they learned to what they want to happen.

Correct means efficient. M&Bs think critically; they analyze information to form a concept based on truth. They preserve pertinent, correct information to avoid wasting time and money reviewing old material for data. The M&B biochemist's brain is hard-wired with decades of data which provides him an advanced platform to develop a viable product to help others.

Who's Right & Who's Wrong

I believed M&Bs only wanted to be correct so they could prove others wrong, or they feel they're better than others. Now I understand they seek and share accuracy so they and others can build upon valid evidence. Lies or misinformation make for an unstable underpinning which will eventually cause damage in any foundation.

Since M&Bs are natural builders, they seek correctness because they want a stable foundation. I know shady people make millions from questionable practices, but they first used the truth to create a lie. Truth is the foundation, because a lie has a little truth, not the reverse. So, cheaters use the truth for a groundwork too.

M&B SELF-CRITICISM

"We all need people who will give us feedback. That's how we improve."
Bill Gates

M&Bs don't take admonition ultra-personally. They are this way because they practice it with themselves first. I overhear them say self-correcting statements such as, "I know that isn't right, come on..." They talk to themselves, "... that isn't the right formula..." or "...why can't I get the right tool..." and so on. They get frustrated with themselves because they know they can do better. They push through until they find the right answer or application.

M&Bs realize if they don't push themselves, then confusion or doubt can overtake them. They hate both. The best way to fight them is to stay sharp by practicing correct. It can easily quash doubt and confusion.

M&Bs have no problem making themselves right, so they have no problem helping others do the same. It isn't about correcting others just to correct them. It's about everyone working from the truth. They enjoy learning the truth, so they expect others to feel the same.

CORRECT CREATES SOLUTIONS

"Your most unhappy customers are your greatest source of learning."
Bill Gates

If M&B parents hear their child isn't performing well in school, they don't respond defensively or blame anyone. Instead, they look for accurate information, review it, and find a solution. Then they address it accordingly.

They follow through with recommendations from teachers and get results. It doesn't kill their ego. They move towards making the situation right which will only benefit them because: Follow the rules and the rules produce good results.

This relates to the Personal vs. Performance concept. Being correct helps M&Bs determine how to perform and what criteria to follow to perform effectively. Rightness doesn't derive from emotions; it's just the facts.

M&Bs also look for what is proper, to provide more opportunity for success in their blind spots. They're aware they have them, so they'll take constructive feedback because it helps them perform better.

CORRECT PAYS

"The only way to get ahead is to find errors in conventional wisdom."
Larry Ellison

One M&B author I worked with asked me to edit his writing for his new book. After I made corrections, his staff told me never to do that again. But he found my editing was accurate, which improved his writing. He then trusted me to do additional research for him and asked me to write a section in his next book.

I think he realized my intention was to provide correct information. It wasn't personal. And it only benefited him. He could trust me to help him write a fact-based book.

Correct is an asset to M&Bs. How valuable is it? It can be worth millions of dollars.

I had lunch with an attorney friend who learned of a recent case ruling. He said it involved three senior business partners who wanted to force a junior partner out of the business with a buyout. It was dubious behavior.

The senior partners decided not to handle the relationship correctly and reinterpreted the contract. The junior partner sued them. The original buyout offer was two million dollars. But because of their behavior, the court awarded the junior partner a ten-million-dollar buyout plus eight hundred thousand dollars for attorney's fees. Why? Because the senior partners presented incorrect information on one aspect of the contract. The judge determined if they could purposefully misrepresent one fact, what's the use in trusting anything else they presented? Case closed.

MATCH RETENTION TO PASSION

I also notice M&Bs, and those who work towards becoming an M&B, build and match their mental precision abilities to their passion. They use it for facts, financial figures, research, and application. It isn't random information. It serves a purpose; they're in industries where customers pay for insight and correctness.

For example, a friend told me of a man's son who has autism. This man didn't force his son to be something he wasn't. He taught him to find a passion, then fed his passion, and now his passion is working for him. The son has amazing mental retention, loves sports, and has a great work ethic.

His father calculated the circumstances; he considered his son's limitations, but he put more faith in his son's passion and capabilities. He found a niche where his son's correctness is appreciated. He is now the quick go-to sports facts guy for a national sports channel. This kid is living his dream.

CORRECT IN ACTION

M&Bs in the world of children's sports is another interesting study. An M&B retired early to spend a few years with his kids one-on-one before they turned into teenagers. His exactness collided with protective fathers who weren't oriented the same way. I watched this biochemist come from a scientifically controlled work environment to one with fathers who had different work ethics.

The sport soon turned political, which appalled him. Little League Baseball is for the kids, not the adults, so he thought.

He witnessed coaches play favorites with their sons and stack their teams to have a better chance at the playoffs. He saw coaches throw temper tantrums on the field.

This was beyond his microscope.

What did he do? He turned to the league rules to find out what was correct. That rule book became his footing for Little League Baseball. Before the rules he guided himself from his own desire for correctness. When he realized others didn't have that same value, he went to a higher power—the rule book.

With the help of the rules and regulations, he could navigate the politics and chaos of Little League coaching. He held some parent coaches accountable by gallantly intervening with the rules. His frustrations subsided because the regulations did the correcting, not him.

I think he spent more time coaching a few of the adults than the children. At one point a coach became belligerent during a game and parents called the police. It's sad when police have to break up fighting coaches at a Little League Baseball game.

The kids of these incorrect coaches suffered the most. Their father-coaches put them on teams beyond their skill level. One father-coach walked a tee-ball stand to his son to use while at bat. This shocked the parents watching the game. Why was a kid, who hadn't graduated from tee-ball, on the team?

Two kids couldn't catch a fly-ball. They stood in fear because their father-coaches yelled at them for not playing up to par. They couldn't because they weren't ready for this level of baseball.

It was awful to see their little faces downcast and heads hung low. They weren't excited to run in from the field when it was their turn to bat. They didn't feel comfortable around their older teammates so they sat alone on the benches.

After assessing the condition of the kids, this M&B did what was right, according to the rules. It offended some parents because it meant removing their kids from advanced teams and fathers from coaching.

But the results were great. His correctly motivated actions released kids from unhealthy parental pressure and allowed them to perform at their age-appropriate level. And it saved them from additional embarrassing experiences.

From observing this M&B father, furious over his coaching experience, I learned the motivation behind correctness. It brings peace and stability to circumstances. It addresses where everyone should be while minimizing no one. It's reasonable.

While on the baseball field he was a coach beholden to the rules. He didn't show favoritism to his sons. When he had a correct understanding of how the role functioned, he then held other father-coaches accountable, which resulted in progress with team attitude and performance.

When he became really upset (which I had never seen him angry until coaching Little League Baseball) he looked for rightness. He went to the rules. This is where he grounded himself. I saw a definitive change in this M&B after he found the rule book. He moved from complete frustration to a peaceful state because he sought the correct way to function inside the world of Little League Baseball.

CORRECT AND KIDS

This M&B also practiced tough love with his kids. While his son was at bat, the pitcher threw a wild ball, hitting him in the shoulder. This traumatized the son. I thought the M&B should let him walk away from baseball, it was for a good reason—he didn't want to get hit by a ball again. Instead, the father found a batting coach to help him learn how to move away from a bad pitch. And he sent his son to a sports psychologist. It seemed extreme to me, but this father didn't want his son to quit because of fear.

Once his son conquered his fear, he was back at bat.

This M&B taught his son he can influence a circumstance. He also proactively showed him how to recover. It was neat to see how he instilled resilience in his son.

QUESTION AUTHORITY

When this father displayed correctness to his children, he gained their respect and trust.

M&Bs encourage their children to ask questions and question their parents' correctness. That wasn't allowed in my childhood so, the first time I witnessed an M&B child questioning his parent, I worried. I expected the M&B to react defensively over the questioning, but that didn't happen. Instead he asked questions to understand what his child wanted to learn.

Most surprising to me was witnessing M&Bs apologize to their kids when they're wrong. They're open to correction, even from their kids. This teaches their children everyone is accountable to truth. Truth is the final authority, not age nor title.

WHAT I LIKE ABOUT YOU

I believe this constant display of openness to correction produced a most authentic response from this M&B's son. One day the son gave his dad a small card. He wrote on it what he liked about his dad. We love our parents, but to truly *like* them is a unique facet to a relationship.

This ten-year-old son wrote he liked how his dad spends time teaching him things and how patient he is with him. His final reason why he liked his dad, he wrote, "You forgive me." I watched this M&B choke back tears as he read that last statement.

I found his son's words stunning. It was a powerful testimony of this M&Bs parenting. I never heard the son ask him, "Will you forgive me?" But the son understood forgiveness by his father's actions.

Like the time his son asked if he could hook up the new printer and program it for printing from cell phones. Chaos ensued. Here sat a biotech M&B on the floor with his son who just scrambled the Wi-Fi system, the computer and the new printer all at once, their cords unplugged and strewn across the floor. (No, they didn't have a Mac.)

This irritated the dad, but he didn't blame or shame his son. He encouraged him, let him take responsibility, read the manuals, and they fixed it together.

I observed this M&B father's relationship with his son for five years. I can say he was bent on having an awesome relationship with his son. He practiced tough love, honesty and forgiveness. Being a father was his thing; being *liked* by his son was priceless.

CORRECT CREATES A CONFIDANT

Kids are little humans; they recognize when they're not respected. After a while they realize what a lie is and when someone lies to them.

I recently overheard a four-year-old (a very intelligent one), say, "I know my Mom lies to me." She openly pondered what other lies her mother told her. She then turned to her friend and said, "Let's lie to my Mom like she does to me!"

M&B's won't risk losing their children's trust, so they give them age-appropriate honesty. They do this because they want to be their children's trusted advisors when they become teenagers. Honesty positions them years in advance.

CORRECT IS A BOUNDARY

"In the end, I always believe my eyes rather than anything else."
Warren Buffett

Correct means specific too. If I recite information, M&Bs quickly correct the accuracy of my statement. There are no "ishes," such as two-ish. The facts are never iffy. They are blunt and accurate.

This bothered me at first. Why does it matter? But then I came to realize facts are boundaries. If a fact is iffy, then so is the boundary. That's why they don't mind investigative questions, because they appreciate clarity. It can provide correctness.

INDIRECT ISN'T CORRECT

M&Bs expect their children to use correct grammar, not obscure words or phrases such as "nah" or "uh-huh." They expect them to answer with, "yes," or "no." This teaches them to show respect to others and to convey correct information. I thought it was excessive at first, but when a child learns to back talk, they can use those little words in a not-so-nice way.

M&Bs envision future conversations with their children. They start at an early age teaching them how to be correct. It helps them have meaningful connections with others.

One day I overheard a non-M&B mother lie to her kids and teach them curse words. I later learned the son was nearly kicked out of school, twice, at eight years old. She's taught him indirect, passive-aggressive behavior is acceptable. This isn't working so well for him outside his home.

M&B parents, from what I've witnessed, don't allow passive-aggressive behavior. They stop it as soon as they see it. They are quick to correct.

M&Bs live a structured lifestyle and teach their kids to live the same way. The kids don't get unlimited amounts of sugar, and the parents never use it for a reward. Positive feedback, a fun activity or one-on-one time with dad or mom is a reward. Getting time with others is a reward, not an entitlement.

M&Bs don't believe in entitlement. They were not entitled, so they don't allow it fostered in their children.

CORRECT IS HONEST

I notice M&Bs are honest in relation to who they are and where they are in life. They don't say positive affirmations to the universe in hopes it will change them or their circumstances. They first seek correctness, and their affirmation is their current reality. Why am I here right now? What did I do to get here? What do I need to do to get out of here?

They use accuracy so they know where to begin. If they aren't honest concerning their circumstances, they can't create a stable groundwork.

My friend, who lost his assets in an unhealthy marriage called me from a friend's home. His friend's couch served as his new bed. His soon-to-be ex-wife emptied their bank account and the house while he was away on a business trip.

I remember when he called. He used concise statements to clarify the situation. First, he told me the events, where he was (homeless and penniless) and how he got there (bad choices). He took responsibility for his predicament. If he didn't, denial could have stunted his potential. He knew his best option was to realign himself with the truth.

He then became a doer. With correctness, he enabled himself to recognize what didn't work and what to do better next time. He then identified where his beginning began.

He moved forward by fully applying himself to a new job. By doing so, he recognized how his boss, the business owner, didn't conduct his business correctly (and refused to receive feedback), which hurt his reputation and business.

The character trait of correct revealed an opportunity for my friend to start the same business but do it correctly. This allowed him to work towards becoming an M&B once again. He now operates a business with satellite offices in different states.

RECAP

Kids need and appreciate correction.

CORRECT:

- Brings clarity.
- Creates healthy boundaries.
- Creates trust.
- Encourages a good foundation for solutions.
- Increases productivity.
- Prevents liability.
- Can launch another beginning.

CHAPTER THIRTEEN:

Clear

"Think of it as you want it, not as it is."
Larry Ellison

"The difference between successful people and really successful people is that really successful people say no to almost everything."
Warren Buffett

"If you don't have a plan for your life, someone else will."
Jim Rohn

DEFINITION:	*free from obscurity or ambiguity, easily understood, not subject to misinterpretation or more than one interpretation*
SYNONYMS:	*keen, cognizable, comprehendible, clean-cut, undisguised, well-defined, straightforward, transparent, unmistakable*
ANTONYMS:	*indefinite, sketchy, cryptic, unclarified, a self-obsessed person, a navel gazer*

CLARITY OF SELF

The M&Bs I work with are integrous. None have infringed on a patent, trademark or stolen someone else's ideas. They are original people. To be original requires honesty and transparency with oneself.

I used to think M&Bs had NPD—Narcissistic Personality Disorder—likely because the movies I watched depicted wealthy people as subhuman, non-emotive, and evil. I can say this isn't true for the M&Bs I know. They are human, emotions included.

I will never forget the first M&B I worked with, he expressed various sentiments and concerns to me. This stunned me. Wealthy people have feelings. I unfairly judged since he had three nice cars, and purchased a two-million-dollar home, that he didn't have problems nor emotions. But I was wrong. He still experienced painful moments as I did. Money didn't make him immune to life.

After many years with M&Bs and later working for someone with NPD, I learned how very different they are from each other. How each one manages beliefs and emotions is a topmost difference.

Life with M&Bs is consistent because they have clarity. In general NPD people have little clarity, so they're internally unstable. Therefore, so is their world.

"Constructive," isn't part of their reality. They're broken children who still seek comfort, reassurance and other needs never properly provided by a parent in their childhood. As an adult, if they don't get what they want, they lash out like an angry child. Seconds later, they curl up in a ball and cry. This isn't what an employee wants to witness.

I found this same NPD person who: says she doesn't want to be a grownup, can't pay her bills on time, is not able to clean her own room, has no political involvement, and has no knowledge there are three branches of government, mention she might run for POTUS, President of the United States. More than once she stated she will run for this office.

Becoming POTUS for NPD sufferers isn't about serving the people; it's about comforting an insecurity by attaining the most powerful position in the world. By choosing a world power position she instantly feels better about herself... before she becomes POTUS. That is self-aggrandizement, or a grandiose perception of Self.

M&Bs don't function this way. They choose a disciplined lifestyle to maintain healthy business and personal relationships. They implement the Five Ps. These bring them to a place of authority or status. *Their hard work creates a grand position. A position doesn't make them grand.*

Additionally, M&Bs believe they are their own heroes. They don't wait around for one, and they do what they can to resolve problems. The NPD doesn't want to be a hero. She wants status to prove how much smarter she is than others. And status will allow her to get long-awaited revenge. It is a glorious thought to become POTUS.

After my experience, I learned NPD sufferers are destructive while M&Bs are constructive. I also learned earning wealth doesn't develop NPD in a person. The saying, "Money only makes you more of what you already are," is true.

Money is an amplifier.

NPD DEPRESSION

M&Bs master their emotions because they believe if they do, they will be more productive. From my experience several people with NPD don't Want for productivity, they Want for never-ending soothing, no matter what it costs others.

But old, deep wounds from yesteryears cannot be soothed today the way they needed to be in childhood. Comfort at an early age felt good, but it also taught resilience. Since comfort may have been limited for the NPD sufferer, now as an adult, she cannot recover from difficulties, thus she is stuck in a negative state of mind bordering on depression.

Meanwhile, since her painful past never resolved, insignificant or undesirable experiences can plummet her into an abysmal cauldron of debasing thoughts and behaviors. Emotions ricochet from bad to worse. I believe this is why NPD sufferers are fragile people, because they fear their feelings may destroy them.

This isn't so with M&Bs. Their Five Ps are boundaries they developed to provide stability and increase resilience. They practice self-soothing techniques found throughout the 13 Cs such as positive self-talk, Scuba Face, rewards, visualization, breathing, movement, and forgiveness. They build perceptions based on facts and what they can do with those facts.

WANTS VS. GOALS

Larry Ellison said, "Think of it as you want it, not as it is." This is the secret of how M&Bs use clear to manage the rest of their world. M&Bs *Want.* They choose to want regardless of a negative circumstance and make decisions to get that Want.

Ironically, I never witnessed an M&B write or use the word "goal." Perhaps because it has no motivational value to them. I also never asked them about goals because they always articulated their Wants. M&Bs use the term "I want" frequently.

From what I observed, "Want" has far more driving power than "goal."

Since M&Bs use "Want" instead of "goal," I compared the two words. Goal seems impersonal. I find it is easy to disconnect from, therefore easy for me to forget. But a Want sounds tangible, maybe because it connects to my emotions. "What do I want for today?" sounds more appealing than, "What's my goal for today?"

When I asked the M&B why he chose not to become a billionaire, he didn't say to me, "Because my goal is to be a father..." He said, "*I want* to be a dad. *I want* to come home to my kids every night..." He started his sentences with, "I want."

Clarity is necessary to determine what "I want" is. It's okay to want. Wants can be beneficial for ourselves and others.

CLARITY RESOLVES CHAOS

Below is the most vivid example I can share about clarity. At the time of this text, I just started working for a new non-M&B client. As I learned her communication style, I found it a challenge because she is very forgetful. Every project needs a detailed recap.

This new client hired painters and electricians to fix electrical problems and lights on an old home. As the projects began, I texted her a question.

After the, "What guys?" response, I thought, "Here we go again, I need to restate the entire project."

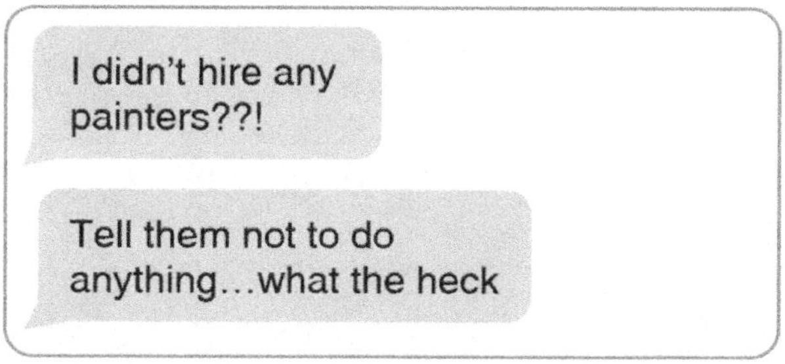

She's been unusually forgetful, I wondered why the extreme response. So, I attempted to clarify the project scope.

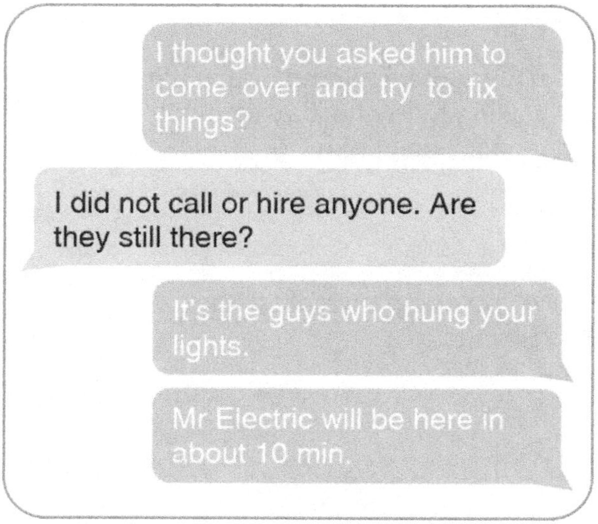

This was too bizarre. It wasn't her usual state of confusion. While I waited for her to remember her plans, I scrolled to the top of the conversation.

I looked at the name.

Wrong client! I texted an M&B on the other side of the world, and it was 2:00 a.m. his time. I tried to explain.

He must have been too tired to read the last text, it wasn't his house.

This was my first time—and last—sending texts to the wrong clients.

THE M&B SECRET TO GAINING CLARITY

Just as all M&Bs do, he immediately worked to resolve the issue, even though it was 2:00 a.m. He didn't allow fear to hinder him, he used it to gain closure. M&Bs don't dabble in confusion. They get clarity, at once.

EMOTIONS AND CLARITY

Most consistent in M&Bs is their desire to kill chaos. Hence why I call the 13 Cs Chaos Cutters. They are strategies M&Bs use to respond to fear and disorder. When turmoil attacks, they act defensively to crush it.

M&Bs refuse to allow anyone or anything to manipulate them. They understand chaos grapples to exploit them, it can grow a small drip of an emotion into a tsunami. Clarity weakens any manipulator's chance at creating a storm.

FUN HOUSE OF CHAOS

When M&Bs know what they want and move toward it, fear no longer can push them into the fun house full of distorted mirrors. "I want" is a quick exit out of anxiety. It's empowering and eases stress.

Chaos causes distortion while "I want," helps bypass it. M&Bs recognize they must find "I want" right away to escape the fun house of chaos. Otherwise, indecision means sitting with confusion longer, making them more sensitive. So, they have a quick internal conversation with Self to identify "I want." This first decision to Want helps them regain a sense of control, which brings stability to their circumstance. It also reduces the impact of shock.

I concluded some people, not M&Bs, prefer living in the fun house. They choose chaos as their companion. Possibly because they're afraid of getting what they really Want. Or maybe because external chaos helps them ignore chaos of the heart.

NO DISGUISED WANTS

M&Bs are clear about their Want. No mumbling, grumbling, or half-hearted requests. Their yes is yes, and their no is no. They decide, then plan for the desired outcome. Sometimes a Want may require additional decisions to attain it. M&Bs choose to handle results of each decision as they happen. With each outcome, they gain a little more certainty and move forward with another choice.

M&B secret: a decision is a work in progress, not the final answer.

WANTS ARE STRUCTURED, STRAIGHTFORWARD, NOT SCATTERED

M&Bs take a methodical assessment of a circumstance to identify what is necessary to achieve their Want. Steps are supposed to lead in a specific direction. For M&Bs so do Wants. They're not random. When they purchase a house for rental income, they look at how much rehab work it needs. That could be a long list, so they prioritize what must happen first.

In one rental home the M&B couple wanted the hardwood floors refinished because they were the best feature. But they knew if they refinished them first, then remodeled the kitchen; the work could damage the floors. So, they chose to refinish the hardwoods after the contractors completed the kitchen remodel.

This is common sense, but I used to assume M&Bs could afford to be scattered, so they didn't regard common sense. They had so much money they could do what they wanted whenever they wanted. If they fancied a new hardwood floor immediately, regardless of the remodel work, they would do it.

This was another lie about rich people I had floating around in my subconscious mind. I deemed they didn't care if they caused mayhem to get what th[illegible]nted. And I believed they rejected sensibility because they l[illegible]ot of money. I miscalculated again.

M&Bs don't practice scatter because it can send them back into the fun house of distorted mirrors. They don't like that place. Thus, they refuse to waste resources on disjointed decisions, no matter how bad they want a Want.

Once they determine their Want, they work strategically and don't mind delayed gratification. Just because they're clear about what they expect doesn't mean they spend cash instantaneously to have it. M&Bs plan from A to Z but may begin their process at Z to achieve A.

START AT THE END TO GET TO THE BEGINNING

M&Bs use alphabet management: they want Z, how do they get Z accomplished? Z can't occur until they first accomplish Y. Y won't materialize unless X happens, and so on, up the alphabet.

The M&B couple's ultimate desire was to refinish the hardwood floors: Z, so they completed A to Y first. This saved them money and prevented problems, two things they love.

In contrast, a non-M&B hired several contractors to complete a home renovation. He expected them to operate simultaneously which caused chaos and shoddy work. He also did his own work, several quick fixes, and six months later, problems erupted.

M&Bs don't waste their time with quick fixes. They choose to do the job correctly with their first opportunity. They hate crises, especially if a quick fix caused them.

I now know five traits M&Bs don't have:

- Can't articulate what they want
- Can't organize themselves to acquire a Want
- Prefer quick fixes
- Don't tolerate delayed gratification
- Work in a scattered manner

CLARITY IDENTIFIES PRIORITIES

M&Bs don't pursue multiple Wants simultaneously because this can promote disorder. When they clarify their Wants, they prioritize them, then start a timeline for each one.

But for an M&B a timeline isn't the greatest influencing factor on deciding what to attain first. They rank projects based on cost. How much will it cost and what return will they receive? What is the financial loss if the project stalls before completion?

An M&B has two projects to prioritize. One is an investment opportunity; she could make a considerable amount of income. But it's a hundred-percent risk, so she could lose her entire investment. The other project is to find a renter for one of her rental homes. Every month without a renter means missed income. Which Want should she want first?

Her conclusion was which one can avert loss of income and cause cash to flow as soon as possible? In this case, it was to secure a rental contract for twelve months. This provides additional funds she can divert to the investment opportunity.

The question, "How much money will this cost me?" clarifies objectives for M&Bs. They calculate and categorize their Wants using the expenditure of capital as their benchmark, not how they feel about the project.

CLEAR CONVERSATIONS

M&Bs practice openness in conversation. They don't leave questions unanswered. They don't read into comments, nor do they strive to interpret what someone might mean. When conversing, they seek clarity.

It used to rattle me how overt M&Bs are in conversation. At first, I assumed they were questioning my integrity or my motives when they asked questions. In frustration I repeated myself, but that didn't help. Then one M&B paused and probed,

"I cannot understand what you are explaining. Can we try it another way?" This question was my epiphany. I realized they contend to find an explanation they can understand. It isn't personal. They'll keep asking until they comprehend.

M&Bs don't care for any shade of gray. They're open about facts straightaway. This practice helped me when I had an opportunity to bring a new product to market in the United States. I read through the contract and found a problem. A clause stated the product owner could communicate directly with my buyers. I wanted to clarify if it meant what I thought it did, so I asked the owner to explain the clause.

She became angry and claimed I insulted her because I didn't trust her. She said to ignore it because it's meaningless. I responded since it's meaningless, let's remove it so we don't invite confusion later. She refused. She emphasized "trust" over and over. It wasn't clear she didn't want to circumvent me, but it was clear she didn't want to remove the clause. Either it's clear, or no deal. I learned it's best to turn down a good-looking opportunity lacking clarity.

SPECIFICS BRING CLARITY

M&Bs refuse to spend valuable time on pointless interactions. As they converse, they resolve a detail and then build upon it with another resolved detail. They place each one in an order they find reasonable to create a concept.

They're ultra-specific, while I used to give random explanations. Sort of like throwing spaghetti on a wall to see what stuck. When I did that, I learned M&Bs review each noodle no matter how long it takes to understand what sticks to what and why. Thus, I appreciate specificity. Fewer noodles means less noodling.

HOW M&BS PRACTICE CLARITY

I assumed since they were rich people, they never had to face undesirable circumstances, so they were all arrogant. Add to that my vivid imagination. I expected them to blow up like Jack Nicholson in the movie *A Few Good Men*. While sitting on the witness stand, he callously barked, "You can't handle the truth!" "You snotty little..."

That's what I assumed M&Bs were like; Nicholson yelling, "... are we clear? Are we clear?"

My Nicholson judgment overshadowed what really happened during times of confusion with M&Bs. I am embarrassed to write how nice M&Bs asked me innocent questions while I felt annoyed because they didn't meet my negative Nicholson notion.

Instead I found M&Bs don't blame or fly into a tirade. They disregard conflict because they're busy at their own business.

I thought this an odd way for a wealthy person to behave. So, after many disappointing interactions, when these M&Bs didn't meet my Nicholson expectation, I relented to observe them. How do they respond to those seeking transparency, and how do they seek it?

When a perceived conflict arises, they begin their clarifying technique from a simple place. It's an "I don't understand, please help me understand," perspective. They start from the first concept that led to confusion.

M&Bs push aside their initial judgments and approach a conflict scientifically, even if they're agitated. They're great at harboring their feelings to resolve an issue. If they escalate, they ask for a break, take care of their emotions, and then come back to the topic with reserve.

I also noticed they don't subscribe to the practice of "getting everything off their chest" during a conflict. They trust conspicuousness, not venting, will reveal a solution.

M&Bs are problem solvers, so they want to fix a matter rather than argue around it. They achieve this by stepping back from emotionally charged topics and use a fact-finding approach to keep themselves unbiased. They pose questions such as, "Why did this happen?" Never do they display an attitude of, "Why did you do this to me?" M&Bs, from my experience, maintain a non-explosive environment by approaching concerns in a neutral way with simple questions.

They don't perceive miscommunication as a personal assault.

If I made a decision an M&B suspected was unnecessary, the M&B initially asked me a sincere question, "I don't understand what happened. Could you explain it to me?" Because we're not competing against each other, he wanted to comprehend how my thought progression brought me to my decision.

Their approach is never accusatory, nor do they exhibit an underlying judgment that my actions are an underhanded effort to thwart them. They don't think that way. Their modus operandi is always an endeavor to make sure we understand one another.

I am convinced M&Bs subconsciously realize accusations don't resolve conflict. To accuse someone turns a conflict into an argument that consumes valuable time. Since their preference is to conclude a problem, they don't shift blame. Instead they're direct. "This is what I want." It saves time and creates a solution.

CLARITY, TRANSPARENCY, AND VULNERABILITY

M&B's expectations are transparent. Some individuals deem honesty is too risky. But I find it's empowering.

High performers prefer to focus on their objectives, so they prefer honest, insightful people around them. This is another secret strategy of M&Bs: they hire intuitive persons who can qualify what others cannot.

I think M&Bs have at least one team member who may be a cousin of Radar from the 1972 T.V. series M*A*S*H*. Radar heard a medivac helicopter coming before anyone else. He finished his commander's sentences and had paperwork ready before requested. He worked for the good of the community and peacefully managed day-to-day operations while the staff focused on performing surgeries in the middle of a war zone. Radar was clear and honest, two things an M&B appreciates.

EXCUSE-LESS

I remember an M&B received a gift from an acquaintance in another country. She didn't understand what it meant, so she researched the culture and how to display it properly. This turned out nicely when her acquaintance visited and found her gift displayed appropriately. The M&B felt proud she honored the giver and the gift. Clarity made her look good.

CLARITY IS AN OUNCE OF PREVENTION WORTH A TON OF PEACE

In healthy relationships clear boundaries exist. M&Bs expect truth and honesty. The only time I've seen them truly upset is when someone misled them.

For M&Bs their front door doesn't swing open for everyone. They define boundaries at a relationship's beginning. If conflict arises, they discuss and resolve it immediately. Transparency brings simplicity, and simplicity stifles confusion.

I spent several years with one ultra-unique M&B couple. I thought, "If these two quirky people could find each other, there is hope for me yet." This was a big lesson for me. It meant they were clear with one another before they married.

Money and having kids can be deal-breakers for a marriage. These M&Bs honestly discussed roles, finances, child-rearing, and long-term desires before marriage. In contrast I knew a couple who married while each one hoped the other one would change. The husband told me he lied to make his fiancé happy so he could "bag the deal." Their hope strategy fell apart and so did their marriage.

CLARITY FOSTERS LOYALTY

Lucidity is deep-seated in M&Bs. They don't buy into useless fads or emotional stimulants because they pride themselves in their devotion to their profession, family and interests. Even if what they prefer isn't popular, M&Bs enjoy having their own style and way of thinking. They promote individuality. I've never seen an M&B snub someone who is different. They appreciate finding others just as distinct as they are.

CLARITY ADVANCES CLOSURE

A non-M&B had gutter problems. He wanted to repaint the exterior of his house first, so he chose to paint first, in the spring, and replace the gutters later. The painters came, removed the gutters and painted. Heading into fall, the non-M&B still didn't have a gutter contractor for the job. Then the heavy rains came. A few months later, the ground swelled with water… under and around his house.

The do-it-yourself sump pump became overwhelmed and sat submerged in a pool of groundwater. The foundation became a thousand dehydrated camels guzzling hundreds of gallons of water. Puddles appeared in the basement carpet. Stored items became thirsty too. It was a waterlogged basement.

When the sump pump couldn't keep up inside its five-gallon bucket from the paint store, the owner decide he needed a bigger one. And he wanted to dry out the basement immediately. He called a remediation specialist. When the specialist arrived, he noticed the house didn't have gutters. He declined the job because he refused to ruin heavy-duty dehumidifiers on water damage from a poorly managed groundwater problem and no gutters.

A cold, snowy winter followed, and not one gutter contractor was available. And so, the house sat submerged.

Almost eight months after painting the exterior, a contractor put up new gutters. Remediation and resolving the groundwater problem have yet to happen because they require a clear plan.

WHITEBOARDING

M&Bs use whiteboarding to help them plan a process to attain a Want. Initially they put a Want in writing, which can bring clarity and fruition.

Life sometimes is overwhelming, possibly because of repetitive thoughts regarding responsibilities. Over-analyzing, or paralysis of analysis, can consume mental hard drive space needed for producing. M&Bs avoid this by writing out problems or projects, in a file, on a list app, or a whiteboard. This relieves the brain of useless loops so it can focus on current projects.

Putting concerns out of their head and onto paper makes an issue seem less formidable. It also helps the brain itemize and organize when it sees a written word.

Every time I visited with a certain friend, he told me how busy he is. He couldn't have a lucid conversation because of his extremely long mental list. So, I asked him to sit with me and write out his mental list. When he did, he found his long list was only five issues. He stared at it, stunned, because he realized how much stress a perception caused him.

Simplicity and clarity helped him relax and feel confident he could complete his tasks.

CLEAR CHOICES, IT'S A LIFESTYLE

Lifestyle is a series of consistent choices that forge a well-worn groove; fashioning a way to live life.

M&Bs define the lifestyle they want to live. They understand simply speaking the words "I want" does not create it. As Jim Rohn said, "If you don't have a plan for your life, someone else will." M&Bs understand they have to make a way or execute a plan for life to happen the way they desire.

One M&B couple retired and wanted a new lifestyle, traveling the world by sailboat. They bought a sailboat, but it didn't magically give them the boating lifestyle. They knew they needed to create it so they took intensive sailing courses, sold their business, rearranged their finances, purchased proper gear, and joined a sailing community.

Since taking the courses, and practicing what they learned, they now live a sailing lifestyle. They were Clear about their Want and created a plan to make it happen. Now they're working on a well-worn groove.

CLEAR ABOUT CONTRIBUTION

M&Bs practice clarity regarding contributing to their work, family and life. They Want their children to be contributors too, so they explain to their them what it means. Either they will be a Taker or a Giver. M&Bs teach them Takers aren't admirable.

M&Bs start teaching them how to be givers by giving them chores. And no family member is a servant to the others, they all pick up after themselves. M&Bs don't allow their children to view others as a personal teat. This behavior unnerves M&Bs. They worked hard for their income level, so they refuse to raise kids without a sense of self-control, respect, and responsibility.

When they grow up and leave home, they don't leave with the millions. They take their small belongings just as other teenagers do. The parents move the kids out or drop them off at college. They're on their own. They may receive some financial help through college, but they don't get a free ride. They must contribute.

I've watched these M&Bs discourage wealth dependence in their children because it can disable development of Self and independence. This was a different story for a friend I met in college. He hailed from a corrupt military-run country. His father was a high-ranking military official, so they were wealthy.

I found it a sad situation because his parents didn't teach him independence. They made him dependent on others to help him. Another friend and I took him to a cheap store to buy utensils and cookware for his apartment even though he couldn't cook. I recall his mother cried when she learned her "baby" made his own bed.

CLARITY REQUIRES SPEAKING UP

M&Bs assert their beliefs and desires, and effect change. They sincerely believe others can too. One day I shared a problem with an M&B. She shot back with a question. She wanted to know what I did to fight for my place in the situation. Short and direct. And no complaining allowed, just, "What will you do to protect your interests?"

We didn't discuss feelings nor perception. The problem was clear, so she asked if I would commit to resolve it. That was the end of the conversation. Clearly, I needed to influence the circumstance.

WHERE THE END BEGINS

A clear Want is the end. Progressing toward a Want requires specific and productive next steps. To generate steps requires planning. It can start out simple, such as wanting to take a vacation. For M&Bs, they initially define what they want from a vacation.

One M&B wished to go to a place that would stretch her mental and physical abilities. She traversed part of a desert in Egypt and hang-glided over Mediterranean waters. An M&B couple brought their teen-age children to Europe for a cultural immersion experience. Another M&B couple wanted to learn more about the culture where their art originated. One M&B wanted quality downtime with his kids, so he took them to a cabin in the mountains. Another M&B wanted to challenge his motorcycle riding skills by crossing the Nevada desert with his brothers.

A vacation serves a purpose, a desire, not just to have fun.

The end begins with a clear Want. Whether it is an attempt to conquer chaos, escape an emotional fun house, or planning a vacation, the M&B responds to them all the same, with clarifying questions, "What do I want?" and "What do I want out of it?"

M&B MEAGER WANTS

What are Wants of an M&B? Their biggest personal Want I identified, is a connected family. So, these M&Bs create family activities to help them define what it means to be together as a family. They initiate a groove early on for their children. They teach them how to ride a bike, so it will become a family activity when they're grown. Ten years later they take a biking tour in Italy.

The second biggest Want: mastery. They enjoy studying and harnessing a challenge. Whether it be gardening, guns, cars, photography, or marathons, they choose to master something.

CUT BAIT AND MOVE ON

If an M&B realizes a Want turns out not to be his thing, he stops pursuing it. M&Bs understand frustration only creates negativity which results in less productivity, so they weed out things which don't bring contentment.

Back in my corporate life, a coworker purchased property with a small river running through it. He didn't do his due diligence by investigating his neighbors before purchasing the land. This was his downfall.

His neighbors were beavers that liked to build dams.

After the first flooding he referred to the beavers as dam beavers. After the second flooding his new "Want" became: deter the dam beavers from building dams. It wasn't a meager Want. After several more dam floods, he turned into a dark resemblance of Bill Murray from the movie *Caddyshack.*

He grew red in the face as he spoke of his next move to outsmart the dam beavers. We worried he'd gone mad because every conversation led back to the beavers. He was on the losing end because he couldn't control his emotions or cut bait and move on.

An M&B handles what he can and then hires the experts for what he cannot. My coworker refused to hire someone and refused to step away from the dam situation. It became a bitter and destructive dam feud, but only for him. The beavers didn't know there was a problem. They continued with their dam projects and attained their Want.

My coworker was no match for the amphibious architects.

RECAP

Clarity:

- Strengthens one's voice.
- Prevents unnecessary mishaps.
- Streamlines plans.
- Creates honesty with oneself and others and encourages boundaries.
- Turns a bland "goal" into an honest, relatable "I want."
- Means less noodling over useless information.
- Empowers and leads.
- Helps complete tasks, which reinforces a sense of capability.
- Helps you cut bait and move on from "dam" projects.

CHAPTER FOURTEEN:

Concise

"Well, I just use the Nancy Regan policy. I just say no."
Warren Buffett

Warren Buffett says his employment form has one question: "Are you a fanatic?" The best investors are.

DEFINITION:	*marked by the use of few words to convey much information or meaning*
SYNONYMS:	*blunt, short, compact, crisp, curt, brief*
ANTONYMS:	*exaggerated, inflated, expanded, repetitious, wordy*

CONCISE COFFEE

When I think of concise, I am reminded of the longest drink order available at Starbucks: The Double Ristretto Venti Half-Soy Nonfat Decaf Organic Chocolate Brownie Iced Vanilla Double-Shot Gingerbread Frappuccino Extra Hot With Foam Whipped Cream Upside Down Double Blended, One Sweet'N Low, One NutraSweet, and Ice.

M&Bs are short with their words, their time and even their coffee. Coffee; it's there to do a job. It's not an experience.

CONCISE STYLE

M&B home décor is blunt. I call it "bare." I considered it odd but now I understand a lean style isn't distracting. It allows them to do in one room what it's intended for or go elsewhere. Succinct living keeps them on target.

NOT NOSEY

M&Bs don't entangle themselves in other peoples' affairs. I think this is because they believe their efforts are better spent on their own projects that can influence society. Conditions that don't assist their impact potential receive curt attention.

M&Bs disengage from useless arguments over issues they cannot influence, such as the past. They don't ruminate over "What ifs." But, away from work or serious matters, they enjoy fun debates.

An M&B told me he argued with his other M&B friends, which would be worse? Fending off a grizzly bear or a cougar if faced with either on a hike. The entertainment for them is analyzing "why."

They ended, for now, with a stalemate, though this M&B is certain a cougar would be easier to fight. It's amusing, but the argument also matters because they enjoy hiking and own property in rural areas. Their debate isn't useless.

Some M&Bs follow a professional sport or two. Their interest isn't in the details of the athletes' lives, but their athletic performance. They whittle a sport down to its key value, the ability of an athlete to execute and win. Because M&Bs habitually critique their own performance, they like to evaluate other high performers' abilities for learning opportunities.

MANEUVERABILITY MATTERS

Since M&Bs are synoptic, they're swift to make decisions so they can advance to the next opportunity. They may come to a conclusion via an imperfect viewpoint, but they don't fear "mistakes." They make choices, not mistakes. If new information reveals an ill-informed choice, they take a different course of action. There is no shame in resetting their course.

LESS WORDS MEANS LESS CHAOS

M&Bs keep dialog pithy because they're processing problems, building projects or finding closure. Concise is about mental efficiency to increase productivity. Ancillary details can derail progress, so condensed is best.

I notice we sometimes use a plethora of words because we're nervous to speak or request what we really want. Or maybe because we fear rejection. In contrast, I watch M&Bs practice shortness to avoid vulnerability, especially when making a request. Pithy is protective. It invites a yes or no without a lot of personal details.

Before my involvement with M&Bs I believed using more words could make my decisions look better. I quickly learned this doesn't work. I must let them decide if they prefer more details or feel satisfied with the shortest answer possible.

While on a building project for an M&B, I teamed up with a nice contractor. One day he looked confused and inquired, "How do I communicate with this M&B?" In my newly developed concise manner, I recommended, "Shorten your explanations to a five or a three-word sentence, preferably three."

He stared at me.

He didn't trust I meant what I said. But because I gave a succinct response, he asked additional questions. After answering each one summarily, he understood. He figured out from my example, if he underwhelmed his client with brief sentences, the M&B could easily assimilate his details at a comfortable speed and avert confusion.

Questions mean there isn't clarity, so allowing someone to lead with questions helps them.

When an M&B stated I didn't present my findings in a format she could process, she asked questions then arranged my short answers in a format she understood.

This I learned: M&Bs seek details for plainness. I also discerned they asked questions to work out a concept they're pondering. They ask questions to cut down on mental chaos, not to blame.

I now use this same understanding with others. I trust if people have questions, they perhaps need closure or want to qualify a decision. If I find someone only uses my answers for destructive purposes, I end that discussion.

Because they're focused on their internal dialog, concise responses help them. And their concise communication style makes discussions more productive. I learned less sometimes is more.

LIMITED EXPLANATIONS

I also learned M&Bs don't desire the backstory of how I arrived at a conclusion. They only care if I have one. If they want backstory, they ask for it. They rarely want one because my succinct answer is a piece to a larger puzzle they're trying to solve. So, my little [illegible]'s all they need.

I think high performers prefer concise answers because first, they're focused people, and second, because details can hold hostage their wildly creative, vivid minds with a new imagination; they get derailed by novel ideas. I can tell they know this about themselves, so they manage it by being concise.

They also talk out loud to themselves, and they're concise with themselves. When I heard their personal, audible concise conversations, I learned not to take their shortness personally. Since they do it to themselves, it must not be a bad thing.

CONCISE: APPLICATION

One afternoon an M&B asked me to send an email on her behalf. Since I was new to summarizing communication, I felt proud when I got my email down to only two sentences. I patted myself on the back. I achieved brevity!

She came to my desk, reviewed my prose and concluded, "It's too long." I frowned. What? I spent a lot of mental energy whittling down my details. I didn't know what to say. Note: Even her critique was brief.

In a few seconds she narrowed down my succinct two sentences to a five-word sentence. I marveled. In that moment she showed me how she practices concise. I read her email. It was short and specific.

Another epiphany happened in that moment. I realized I added words because I worried I might hurt someone's feelings. M&Bs don't worry about offending others because that isn't their intention. If it happens, they clarify their communication with the hurt party. Otherwise, they assume people are professional and won't take curt messages as an affront because they don't.

SHORT IS SWEET

One afternoon while with an M&B, he looked puzzled, then asked me a direct question, "I want to know why you've been doing…" I gave him one succinct sentence to explain. I didn't blame, or defend, nor did I give a backstory. I trusted if he needed more details, he would ask. Via my short response, he understood my actions; they derived from a limitation I couldn't control. He shot back, "Got it," and walked away. He resolved the limitation.

SCUBA FACE AND CONCISE

I realized M&Bs seldom respond quickly to serious questions. Instead, they initially have a conversation with Self. They think through minutiae—determine what precise information someone seeks, formulate the initial communication, evaluate it, and shorten it to the facts. Then they answer.

I've learned M&Bs communicate with their clients in the manner the client prefers. They easily match their client's style. But in their personal lives they're brief. They're not chatty people like my family. We have a story to tell with an answer. We enjoy telling them with a "no way!" ending. Similarly to a musical, an answer comes with a song and dance. We make everything fun and dramatic.

Engaging with M&Bs has changed me. It used to offend me when they didn't want to sift through my stories for answers. That's half the fun of a conversation. It took plenty of practice for me to learn how to be Concise. Now I save stories for story time.

CONCISE DROPS BUT

An easy way to practice Concise is when asked a yes or no question, respond without adding on a "but." For example, "Did you…?" The answer is: "Yes." Not: "Yes, but…" They don't ask for "but." I drop the but and wait for the next inquiry which usually starts with "Why…?"

We only remember about thirty percent of what we hear. I don't want to overwhelm an M&B with details because more means they can easily forget what I want them to remember. When I am concise, it means I can make that thirty percent more valuable.

There are many books written about the importance of brevity. The book *Brief: Make a Bigger Impact by Saying Less,* by Joseph McCormack gives great examples of how important pithy is in business. He also makes suggestions on how to practice it.

I'd like to add to his suggestions "Scuba Face." Practice it by developing a sentence, then cut it down to a basic three or five-word sentence. And always drop the "but." Then fill in details when asked.

RECAP

Concise saves time and prevents chaos.

Fluff can minimize quality.

Concise is always amendable.

Scuba Face helps shape information into pithy responses.

Concise makes communication impactful.

Dropping the "but" allows others to find what they need.

Use bullet points to help condense communication.

Concise takes practice. Edit communications you overhear or read and ask yourself how to make them pithy.

Ask trusted people to critique your communication style.

GETTING DIRTY HAS BENEFITS

If M&Bs can fix something, they will, because they revel in their abilities. Practicing CC&O creates a sense of independence, empowerment, and control. They are motivators and confidence builders.

I once read various addiction rehabilitation programs use this trio to rebuild individuals destroyed by drug abuse. Those who suffer from severe addictions lose a sense of self, time, structure, boundaries, and self-love. Relearning to care for oneself with CC&O ignites faith, hope, and self-love.

WEEDING THE CLUTTER

M&Bs weed out their homes more often than they weed out a garden. This was odd to me too. Before working with them, I believed M&Bs bought and kept as much stuff as possible. I applied the saying, "The person with the most toys wins," to M&Bs.

Then I realized this saying contradicted what I observed. Since they believe their income tracks if they're winning or losing at their game, they don't spend it on things they soon throw away. Possessions must add value, not waste it.

Their first, and favorite space to clean, is the refrigerator. They regularly check for and abide by product expiration dates. This routine differed from my experience. I grew up in a large family. We never checked for dates because we consumed the food long before it could go bad. So, I didn't understand why these M&Bs were so adamant about expiration dates.

I remember my first observation of an M&B with an expired expiration date. It was interesting. He opened the refrigerator, picked up the milk carton and stared at it. As I watched, I thought, "What. is. he. doing?" Then I rolled my eyes,

"Sheesh, just sniff it, if it smells bad pitch it. If it doesn't, drink it." It was that simple to me.

But later I thought about what he did and why.

On an early morning, still groggy from sleep, he stared at the expired expiration date. He first had to recall what day it was, then calculate how many days the milk was past expiration. Annoyed, he wondered if it was too far, would it taste bad? This needled him from his sleepy state and devoured part of his morning. M&Bs hate this. So, to avoid frustration, he now wholly abides by expiration dates.

THERAPEUTIC HOT SPOTS

M&Bs each choose what I call a Hot Spot. They use this technique instead of succumbing to the Kick the Dog Syndrome which occurs when a person has a frustrating experience and waits until he arrives home to erupt and kick man's best friend, the faithful dog.

It is unfortunate this syndrome exists, although I never witnessed it around M&Bs. They subconsciously comprehend they don't have to pick their poison by continuing to feel frustrated or by mistreating someone they love.

To avoid those poisonous options, they focus on a space where a small mound of clutter might amass between cleanings. They determine to keep it CC&O every day. Hot Spots may be a dirty floor, a counter, or disheveled cubby hole.

I surmised Hot Spots are places they project their fears and frustrations. If they can keep it CC&O then they're confident they can resolve bigger challenges.

Because:

- One small accomplishment makes way for a bigger one.
- Organizing a small area helps stimulate a problem-solving perspective.

I've never discussed my theory with a psychologist, so it's only my opinion that this is a self-soothing technique they use to rebound, take control and get results, without regret.

Psychologists might not agree, but dogs do; Hot Spots are best.

CLUTTER CONSUMES

I recently worked with a client who doesn't have an M&B mindset. She has the most clutter I have seen yet. One afternoon she asked me to help her prepare for a last-minute party that evening. As I reorganized furniture to accommodate the crowd size, she disappeared downstairs. To declutter a closet.

I found this perplexing. Why did she go downstairs when the party is upstairs? And why clean out a closet that had nothing to do with the immediate need? I realized her subconscious mind chose the old stuff, since it had been on her list for years.

This is an extreme example of priorities gone wrong but validates how mass accumulation of stuff can cause stress and hinder us from completing important tasks.

MORE AND LESS

I believe M&Bs minimize loss by having less. They know "more" means "more mess," "more dust," or "more distraction." And "more" requires more resources to care for "more." They don't like that either.

The M&B who headed out on a friend's yacht chuckled, "It's better to know someone with a yacht than to own one." He wasn't into yachting and recognized yacht-owners can spend more time maintaining their vessel than enjoying it. Since he didn't have a boat, he had more time to float with someone who did.

EXTREME CLEAN IS OVERKILL

I believe there are two types of OCD, Obsessive Compulsive Disorder and Obsessive Cleaning Disorder. The M&Bs I know have neither. This surprised me because I assumed they all had one or the other.

I didn't understand these disorders until I became friends with someone with both. When I opened her refrigerator, it resembled a magazine ad: Perfect. Nothing used, every item in multiples and they neatly fit the shelves. Whatever she used for the day; she went to the store that evening to replace it for the following day. Every day.

Her husband worked while she spent fourteen hours a day scouring a six-hundred-square-foot condo.

When they had their first child, it interfered with her disorder, which destroyed their marriage. They divorced. Two years after the divorce, I asked her if she's cleaning as much. She yelped, "No, I don't have enough time, I have to work to pay my bills!"

Cleaning is a tool, not a master.

CC&O CASE STUDY: PRIVATE CAR COLLECTION

As I wrote this chapter, a friend invited me to visit a multimillionaire's private classic car collection. I thought it a good opportunity to test my CC&O theory on a random M&B while he was unaware.

When we arrived, I noted the showroom didn't have windows, nor frequent visitors, but was CC&O. Not a dust bunny found. I looked.

The original engine blocks sat out in the open air; they showed no signs of dust. I know because I swiped my pinky across them to confirm. I complimented the curator on the cleanliness. He looked puzzled when he thanked me.

My visit proved to me M&Bs maintain CC&O: it's not just for show.

There was one car I didn't touch. Per the curator, it's worth $75-$100 million. I stood at a good distance.

COMPARTMENTALIZED: CC&O IN THE HOME

From my observations, "home space" signifies mental space. If an M&B's home is in disarray or cluttered, so is his mind. So, they create compartments to stymie disorder.

Creating compartments helps them transition to different roles with ease. It's like the T.V. show *Mr. Rodgers Neighborhood.* When Mr. Rodgers arrived home, he took off his suit jacket and put on his house sweater. Then he sat to change his shoes. His sitting area was a place of transition; it symbolized switching gears, from business to personal. M&Bs do this too.

LAYOUT MATTERS

M&Bs work in defined sections or categories. A home office is for business, not rest. And a bedroom isn't a workstation. They assign each room a purpose. It contains only what they need to keep productivity at a maximum.

If a compartment doesn't exist, they create it. One M&B's home has eight entrances. The primary entry has a sitting place like Mr. Rodgers does, but she preferred a side entrance. It is closest to the most likely place her son would be—the playroom. And the path to it weaves through part of her garden. By using this service door, she enjoyed her garden and met with her son sooner.

Since it didn't have a spot for her to switch from a corporate president to Mom, she moved an ottoman by the entrance. She now has a place to set down her satchel, take off her coat, and sit to change her shoes. She created a compartment to transition.

An M&B couple arranged their twenty-five thousand-square-foot mini-mansion for entertaining large crowds. They didn't waste valuable floor space on sleeping quarters. The second floor accommodates only three bedrooms: The Master Bedroom is approximately one thousand square feet, while the two bedrooms are large enough for a double-sized bed, a nightstand, and dresser.

After one M&B couple, new to town, moved into their home, I checked to see if they needed help organizing their kitchen. I opened cupboards and drawers only to find every item had its own space. Even the children's odd-shaped dinnerware had a place. This surprised me. I wondered how someone with such an abundance could make every piece fit as though she designed the kitchen for them.

While filing their paperwork, I found a schematic of her kitchenware. This M&B measured pots, pans, dishes, cups, tools, everything, for their space requirement. Then assigned them to a place on the diagram. I rolled my eyes and filed it away. I thought it was extreme.

WHEN LAYOUT DOESN'T MATTER

A few years later I worked with a non-M&B client who owned hordes of kitchen tools. She purchased a 1920s house with a tiny kitchen. Her shelves and drawers overflow with three generations of kitchenware, while her countertop appliances sit in a downstairs storage room.

One day she lamented how her purchase of the home was an emotional decision—it was her childhood dream home. When she said this, the memory of the schematic and my opinion of it returned. It didn't seem extreme now compared to the non-stop annoyance of an overstuffed 1920s kitchen.

And, an M&B schooled me yet again.

Until this experience, I didn't realize I pigeonholed M&Bs. I theorized since they have money, they can afford to, and choose to, make emotional decisions no matter how much it costs. But the schematic killed my theory. The M&B knew if the home didn't suit her family's lifestyle, and the kitchen wasn't large enough, she wouldn't buy the home.

ORDERLY: EVERYTHING HAS A HOME

This is a phrase I try to remind myself; Everything has a home. So, put it back where it belongs. Otherwise, when focused on an important task, an out-of-place object can trigger a rash of thoughts. It's like the traveling gnome. He pops up in the most useless places.

Therefore, M&Bs systemize their environment because they discern if they don't, it can distract them from their groove. An object only gets attention when allowed. Otherwise, it remains out of sight.

MINIMAL QUARTERS

I assumed M&B homes resemble hotels because they sometimes spend frequent stints in hotels. So, they must no longer distinguish a difference between home and work. Then I contemplated why. Perhaps since they're so busy and transitory, they have limited awareness of their surroundings. I supposed if they really lived here, it would look different.

I then wonder if they were image conscious? Were they trying to match what they saw on the front of a magazine? My OCD friend did this. She bought a curio cabinet from an advertisement, including the items in the cabinet.

But I was wrong again. I recognized M&Bs are subconscious minimalists. Because they're always in motion, in thought and deed, a minimal configuration doesn't meddle with their movement.

When furniture is slight, a room feels spacious. Otherwise, more stuff means stuffy, too close and nowhere to walk. I believe their entrepreneurial spirit refuses restriction. It expects respect.

ORDERLY OFFICE

M&Bs simplify office organization to a "one-touch" strategy. If they touch it, they do what is necessary to resolve it. If information is not needed daily, it gets archived in cabinets away from the desk. But, they keep items of importance in direct view.

Their desktops aren't empty. Usually, significant research papers or pending issues remain in what I call "priority piles." Piles exist because "out of sight" goes "out of mind," and they don't like that. They also don't like piles, but they greatly dislike forgetting. So, they use piles as a strategy to annoy themselves to perform.

MINDLESS PAPERWORK

Systemizing processes makes simple tasks "mindless," which allows them the opportunity to make better use of their minutes. Rather than searching through every drawer for a stamp, they keep them in an assigned location, so the effort to find one becomes second nature.

More paperwork; incoming mail, can steal scads of time. So, M&Bs organize it into categories. The most important is Urgency items such as bills, work communications, and letters from friends and family. The next is Solicitations, also known as the "Place on the do-not-contact list" items. Another is "Event Notifications," such as industry or local events. The least important is "Catalogs & Magazines." Catalogs go to the bottom, industry magazines on top, with enjoyment magazines in the middle.

M&Bs spend a sliver of time systemizing what could pilfer more of it.

CC&O AUTO-PILOT

CC&O for the M&B creates an auto-pilot mode to minimize time consumption. This trio frees up the frontal cortex to focus on more important matters.

The compassionate ex-M&B doctor made house calls to homebound and bedridden people. Once when he was in my neighborhood on a house call, he came to my place for my appointment. When he arrived, he opened his medical bag, and I noticed how each medical device had its own pocket. It was CC&O.

When he walked away, I moved a few small supplies, then waited to see if he might notice. Oh, he noticed. Immediately. And he became upset. Although I didn't understand why, I decided *never* to do that again.

As he put his bag back in order, he clarified his irritation. He memorized where he placed medical supplies so he didn't need to wonder where one might be during an emergency. Auto-pilot mode made him more efficient for the patient, and the next one awaiting him.

TIME: THE NON-RENEWABLE

I notice M&Bs operate under the supposition that time is a non-renewable resource. They understand it disappears every nanosecond, and they can never get it back. That's why they never convey, "I have all the time in the world."

I believe M&Bs make peace with this by creating markers and a catalog for when time existed. When it dissolves, in its stead remains a physical memory or something of value.

HISTORY MAKERS

M&Bs record time with photos of family and friends at events and places. Doing so is fun, but they also use the photos to chronicle the history of a life lived. They acknowledge a moment existed and mattered.

Likewise, they build an entity to catalog moments and history. It's the business they established, a philanthropic cause, or maybe a community. It's the year they planted their living Christmas tree in the yard that now stands twenty feet tall. Or it's a painting that matches none of the furniture.

One M&B had an old oil painting of a Jersey milking cow. I thought it was odd. I later learned family members coveted the painting because of its symbolism. It was the first cow their great-grandfather bought to start their family farm over one hundred years ago. It's a marker, a physical reminder of time spent on a family business now vanished.

ART OBSERVES TIME

Even though M&B homes are minimal, they don't lack personal taste or ambiance. One wall may remain bare for months until they find a piece of art that resonates a desired feeling or concept. They're aware art impacts their mental space, so they make a judicious selection.

I've asked several M&Bs why they have a certain piece of art. Each one told me a story. It wasn't, "This is the day I bought this piece of art," but rather, "This art reminds me of the day when..." Art is personal because it marks a place in their catalog.

M&Bs also catalog time by honoring their children's presence in the world. They frame and hang art their children create in junior or high school. They keep pieces of memorabilia, along with photos and sentimental items. Family made items make great markers.

HOLIDAY DECORATING: TRACKING LIFETIME

Not only for enjoyment, decorating is a great way to stay present, build memories, and prepare for the next season. M&Bs use seasonal and holiday decorating to remind them of upcoming events such as planting the garden in the spring, harvesting in the fall, or preparing it for the winter.

When decorating for a holiday, they choose a simple decoration plan they can manage on their own. Even if it's a little one, they feel accomplished when they see their work on display. It's a confidence boost. And it gives them a Twofer, the opportunity to create memories by decorating with family and friends.

TIME ARRANGEMENTS

CC&O applies to time too, not only space. If M&Bs don't waste a minute either staring off into space, or on reoccurring messes, chaos, or a frivolous debate, it means they spent time well.

If they have five blocks of time per day, they question how can they fill and arrange them? This is how they live, with intention.

This arrangement keeps them on task throughout the day and creates value as time dissolves.

MINUTES MATTER

We all exchange our minutes for something. Regardless if we want to or not. It's a harsh reality.

I didn't realize this until I worked a retail job. My employer didn't disclose their micro-management style until I got the job. Then I found out they controlled each minute of my nine-hour workday.

They allotted fifteen minutes to balance the cash drawer and three minutes to sweep up dust bunnies. I didn't know an employer could be so *precise.*

Though monotonous, it is a treasured lesson. I learned how not to let one minute disappear without having something of value in its stead.

M&Bs do this too. They contemplate, "What can I do in the next minute that might return a profit?" "How many minutes do I have before ______ to complete a project on my list?" This proactive thinking positions them to create value as time dissolves.

CC&O CORPORATE CULTURE

Sustaining a corporate culture is vital to a company's success. Who M&Bs hire will certainly influence it. As an old saying goes, "it only takes one bad apple to spoil the whole barrel."

In my last corporate job, I remember a pleasant coworker who was in good shape and drove an expensive sports car. It was odd to hear someone caught him stealing food from coworkers' lunches in the employees' refrigerator.

Management couldn't catch the thief for quite a while because he never stole a whole lunch. When caught, they reprimanded him, but no one knew why he stole. I contemplated the circumstance. I found it bizarre, so I asked him why he did it. "You drive this great car, you earn great money, you can certainly afford to buy a lunch or pack one, so why do you steal other peoples' food?"

He bemoaned how long it took him to lose ninety pounds of weight and feared gaining it back. He determined if he didn't take a lunch to work, he could limit his caloric intake. Stealing from others would also limit his intake. And, since he didn't find many of the lunches he perused desirable, he lost his appetite for a full meal.

I stared at him, dumbfounded by his response. He didn't see how his fear mastered him and drove him to theft. What he practiced at home, fear of weight gain, followed him to the office.

Personal habits impact professional life. M&Bs recognize this, so they choose and practice habits they want. They are the same at home as they are at work. It isn't a façade. CC&O is their lifestyle. To them, CC&O makes a person acceptable, correct, and available, and therefore headed toward productivity.

M&B KIDS AND CC&O

M&B parents groom their children to practice CC&O in their early years. They start by showing them how to put their toys away as soon as they can walk.

Training children to keep their space orderly teaches them patience and a good work ethic. They can see the fruit of their own labor which helps them assert their capabilities. Do M&Bs consciously know this helps their children? Or does it emanate from an unintentional inclination to be orderly? I don't know. But I never heard an M&B discuss the profound benefits of CC&O.

GIVING GIVES

When M&B children receive new toys, their parents encourage them to give away toys. They use this opportunity to walk their children through loss; how not to fear it, and how to recover from it. Mom or dad holds their hand and uses positive reinforcement to empower them to give.

They remind their children how they felt when they received a toy, and that because of them, when they give this toy to another child, he will feel the same way. This stimulates their children to have a positive emotion attached to giving. And, it also teaches them they matter to others, and their actions matter. That feels good too.

M&Bs also tell their children they are good people, and good people give. One M&B couple started a gift allowance for their son when he turned five years old. He determines how to spend it on other children. They taught him how to consider others, budget, and be generous. They wanted him to give freely and enjoy doing it. Now when he looks at toys, he discusses his gift allowance and what he can buy for someone else.

SENTIMENTAL BOUNDARIES

Stagnant stuff can become a counterfeit source of security and stability. When kids learn to give, they discover possessions don't possess their identity.

I witnessed a non-M&B encourage her children to develop attachment to every piece of paper they scribbled on from the age of three. Their room is a fire hazard, overflowing with crumpled and torn pieces of papers stuffed in corners, bookshelves, dressers, and spilling onto the floor. The storage room contains several bags of these papers.

This mother never taught her children to separate themselves from these scraps. Now they don't understand the paper isn't them, and they aren't the paper.

Alternatively, M&Bs have a few sentimental items and valuables such as art or collectables. But they don't allow themselves to grow attached to every belonging.

This innate detached value system influences their children. M&Bs perceive if kids don't learn to release belongings, they may never learn how to recover from loss and thus may never develop healthy risk-taking behavior.

ESTABLISH IDENTITY

M&Bs encourage their children to value their capabilities and discover what they can give back to society. This helps them develop a sense of self-worth and confidence in themselves, not their stuff.

M&Bs engage their kids in good conversations, exploration and learning so they value these above "having stuff." Because of this training, I've not seen their children fret over what they don't have.

Capabilities create possessions; possessions cannot create capabilities.

OUTSIDERS

Before my work with M&Bs, as an outsider, (one who is unfamiliar with personal lives of M&Bs), I found it odd they didn't buy their kids everything they wanted. Instead, they limit fads, junk food, junk toys, internet, and television.

They control the influence television has over their children. They refuse to allow it to teach them what they need. Instead, M&Bs show their kids what their needs are and how they meet them. When children understand their needs and have them met, a healthy self-esteem begins. They realize stuff isn't a real need. It's a Want.

Some outsiders assume the healthy self-image they see in these M&B children has its roots in money. Maybe because they assume that since the parents have money, the kids know it, so they find their identity in it.

The M&B kids I watched grow up didn't know their parents were wealthy. They each received two pairs of shoes, wore hand-me-downs, and received re-used items. And their parents didn't shop at expensive clothing stores for them either. Yet some outsider parents without a millionaire's income go into debt buying too many overpriced, new items for their kids. One non-M&B couple told me they refinanced their home to an adjustable mortgage because they wanted to buy more clothes and toys for their two kids.

PRIVATE SCHOOL

We didn't have private schools in our town. I struggled in the haves and have not circles in a small public school, just as some of these M&Bs did. They too had to cope with bullies, went through puberty, and experienced rejection. So, they send their kids to private schools to teach them not to judge others based on haves and have nots.

When I walked into one M&B's child's classroom, I realized the children on scholarship (several private schools offer scholarships to families that can't afford a private education) look no different from the kids of hyper-wealthy parents. Similar attire helps children learn to appraise others as equals. So, they learn to develop relationships based on personality, not clothing.

I remember I heard people from the outside quip, "They send their children to a private school because they think they're better than everyone else." But I learned the truth, M&Bs send their kids to a private school to wear the same uniform as everyone else so they don't think they're better than anyone else.

RECAP

CC&O: Clean, Compartmentalized, and Orderly decrease distractions and time loss.

Use CC&O to control a small project to decrease stress and build confidence.

Hot Spots can be therapeutic for you and your loved ones. And they're pet approved.

Our brains and bodies crave cleanliness. A clean environment encourages productivity.

Twofers and Morefers add value.

What happens in one room, stays in one room. Compartmentalization improves efficiency.

Less means more; less stuff to manage means more time available to be productive.

Record time with memorabilia, events, or decorating.

Build confidence in capabilities, not stuff.

Give. It gives back.

Practice minute awareness. Time how long a minute lasts.

Make your bed. M&Bs make their bed every morning. Even when they're sick. It's a good start for the day.

CHAPTER SIXTEEN:

The Game

Principles are concepts that can be applied over and over again... Every game has principles that successful players master to achieve winning results… those who understand more of them and understand them well know how to interact with the world more effectively than those who know fewer of them or know them less well.

Ray Dalio

"If women didn't exist, all the money in the world would have no meaning."
Aristotle Onassis

"Money was never a big motivation for me, except as a way to keep score. The real excitement is playing the game."
Donald Trump, The Art of the Deal

"A game is a system in which players engage in an artificial conflict, defined by rules, that results in a quantifiable outcome."
Salen & Zimmerman

As the former chapters derived from my observations, so did Chapter Sixteen. This chapter is not a theory I developed, but actual behaviors and attitudes I witnessed and documented.

When people spoke of "The Game," I didn't comprehend what they meant. It was illusive until a few years ago when an M&B said, "I love to push the envelope to get a good deal." Her words gripped me; they interrupted my thoughts. I realized, in more than a decade I never heard her use the word love, other than with family. Her use of it in this manner pierced my ignorance.

My brain froze, it didn't have information to make the next connection. Why? What was I missing? As I stared at her in surprise, my mind slowly revealed flashes of memories. Then the spark happened, and my mind made the connection. I understood what those memory snippets were: pieces of The Game.

It's amazing how the brain can choose when and where an epiphany will happen. In those few seconds one sentence resolved many years of confusion. It revealed The Game, its rules and how simple it is:

The Game: ... make great deals... you decide the deals.

In this chapter I share three insights about "The Game."

1. Anybody's game isn't everybody's game. An M&B plays it in his or her own field.

"A few sons set out to outdo their fathers at the same game..."
Donald Trump, The Art of the Deal.

2. The reward of winning The Game is "crushing it."

"After a certain point, money is meaningless... The Game is what counts."
Aristotle Onassis

3. There is a double reward. It is money.

"The money has been an accident. I mean, it's a good accident, but I happened to be playing a game that I love."
Ray Dalio

ANYBODY'S GAME ISN'T EVERYBODY'S GAME

Different games have different struggles, and competitors. The M&B real estate agent works to create the best arrangement for her client on a house or building. Her game is if she can she make the real estate deal happen. The financial portfolio manager competes in the markets; can she structure a portfolio for the best returns with minimal risk? The pharma scientist competes against death. His game is if the drug he created can prove in clinical trials it can destroy cancer *without* side effects?

M&Bs play The Game in the third P, Position, a field of study or expertise. Passion, Purpose Practice and Prune improve their ability at playing The Game.

The Game need not be multi-million-dollar acquisitions every day. M&Bs create and play games of all sizes daily.

THE REWARD: CRUSHING IT

The competition taunts, "Not gonna happen." But the M&B crushes it, the competition, by doing what it said couldn't be done. This is the first reward of playing a game well: victory.

THE DOUBLE REWARD:

What I call the double reward is getting paid handsomely for crushing it. The Game is not personal to M&Bs. To them it's about beating "not gonna happen," no matter who or what says it. For them money is their measure of how good they are at crushing it again and again.

"What's the quickest way to become a millionaire?
Borrow fivers off everyone you meet."
Richard Branson

This is my favorite quote regarding The Game. It's funny, but it also validates M&Bs belief that money is a reward for a game well played. It isn't *The Game.*

Branson created a game to attain a Want. The Want: status. The Game: to borrow. The reward: crushing it. The double reward: money. Earning a million dollars proves the person played The Game well.

MONEY IS A MEASURE

There are people who believe they become wealthy by spending their income accumulating stuff. They determine they can spend their way to prosperity.

For M&Bs, The Game is not earning a million dollars so they can spend a million dollars. As noted in Branson's quote, money must be accumulated, not spent, to become a millionaire because money is a measure. It confirms exceptional skills helped them obtain the status. Keeping wealth helps you win at The Game:

"The whole thing is a big game to him. Dollars are the mark of the winner. He doesn't spend anything. He'll drive his car and wear his clothes until they fall apart."

Susie Jr. Buffett on her father Warren Buffett

THE GAME: A BRIEF CASE STUDY.

Michael Phelps is the most decorated Olympian in history, holding twenty-eight medals. He owns twenty-three gold medals, while the second-most decorated Olympian has nine. Phelps holds twenty-six Guinness World Records.

ANYBODY'S GAME: His game, swimming, isn't everybody's game.

He is built for this game, and his physique makes him hard to beat. Phelps' torso is long and slim, and his arms span six feet, seven inches while his height is only six feet, four inches. His size fourteen feet are as good as flippers. Their size, plus hypermobile ankles, provide him greater propulsion.

THE REWARD: Winning.

Phelps competed and broke records when others said, "Not gonna happen." Phelps' idol Ian Thorpe didn't believe Phelps could win eight gold medals in the 2008 Olympics, "... I don't think he (Phelps) can do the eight... It's sad, but I just don't think it will happen." Phelps used Thorpe's "not gonna happen" words as motivation. He taped them to his locker. Phelps crushed it at the Olympics, taking eight gold medals and beating a 1972 Olympic record.

In 2012 Michael Phelps retired.

He's competitive. In 2014 he left retirement to win back a butterfly title he lost. At the 2016 Olympics he won it back by 0.04 seconds.

THE DOUBLE REWARD: Money.

Money is a vehicle, not the destination.
Laine

The endorsements from crushing it earned him over sixty million dollars. He retired from Olympic competing, volunteers as a swim coach, and created a foundation to promote *his game;* swimming.

Money became a vehicle to promote his love, his game.

RULES OF THE GAME:

These are the primary rules I identified after fourteen years around M&Bs.

RULE #1 <u>FUN</u>:

"A business has to be involving, it has to be fun, and it has to exercise your creative instincts."
Richard Branson

"Always wake up with a smile knowing that today you are going to have fun accomplishing what others are too afraid to do."
Mark Cuban

It's not that I want money. It's the fun of making money and watching it grow."
Warren Buffett

In business fun doesn't mean easy. Nor is it a trip to the movies to sit back and feel entertained. To an M&B, fun is a challenge of their abilities. It's a legal conundrum for the attorney, a shift in the markets for the financial advisor, or a bug in a code for a programmer.

A thrill comes from actively engaging in conquests because high performers condition themselves to problem-solve. That's exciting.

It's important to note, Rule #1 applies to a field of expertise. If you're not passionate about coding, then fixing a bug won't be enjoyable.

M&Bs can play The Game and follow the rules because they devote themselves to the 5 Ps. They identified their Passion and Purpose, which inspired them to choose a Position, where they Practice, and have fun. The fifth P, Pruning helps them attain Rules #3 and #4.

The 5 Ps are tools to find The Game, (your game), and play it well.

RULE #2 YOU GOTTA LOVE WHAT YOU DO:

"(I) enjoy the process far more than the proceeds, though (I) have learned to live with those also."
Warren Buffett. Forbes 400, October 22, 1990, p.122.

"... I certainly never expected to become rich... This is surreal. And it has nothing to do with money. I mean, you buy clothes with money, and cars. But I really wanted to work with people I enjoyed working with..."
Larry Ellison

Every self-made M&B I worked with LOVES The Game. Each one has one. As I stated earlier, they don't live for the weekends or paychecks because they know what they love about their work. And, they live to conquer the daily challenges in their Position.

In Steve Jobs' 2005 Stanford speech, he shared when Apple fired him, and how it was the catalyst he needed to identify what he loved, which was working with those he admired. Jobs stayed in The Game, his game, until he died.

> *I really didn't know what to do for a few months… I even thought about running away from (Silicon) Valley. But something slowly began to dawn on me. I still loved what I did. The turn of events at Apple had not changed that one bit…*
> *I didn't see it then, but it turned out that getting fired from Apple was the best thing that could have ever happened to me... I'm pretty sure none of this would have happened if I hadn't been fired… It was awful tasting medicine… Sometimes life hits you in the head with a brick. Don't lose faith. I'm convinced the only thing that kept me going was that I loved what I did. You've got to find what you love.*

RULE #3 PRODUCTIVITY, CAPABLE TO PRODUCE (BECOME AN EXPERT, THE BEST YOU):

"Money is a by-product of doing something I like doing extremely well."
Warren Buffett

"If you do everything that everyone else does in business, you're going to lose. The only way to really be ahead, is to 'be different.'"
Larry Ellison

"The single best piece of advice: Constantly think about how you could be doing things better and questioning yourself."
Elon Musk

"They're productive, and they don't expect to just be some rich guy's kid."
Warren Buffett on his kids

Rule #3 also involves the 5 Ps. Passion and Purpose identified and applied to Position results in finding a niche to become the best you. The fourth P, Practice is building skills to become an expert to produce high-quality deliverables. M&Bs harness the fifth P, Prune, to hone their skills and habits to increase their productivity.

The 13 Cs are an M&B's accountability partners.

RULE #4 COMPETITION

Even the famous Billionaire Warren Buffett who is quiet and mild-tempered is also competitive.

"If past history was all there was to the game, the richest people would be librarians."
Warren Buffett

Competition can be a healthy stimulant used to improve knowledge and abilities. Creating and delivering good products can be fun, but M&Bs find it more so when they have someone to compete against. It keeps them sharp and in good shape.

"... in business we cut each other's throats, but now and then we sit around the same table and behave – for the sake of the ladies."
Aristotle Onassis

HORSEMANSHIP AND THE RULES

On a walk, I met a retired mathematician with a computer science background. He is a Cal Poly graduate, seventy-four years old, and smart. As we walked, I commented on his equestrian sponsorship t-shirt which made him proclaim of his newfound love of horses. At age seventy-two he took his first riding lesson and is learning to compete. His dream is to beat William Shatner, who at the time of this writing is eighty-seven years old and still rides and competes.

This Cal Poly mathematician is playing a new game, and he's following the rules:

1. FUN: He finds horsemanship fun (challenging) and rewarding.
2. LOVE IT: He loves caring for horses and sponsoring fundraising events for horses in need.
3. CAPABLE: He builds his expertise. He learns breeds, their needs, and how to compete.
4. COMPETE: He found a competitor, Captain Kirk of the Starship Enterprise.

After he told me about Shatner's age and riding, I told him of a video I watched of a one-hundred-and-two-year-old woman riding a horse. His chin dropped, he stopped walking, put his index finger to his lips and whispered, "Oh, I've got some planning to do."

M&Bs Ponder

They wonder:

"There is limitless cash available, flowing throughout the world. How do I tap into that flow?" And, "How do I create Win-Win situations so we can keep this game rolling?"

They reason:

"Money is just a thermometer because I am the thermostat!"

(Money is a measure of my ability to change dynamics to create productivity).

They consider:

Where do I do business (oil the wheels, get the lead out, shake it up, build it up, rub elbows with, and so forth) to create more, or produce products others want? Because, when I do this, others will say, "Well done!" and "I love it!"… *with their cash!*

M&Bs trust society needs and wants what they produce. They have the world's money to prove it. Therefore: *Money = Confirmation. Confirmation = Feel good! So, play it again!*

That's a fun motto to have every day.

THE GAME: A PROFESSIONAL OPINION

I spoke with an estate planner who structures and manages legal aspects of multi-millionaires' estates. He is still in practice after thirty years. I asked him what he thinks his clients' perception of money is. He sat up and spouted, "It's a game." I laughed.

I asked him to extrapolate on his opinion of, "The Game," and send his response to me by email. Below is what he wrote, verbatim:

> *I don't work with the super mega-wealthy, but I do have clients that are in the $15 to $50 million range and have a few over $100 Million.*
>
> *Most of these folks could retire and hang out on the beach or wherever, but, assuming good health, many continue to work beyond Social Security retirement age because:*
>
> - *they enjoy the challenge of the projects and pursuits ahead of them;*
> - *they enjoy the focus, adrenaline and gratification that they get from working hard to produce successful results;*
> - *they are very good at what they do, and in some cases are "Masters of their own business universe" and get gratification from continuing to pursue their business;*
> - *they enjoy what they do.*
>
> *Very few M&Bs focus on money. Rather, money is just a by-product of the "machine of excellence" that they have created in their niche in the business world. They treat their business as a game that they work hard to master and once they have done this, typically financial rewards follow. Similar to a chess game, after they establish a "win," (i.e. complete a project, achieve a milestone, etc..) they establish a new goal or object and play the game again.*

> *There is obviously some luck involved to get mega-wealthy, such as being in the right place at the right time, but even then, they had the skill set, discipline, hard work and perseverance to master their job or business.*

His perception confirms precisely what I wrote in Chapter Six: Calculated. M&Bs take calculated risks to increase their chance at "good luck." They are masters at and pursue their own business universe. They mastered their industry and created their own game in it.

This attorney used the word "enjoy" several times. His synopsis covers all four rules: Have Fun, Love it, Produce, and Compete.

MILLION-DOLLAR TRADER

A little over ten years ago, an M&B introduced me to a man who was a hedge fund back-office trader. The hedge fund company gave him a million-dollar bonus when he mentioned he was ready to retire, in his thirties. He owns a gorgeous home on a multi-million-dollar lake-front property with a boat and two jet skis.

When he invited me to his new office, he greeted me at the elevator wearing beige cargo shorts, a plain white t-shirt, and sneakers. His hair was unkempt.

It was an amazing setup in a prime location.

His office was no larger than six feet by ten feet, and he shared it with another trader. It was a HOLE.IN.THE.WALL. So much for the glam life of a billion-dollar trader. I realize these people can live extravagantly, but the ones I know don't make "spending money" The Game. They understand income will not flow at the same volume every day for the rest of their lives.

During my visit, my curiosity took over, I had to find out how it felt trading millions of dollars of other people's money. When I asked, he didn't flinch, because he didn't think the way I did. Me:

I'd worry all day all night and feel sunk if I lost in a trade. Him: No guilt, no worry, he felt no turmoil (which I learned is a trait of excellent traders; they're not controlled by their emotions).

I then asked him what was the biggest loss he suffered in a trade. In a deadpan tone with no shame, fear, or blame, he replied, "Around three million."

Whoa! He was calm, I was not. I spouted, "How in the world did you go to sleep that night? I couldn't do it."

His mellow response, consistent with M&Bs: concise, clear and confident was, "If I lost it that fast, I can make it back that fast."

I think my chin dropped. I am not as fearless as this guy.

He pointed out the money wasn't "lost." Someone else was on the other side of that trade. He said it's simple. He only needs to be on the right side of the trade next time. And he was, hence the million-dollar bonus.

He's been at this for many years, so his security is in his skills. He is an expert. But then I wondered if he had inside information. Maybe that is why he's mellow. I quizzed him on how he traded, if he had connections. No. No angles. Just pure love for The Game.

So, I inquired about his routine. It included reading the industry newspapers every day, even though he used the internet for research. He spent his morning hours crunching data. He was an expert and a fabulous trader because it wasn't all about the money. If it was, he probably would have quit after that huge loss.

GROW THICK SKIN AND PUSH BACK

Part of The Game is developing thick skin. How do M&Bs do that? By pushing back against the "not gonna happen." A multi-millionaire had a round table meeting with a few women after his presentation. He explained how to develop thick skin.

He said he believes women have it tougher in the workplace. His two daughters work in his business now, so he notices how some men treat them worse because they're women. So, he teaches them to develop thick skin by pushing back.

"Push Back" is to fight against negativity, speak out if someone tries to hold you down, and speak up for what is right. Stand firm, if you believe you're right. Don't back down because you're a woman. Perform well.

He said thick skin develops from becoming excellent at your job, using your voice, and fighting for your place. Use your excellence. Set boundaries and hold to them in the face of criticism. Keep moving and doing regardless of attacks.

AMPLIFY YOU

Last, in The Game, money is a personality amplifier. It only makes you more of what you are. The first time I heard that saying I worked in a corporate setting with a few self-made millionaires. I knew them before they became wealthy.

The one coworker who became a millionaire in front of my eyes, turned two thousand dollars into two million dollars in two years. This didn't change her personality. And she didn't quit once she made her million because it wasn't about the money. It was about The Game. She still plays her game and teaches others how to play it the way she does.

Finally, when we play The Game with the right principles, as Ray Dalio says, then money is the reward for playing well. Find a game to love, follow the rules, practice the 5 Ps, and make more money.

RECAP:

What's *your* game? Find it in your passion and purpose.

The Game isn't personal. It's using your expertise and resources to crush the competition or, "not gonna happen," whether it be a circumstance or a person who says it. It's a challenge, it's fun, so love it like they do.

The ability to play any game well develops from practicing the 5 Ps.

What's *your* game? Find it in your passion and purpose.

The Game isn't personal. It's using your expertise and resources to crush the competition or, "not gonna happen," whether it be a circumstance or a person who says it. It's a challenge, it's fun, so love it like they do.

The ability to play any game well develops from practicing the 5 Ps.

Develop thick skin: take a debate class. Learn to argue professionally.

Push Back: Use your voice, speak up, hold your ground.

Rules of The Game:

1. Have Fun!
2. Love What You Do.
3. Be Capable, be an Expert at Being Different.
4. Get Competition.

How do you know when you won The Game? Review Chapter Ten, Compete.

Since money is the vehicle, what's your destination?

DOSSIER 2.0 POTUS
#45 DONALD J. TRUMP

Billionaire Donald J. Trump becomes the 45th President of the United States of America

Billionaire POTUS

"I have an almost perverse attraction to complicated deals, they're more interesting."

Donald Trump, The Art of the Deal.

For the first time in the history of the United States, we have a president who is a self-made billionaire. Per research, President Trump's fortune is greater than the combined wealth of all forty-four prior U.S. presidents.

Over two-hundred years of presidential prosperity is shadowed by the wealth of one.

As of March 2018, six hundred and seven billionaires live in the United States. Only fifty-seven percent of these are self-made billionaires. This is a small group of unique people who understand what Donald J. Trump accomplished before his presidency.

The 5 Ps Trial Run

When I finished articulating the 5 Ps I wanted to test them, to verify I didn't create "fake" information or write from inside an echo chamber. Since I tested my CC&O concept on an unsuspecting M&B, I decided I should qualify the entirety of my observations on another M&B I don't know.

How would I find an M&B I could use as a measure? M&Bs are private people so it would be difficult to find one. Then I remembered I still had the book *The Art of the Deal* by Donald J. Trump, from a college course. I wondered if I would find my 5 Ps in Donald Trump.

I read it again but this time with a new perspective. Now, after fourteen years of working with M&Bs and pinpointing the 5 Ps, I no longer read just a storyline. I can identify the subconscious traits that influence deals and decisions.

Past and Present

The past is a good indicator of the future, even for identifying behavioral patterns. Self-made people included. They've worn their grooves to earn exponential wealth. POTUS #45 is no different. If we know how he conducted business in the past, it's likely he will continue the same processes.

By gleaning subtle details from Donald Trump's book, we can understand how his billionaire mindset functions in the office of POTUS. I thought sharing them might be useful for others to identify how subconscious commonalities express themselves in the now globally public, daily life of a once semi-private billionaire.

I hope the 5 Ps and this dossier bring clarity to our country's unique experience with President Donald J. Trump.

5 Ps and POTUS #45

Passion | Purpose | Practice | Position | Prune

There are numerous expressions of the 5 Ps in *The Art of the Deal,* but I will leave many of them unacknowledged so readers can test their newfound understanding of the 5 Ps. I recommend reading the book alongside these excerpts, so context is kept intact.

Passion

"The most important thing in life is to love what you're doing, because that's the only way you'll ever be really good at it."
Donald Trump

Page:

43–44…	"Money was never a big motivation for me, except as a way to keep score."
44…	"The real excitement is playing the game."
54…	"… violent at worst and unpleasant at best… It just wasn't worth it."
124…	"They don't make doing business fun."
125…	"And while I can't honestly say… I do get a kick out of having one."
133…	"… I have an almost perverse attraction to complicated deals, partly because they tend to be more interesting…"
242…	"… that would take half the fun out of it."

Purpose

Page:

50... "... where I was headed. One day we were in the playroom... I wanted to build a very tall building..."

54... "The real reason I wanted out of my father's business... was that I had loftier dreams and visions."

64... "I found myself dreaming..."

70... "I found myself dreaming about what could be built there."

70... "I believed... Manhattan was always going to be the best place to live."

70... "What other city was going to take New York's place?"

172... "I buy buildings in my own name, and I have a reputation to uphold."

Practice

Page:

66... "... I'm not very big on sitting around."

69... "... everything runs in cycles and real estate is no different."

69... "... I got to know properties..."

74... "I put in enough time and effort... very serious and very committed."

76... "... I became an expert..."

Position

Page:

64…	"… moved to Manhattan… for a reason…"
65…	"One of the things I did was join Le Club…"
81…	"… defaulting on its property taxes… that was the best news (luck)…"
81…	"… I got more and more friendly…"
100…	"… sometimes making a deal comes down to timing…."
108…	"It was then that I thanked my lucky stars…"
115…	"… and that if I got lucky, she might write something that would help."
120…	"… it was the right product done by the right guy at the right time."
120…	"… through some blend of design, materials, location, promotion, luck, and timing…"
132…	"I knew that if I were patient and kept my eyes open, a better opportunity would eventually arise."
140…	"… I was lucky to get financing at all."
172…	"By building a close relationship…"

Pruning: The 13 Cs.

"His specialty was something called pruning…"
Donald Trump, The Art of the Deal.

The fifth P, Pruning, is disseminated throughout the book. Below are more than three hundred moments when Donald Trump subconsciously expressed one of the Crucial Commons in the book *The Art of the Deal.*

1. CONFIDENCE: 35
2. CONTROL: 18
3. CAUTIOUS: 19
4. CALCULATED: 56
5. COST-CONSCIOUS: 31
6. CONSISTENT/COMMITTED: 30
7. CLOSURE: 12
8. COMPETE: 23
9. CREATE WIN-WIN: 21
10. CORRECT: 18
11. CLEAR: 26
12. CONCISE: 18
13. CC&O: 11

Confidence

Page:

41… "… when you become successful… jealousy and envy inevitably follow."

42… "I promoted the hell out of Trump Tower, but I also had a great product to promote."

43… "… when I finally couldn't stand it anymore… offered to do it myself."

44... "I don't spend a lot of time worrying about what I should have done differently..."

53... "In my opinion, that degree doesn't prove very much,"

62... "Now, I'm someone who responds to people I have respect for, and I listen."

69... "... New York was suffering from a crisis of confidence."

70... "Even on the tough side streets..."

70... "Even so, you didn't have to look very far to see how easily it could all change."

70... "I believed... Manhattan was always going to be the best place to live–the center of the world."

70... "I don't believe that you can ever be hurt by buying a good location at a low price."

70... "I found myself dreaming about what could be built there."

70... "It was only a matter of time before people discovered the value."

74... "I can't say that any of this made me truly fearful about the city's future."

75... "I always thought... The problem was everyone else had other ideas."

76... "I also told anyone who would listen..."

76... "To me that was classic shortsightedness."

78... "... I earned much less than I deserved–and nowhere near enough to justify the effort financially."

78... "I would bring the entire job in... any overruns... I'd pay for them myself."

78... "I've been criticized... but I have no apologies... there wouldn't be a... center... if it hadn't been for the Trumps."

79... "I offered, this time for no fee at all..."

81... "... defaulting... that was the best news... I decided... had potentially the best location..."

82... "... everyone else considered it a loser."

82... "To most people it would have been a very depressing scene."

89... "To most people, that would have been ridiculous."

102... "I was confident I'd be able to..."

116... "... I hired... Barbara Res... the first woman ever put in charge of a skyscraper in New York."

117... "... I'm not looking to be a bad guy..."

121... "... we were a natural choice for people connected with show business..."

127... "I'd probably succeed... even if I didn't get a tax exemption."

134... "... it is more likely you can a good price on a difficult deal."

135... "... but I was very confident that if I wanted to..."

148... "Perhaps no one was better rewarded... than I was."

171... "I saw the city's trouble as a great opportunity for me."

176... "I'm a practical man."

Control

Page:

57... "... we could focus a lot of energy without feeling we were wasting our time."

66... "... I'm not very big on sitting around."

67... "... I went out at night, but I was also working. I was learning..."

79... "For a second time I offered..."

94... "... as long as I own fifty percent owner..."

94... "... I still had a 50 percent interest, and I'm not exactly the hands-off type."

100... "At nine sharp, ... I got Hanigan on the phone."

101... "drew up the letter of intent right then and there."

103... "I'd seen him at parties, and he was a man with impeccable manners."

103... "I was very polite and very respectful..."

118... "So we ended up going to the quarry... marking off the slabs that were the best."

132... "I knew that if I was patient... Nearly three years passed..."

135... "... but I controlled the best site..."

137... "What I needed was someone totally competent, totally honest, and totally loyal..."

139... "In our organization, anyone with a question could bring it direct to me..."

145... "... that's just not the way I do business."

146... "... it assured I'd sleep better at night..."

147... "The other was to go for control."

Cautious

Page:

58...	"But it's a mistake to be lulled by good times."
62...	"I listen. Again, it's instincts, not marketing studies."
68...	"... so I would always question..."
78...	"... and is virtually uncontrollable."
83–84...	"... I wasn't too eager... so I stalled."
87...	"... he doesn't much trust people in business..."
87...	"... he's tough and sharp, and he plays very close to the vest."
101...	"My most immediate problem was trying to keep the deal secret."
121–2...	"It's a license to discriminate... It's probably illegal."
131...	"Was the timing right, was the price of entry reasonable, and did the area make sense..."
132...	"I didn't like the idea of putting up a lot of pure risk money."
133...	"Every lawyer and real estate broker I spoke with..."
135...	"Fortunately, I didn't feel pressed to make any quick decisions."
136...	"... I couldn't afford to sacrifice anyone."
136...	"I had to demonstrate an absolutely unblemished background."
137...	"I didn't want to put... dollars at risk..."

137... "Once you've begun investing huge sums of money, it's very hard to say no to things they ask for."

154... "We had our disagreements, but the bottom line was that we were friends."

164... "It pays to trust your instincts."

Calculated

Page:

45... "... I learned about efficiency: get in, get it done, get it done right, and get out."

57... "... success became a matter of management and marketing."

59... "... it's not how many hours you put in, it's what you get done while you're working."

59... "That meant I only had to keep my eye on *him*."

61... "You can't be scared. You do your thing, hold your ground, you stand up tall, and whatever happens, happens."

63... "... and spend my time learning everything I could about what I was thinking of buying."

63... "... it never pays to be in too much of a hurry."

64... "... moved to Manhattan... for a reason..."

66... "... if that was the case, I was going to have a big advantage."

71... "... what I did have was the willingness to go after things people in a better position... wouldn't..."

73... "I had a lot riding on those first projects."

75... "... but people I knew told me..."

75...	"I immediately hired... a talented attorney who specialized in zoning..."
75...	"... I hired, a woman... who had extraordinary political connections."
75...	"If I was going to attract attention for my site and win support for it, I had to raise my profile."
76...	"A nonnavigable permit... I became an expert..."
76...	"I also circulated a state study which concluded that building..."
81...	"I got more and more friendly..."
81...	"... defaulting that was the best news [luck]..."
82...	"... walking over to look... the day Victor first mentioned it to me."
82...	"I wasn't naïve. I saw potential. But I also recognized a downside."
82...	"... I also knew that failing could bury me."
82...	"... millions of affluent people... passing by this location every day."
85...	"From the start, Hyatt was at the top of my list."
85...	"... I thought I might have more leverage with them in making a deal."
87...	"... hired... broker with a special expertise in financing."
87...	"... I knew the banks were scared to death of cost overruns..."
93...	"It's strange how things can turn around."
95...	"... he got what he wanted not by fighting but by being positive and friendly and solicitous."
108–9...	"But I decided to take a calculated risk."

100... "... sometimes making a deal comes down to timing."

100... "I asked... to speak to her friend... whose husband... owned..."

101... "In my mind... In order to put up the building... I was going to have to..."

101... "... even in the middle of a depression there'd still be people lined up to buy it."

102... "... since I already had a great relationship..."

103... "I found myself juggling provisional commitments."

103... "By purchasing those rights I'd get..."

107... "I was reviewing my air-rights contract..."

108... "Leonard... put the land in the hands of someone he thought would get the most value from it..."

110... "I knew it was going to be an uphill battle."

110... "... the better the return I could hope to get on my investment."

115... "I took a calculated risk..."

119... "... all things you want people to feel when they shop: comfortable..."

120... "... through some blend of design, materials, location, promotion, luck, and timing..."

120... "... it was the right product done by the right guy at the right time."

122... "... they want the best, not the best buy."

129... "... I wasn't about to tamper with something so successful just to save a few bucks."

132... "The timing couldn't have been better."

132... "... but I thought it was better to pay more for a sure thing."

134... "... find myself squeezed... by one holdout... who understood the value of controlling the final piece of the puzzle."

148... "... I wasn't particularly eager to spend my life in the court with these guys."

154... "There are times when you have to be aggressive, but there are times when your best strategy is to lie back."

158... "... no time to be cute, and no room to be tough in this negotiation."

167... "I was prepared to be as patient–and as persistent–as I needed to be."

173... "Stupidly, we also brought several cases that were flawed."

176... "If an older look is what people want, that's what I'm going to provide."

Cost-Conscious

Page:

39... "My point is that the real money isn't made in real estate by spending the top dollar to buy the best location."

42... "The dollar always talks in the end."

43... "... the day... to save $10,000 is the day I'm going to close shop."

43... "That's when I learned to be cost-conscious."

43... "The point is that you can dream great dreams, but they'll never amount to much if you can't turn them into reality at a reasonable cost."

48... "... we never thought of ourselves as rich kids. We were brought up to know the value of a dollar and to appreciate the importance of hard work."

51... "He'd negotiate just as hard with a supplier of mops and floor wax as he would the general contractor..."

51... "... hunting for empty soda bottles, which we would take to the store for deposit money."

51... "One advantage my father had was that he knew what everything cost."

52... "Because he built the projects so efficiently..."

54... "It was a classic Fred Trump... trying to save a few bucks."

78... "but in my view he often chooses the most expensive solution to a problem..."

78... "... most difficult to build... vulnerable to cost over runs."

79... "When you add interest–the carry cost for all of those years of construction..."

79... "... all the money that was unnecessarily squandered..."

81... "... likely more money than I wanted to spend."

114... "I'd paid... mortgage, carrying costs, getting back... a profit."

116... "... I felt I could afford it."

134–5... "My strategy was to keep my up-front investment down..."

140... "... to assure any lender that we'd come in on time and on budget."

141... "... because of my reputation as a builder who came in on time and on budget."

143... "... and even under budget, based on how carefully we'd done our planning,"

144... "Through value engineering..."

144... "When you have incomplete drawings, a smart contractor will often..."

144... "The second way we saved money..."

145... "One reason I... particularly like owning the facility... value of depreciation."

146... "... the real issue is the spread between the revenues and costs–because that's your profit."

172... "The doormen were taken out of their fancy uniforms... saved a small fortune..."

172... "... free telephone... calls to Gstaad and St. Moritz."

172... "High wattage lights... replaced with lower-wattage bulbs..."

172... "... as any cost-conscious landlord will tell you..."

Consistent/Committed

Page:

41... "But my experience... fighting for something you believe in... means alienating some people along the way..."

50... "... along the way I learned a lot about discipline, and about channeling my aggression into achievement."

51... "... by being very tough and very relentless."

51... "Almost from the time I could walk, I'd been going to construction sites with my father."

52... "Every morning at six, he'd be there at the site..."

52... "... my father would step in and buy them out."

52... "... at the site and he would just pound and pound and pound."

52... "... managed to earn through hard work and competence."

66... "And I'm as much of a rock as my father."

67... "I'd rather fight than fold..."

69... "... long after everyone else had bailed out, literally standing by you to death."

74... "... I'd put in enough time and effort... I was very serious and very committed."

77... "In the end, we won by wearing everyone else down."

87... "... a tentative agreement was the fact that from then on I was able to..."

87... "... he was unrelenting in his quest for financing this job."

92... "The battle was more than worth it."

94... "... I like Pat... he'll know everyone's name... everyone feels uplifted..."

95... "I was taking a chance... the whole financing could have fallen through."

97... "There are some people... you just want to pay your respects to... no matter what it involves."

99... "Even so I didn't give up. I was relentless even in the face of a total lack of encouragement..."

99... "... because more often than you'd think, sheer persistence is the difference between success and failure."

105... "'... I shook hands with this young man over a month ago.'"

108... "I'll be fighting like hell for the Kandell family."

130... "For nearly two years, I'd been working day and night to build..."

131... "... I tend not to give up on something I've started."

131... "For nearly two years, I'd been working day and night to try to build..."

145... "... a deal is a deal, and I live up to what I've agreed to... even if..."

150... "... and then started again half-heartedly. By the time Hilton finally committed..."

158... "This time the risk was entirely mine."

160... "We'd been in the offices around-the-clock for nearly forty-eight hours..."

<u>Closure</u>

Page:

80... "... I reluctantly let my option on the 60th Street yards expire so that I could concentrate..."

100... "As soon as possible..."

107... "'... so would you mind if I also bought your option, as part of my deal?'"

113... "... we got the variance that allowed us to create our spectacular entrance..."

Concise

Page:

71... "The simplest approach is often the most effective."

79... "... disaster of delays and overruns..."

79... "... to assure that it would get completed quickly and without cost overruns."

101... "Listen, I'd like to draw up a quick letter of intent that says..."

106... "It was very simple and very elegant."

107... "... and in no more than twenty minutes..."

110... "'If you want sunlight move to Kansas.'"

111... "Immediately, I told him to transform it..."

112... "... I picked the best elements from each one."

116... "I made a deal..."

116... "... she knew how to get things done."

118... "Controversy, in short, sells."

127... "I called Koch and told him I thought the ruling was unfair..."

135... "My pitch was very simple..."

138... "I was very respectful, but I was also very blunt."

155... "... when Conrad died... he totally screwed Barron. There is no nicer way to say it."

158... "... and after two minutes he said, 'We have a deal.'"

158... "I'd like you to lend me the money, and I'm going to need it within a week."

Clean, Compartmentalized & Orderly: CC&O

Page:

58... "Markets always change... cleanliness becomes a major value."

58... "I made sure the whole complex was very clean..."

58... "I've always had a personal thing about cleanliness, but I also believe it's a very good investment."

68... "We wanted tenants... who would be neat and clean and good neighbors..."

82... "The brick facade... absolutely filthy..."

85... "Their hotels... clean... glossy..."

94... "... see dust in the corner... clean it up."

106... "... Trump Tower is kept clean, pristine..."

111... "The typical suburban mall is clean... antiseptic..."

129... "... so impeccably well-run."

164... "The facility is always spotless..."

Fast Forward Thirty Years Later

As we review the past few years with Donald Trump as POTUS, we find the same characteristics in his commentaries. Below are categorized quotes from POTUS #45. They validate the subconscious Crucial Commons continue to govern his mindset.

Confidence

"I've done more damage to ISIS than all recent presidents....not even close!"

"... Actually, throughout my life, my two greatest assets have been mental stability and being like, really smart..."

Control

"The U.S. will soon control 100% of ISIS territory in Syria"

"Last year was the best year for American Manufacturing job growth since 1997, or 21 years. The previous administration said manufacturing will not come back to the U.S., "you would need a magic wand." I guess I found the MAGIC WAND – and it is only getting better!"

Cautious

"I hope the people over at the Fed will read today's Wall Street Journal Editorial before they make yet another mistake. Also, don't let the market become any more illiquid than it already is. Stop with the 50 B's. Feel the market, don't just go by meaningless numbers. Good luck!"

"Starting the long overdue pullout from Syria while hitting the little remaining ISIS territorial caliphate hard, and from many directions. Will attack again from existing nearby base if it reforms. Will devastate Turkey economically if they hit Kurds. Create 20 mile safe zone.... ....Likewise, do not want the Kurds to provoke Turkey. Russia, Iran and Syria have been the biggest beneficiaries of the long term U.S. policy of destroying ISIS in Syria – natural enemies. We also benefit but it is now time to bring our troops back home. Stop the ENDLESS WARS!"

Calculated

"We have defeated ISIS in Syria, my only reason for being there during the Trump Presidency."

"No, Amnesty is not a part of my offer. It is a 3 year extension of DACA. Amnesty will be used only on a much bigger deal, whether on immigration or something else."

Cost-Conscious

"Drug makers and companies are not living up to their commitments on pricing. Not being fair to the consumer, or to our Country!"

"Jens Stoltenberg, NATO Secretary General, just stated that because of me NATO has been able to raise far more money than ever before from its members after many years of decline. It's called burden sharing…"

Consistent/Committed

"I will not be going to Florida because of the Shutdown – Staying in the White House!"

"I inherited a total mess in Syria and Afghanistan, the "Endless Wars" of unlimited spending and death. During my campaign I said, very strongly, that these wars must finally end. We spend $50 Billion a year in Afghanistan and have hit them so hard that we are now talking peace..."

Closure

"I think we've done more than perhaps any president in the first 100 days."

"When I became President, ISIS was out of control in Syria & running rampant. Since then tremendous progress made, especially over last 5 weeks. Caliphate will soon be destroyed, unthinkable two years ago…"

Compete

"Will someone from Kim Jong-un's regime please inform him that I too have a Nuclear Button, but it is a much bigger & more powerful one than his, and my Button works!"

"The United States has a great economic story to tell. Number one in the World, by far!"

Create Win-Win

"Be a TEAM player & WIN!"

"Volkswagen will be spending 800 million dollars in Chattanooga, Tennessee. They will be making Electric Cars. Congratulations to Chattanooga and Tennessee on a job well done. A big win!"

Senator Lindsey Graham on Trump 1/25/2019 "To my Democratic colleagues, this is the best chance I've seen since 2006 to get a deal that is a win-win for all of us."

Correct

"Not only did Senator Burr's Committee find No Collusion by the Trump Campaign and Russia, it's important because they interviewed 200 witnesses and 300,000 pages of documents, & the Committee has direct access to intelligence information that's Classified"

"Best line in the Elizabeth Warren beer catastrophe is, to her husband, 'Thank you for being here. I'm glad you're here' It's their house, he's supposed to be there!"

Clear

"Lets just call them WALLS from now on and stop playing political games! A WALL is a WALL!"

"Just a son who loves his Dad. Nice!"

Concise

"BUILD A WALL & CRIME WILL FALL!"

CC&O

"The Red Hen Restaurant should focus more on cleaning its filthy canopies, doors and windows (badly needs a paint job)…

"No president ever worked harder than me (cleaning up the mess I inherited)!"

And Have Fun!

"Why would Kim Jong-un insult me by calling me "old," when I would never call him 'short and fat?' Oh well, I try so hard to be his friend- and maybe someday that will happen."

"The Democrats are so self righteous and ANGRY! Loosen up and have some fun. The Country is doing well!"

"In the beautiful Midwest, windchill temperatures are reaching minus 60 degrees, the coldest ever recorded. In coming days, expected to get even colder. People can't last outside even for minutes. What the hell is going on with Global Warming? Please come back fast, we need you!"

Globalizationism and POTUS #45

Globalizationism is neologism, or a new word I coined to embody the concept of how the destructive "Isms," such as Communism, Marxism, and Socialism, have veiled themselves in a not-so-scary Ism to manipulate people to acclimate to them and accept them. These Isms hide in Globalization: The "integration of people" into a "unified" process. Usually we think this only applies to the business world and doesn't impact us personally. But, for instance, when the E.U. governs immigration policy, trade, travel, media and more for each of its members, globalization can impact an individual directly.

We can identify these destructive Ism themes in phrases such as: "global economy," and "global health initiative." These Isms are slowly integrated into our personal lives through organizations such as the World Health Organization as it attempts to standardize the care of every human being. It's no longer Socialism, but Globalization. What's best for your comrade on the other side of the planet is what's best for you.

Ruling bodies practice and enforce these Globalization principles, which are similar to the destructive Isms, therefore Globalization is a method, or practice just like Marxism. It's simply another Ism from the old, failed Isms that didn't accept Individualism as the only successful Ism.

Individualism is the only Ism that works. otherwise empires never would have died. Truly, Individualism is the foundation of all social Isms because when the empires crumble, we're left with individuals who rebuild powers and empires through their Individualism. We must preserve our individuality, it preserves cultures, people and independent, constructive thinking.

Soothe us to Death

I wonder how many policymakers understand economics, or even finance. Do they misrepresent government on purpose? Do they not know the basics of borrowing?

I heard four legislators say federal funds are "free money," "like a grant, you don't pay it back," "so let's get more of it!" I heard those words with my own ears from state representatives at a town hall meeting. The Director of the Department of Transportation stood up and corrected them, telling them federal money isn't a grant, nor free money but it is a loan the state must pay back at the current interest rate. Were the representatives lying to the people or do they not comprehend how the government they represent works? Either way, not good.

As we know, some politicians try to appease everyone to get votes. Thanks to some social media platforms we can see their duplicity. Politicians whose priorities are not for The People are smooth talkers, they tell us not to worry as our sovereignty slips away. They soothe us to death.

The eagle was stunned.

Just like a stunned bird when it hits a glass wall, so was the United States.

Watch what happens to a bird after it flies into a glass wall. If the bird doesn't die from the impact, it may survive. But if a person comforts the bird, this will most likely kill it. The worst thing to do to a stunned bird is to comfort it. Doing so will instruct it to stay that way. "It's ok," you coo while you gently stroke its feathers. Then it dies.

The best thing to do is put the bird in a safe, dark, quiet location and let it fight to recover. You must let the bird struggle through the trauma. It will have a better chance at living if no one comforts it while it struggles to recover.

Years of globalization policies (glass walls) stunned U.S. productivity, nearly destroying our economy. Global policies striped us of our ability to harness natural resources, forcing our dependence on other countries. This weakened our sovereignty. And, all the while grand politicians told us how killing our economy was for the global good.

And the eagle recovered.

November 8th, 2016.

When elected, President Donald Trump unleashed the power of this nation to produce for itself. Now we fly again, limitless.

The Great Equalization

I believe in our individuality as a nation. We are many people from diverse cultures and beliefs, yet we agree to have a common faith in the Constitution of the United States of America. It is an agreement that freedom is granted by God, not a government, therefore the people elect the government to secure this truth. Government is not elected to usurp it.

Many countries dictate their citizen's freedoms. In the United Kingdom the government controls a socialized health care system. It dictates who receives care. Also, the U.K. authorities, not a parent, determines how to care for a child. This right doesn't come directly from the government's constitution, but from their ratification of the UNCRC.

The UNCRC is the Convention on the Rights of the Child, a United Nations treaty which gives countries (states) authority to decide how to care for a child, usurping the rights of the parents. It confirms *children are children of the state, not of the parents.* The U.K. ratified this treaty by signing it in 1991.

Son of the State

Most shocking is the story of Alfie Evans from Liverpool, England. When the cost of life support for Alfie became too great for the U.K.'s socialized medical system, the U.K. court ruled to take Alfie off life support. The government chose to "help" Alfie "die with dignity."

But when the doctors removed Alfie from life support he continued to live. Many people hoped the U.K. government would help Alfie survive. Instead, they ruled to give the doctors the right to stop treating Alfie, to end his life. After several hours, little Alfie died due to lack of food, water and oxygen.

I find no dignity in forcing his parents to watch him starve and suffocate to death.

Before Alfie died, Italy granted him Italian Citizenship. This entitled him to receive expert treatment from hopeful and competent Italian doctors. But alas, the U.K. court denied him this opportunity. Alfie was *their* child, *their* state-son. The government knows best, therefore ended their state-son's life.

Alfie's parents couldn't fight for him because Alfie first belonged to the state, per the UNCRC.

I find it shocking 193 nations of 195 signed the UNCRC. Maybe because it suits Socialism, and other destructive Isms because it gives governments (a few people) control over its many people. This is probably why the U.S. has not signed it, because it would turn our government against our Constitution, our God-given freedom. Freedom from evil Isms.

Non-Conformity

Conformity is the demand of the "universal government" of the United Nations.

From its inception, the United States of America is considered the Wild West of the world. It's been the non-conformer to the global agenda of Socialism, Marxism, Communism and every other destructive "Ism." But it seems we are losing sight of our "anti-Ism" agenda through Political Globalization. It's another cloaked "Ism."

Political Globalizationism is pressure from U.N. members to force others to conform to their global idea of "fair" and "common good for the world." Yet how does the U.N. define "fair" and "good" when (at the time of this writing) only 87 member countries of the 195 member countries are democracies?

How good is a true democracy? The U.N. is an example of a true democracy. Each member-nation has one vote, each vote is equal. Therefore, the anti-democratic states are its ruling body. They do not think as we do.

I see many politicians who don't grasp this anti-democratic environment. They adore the conformity game. They minimize history and have limited respect for the wisdom of our Founding Fathers who fought and triumphed over Political Globalizationism.

The Constitution of the United States is the first document of any country allowing its citizens to choose its own method of governing. It is so because our Founding Fathers suffered when an empire stripped them of their independence. Hence, they wrote the Declaration of Independence to separate the colonies from a ruling empire, or Political Globalizationism.

The Constitution of the United States of America is an anti-One World Order document.

Shame; a Favorite "Ism" Tactic

Today Political Globalizationism is cooing from a distance. The U.S. welcomes it in the form of trade deals that allow free imports but demand export tariffs. These deals scream, "You're bigger than we are so it's only fair you pay more."

Who made that rule?

Shaming is a favorite tactic of Political Globalizationism promoters. It says Americans are too proud, they should be ashamed. It says, "You should do better," and they'll tell us what better is. People who shame others assume they make the rules. We shouldn't listen to them anymore.

Tying up a country's natural resources and reducing manufacturing through hyper-stringent regulations can cripple a country. But it's better for everyone they say. By not producing enough for ourselves, it forces us to rely on other countries or go without. We end up buying more than we produce, which isn't prudent and certainly isn't acceptable to an M&B.

Fear; Another Favorite "Ism" Tactic

MEDIA HYPE:

I believe when we understand the unique M&B mindset of President Trump, scare tactics won't be so bothersome. Insight empowers us against those who use fear to manipulate us.

Two earlier fears the media propagated against #45 were "going rouge," and "loyalty." Both were to entice us to believe the billionaire-president would go against the rule of law and become a dictator. That was fantastical promotion, and unlikely since we have a co-equal, three-prong government: legislative, administrative and judiciary, designed to protect us from such injustice.

HYPE #1: BILLIONAIRE GOES ROUGE

"I'd rather fight than fold, because as soon as you fold once, you get the reputation of being a folder."
Donald Trump Art of the Deal.

Never has a self-made Billionaire held the highest political position in the United States of America. Billionaire Donald J. Trump became the 45th POTUS, took his position in the White House, and a few polished politicians panicked. They exclaimed, "Billionaire goes rouge!" Maybe it's rouge to them because billionaires don't do business the way politicians do.

I'm not surprised to see the conflict because most people, including career politicians, have never worked daily, or even directly, with a billionaire. They have never experienced that steely drive ever-present in the M&B. And this billionaire-POTUS is no different.

As presented in recent quotes and many from three decades ago, we see a consistent personality. One that lives and draws life from the 5 Ps.

HYPE #2: LOYALTY AND PRESIDENT DONALD J. TRUMP

"He was a truly loyal guy–it was a matter of honor for him."
Donald Trump, Art of the Deal

Loyalty and POTUS #45 are an interesting combination. The media have quite the tussle concerning his loyalty expectation. But why does the media take issue with his expectation? I am certain every government leader, business owner, team member, sports fan and devoted couple expect loyalty.

So why their frustration with #45? He simply perceives loyalty and honor are mutually inclusive. They are equal and bound to one another. His vision of the office of a POTUS (role) is philanthropic; the POTUS works for the people. #45 donates all income he earns as president back to the citizens because he is loyal to this role of loyalty and honor. He expects those around him to do the same. He may be far more altruistic for D.C. than it likes.

President Trump believes he is acting out altruistic motives, to fulfill a role, so loyalty from others is a non-negotiable.

Media recently revealed several government employees are still loyal to an expired regime, a memory. (Yet the media has no problem with their loyalty). This is disloyalty to the rule of law in our county. Our law requires a presidential election, a new administration every four years. Anyone who attempts to usurp a new administration commits treason. Therefore, his expectations are correct, and appropriate.

Loyalty in The Art of the Deal

On page sixty-nine of *The Art of the Deal,* you will find Trump explains his friendship with attorney Roy Cohn. He said, "He was truly a loyal guy–it was a matter of honor with him... You could count on him to go to bat for you, even if he privately disagreed with your view, and even if defending you wasn't necessarily the best thing for him. He was never two-faced. Just compare that with all the hundreds of "respectable" guys who make careers out of boasting about their uncompromising integrity but have absolutely no loyalty. They think only about what's best for them and don't think twice about stabbing a friend in the back..."

Per #45, a person is a professional when he acts loyally even though he disagrees. You can have integrity yet not agree. But to commit to a plan and secretly turn against the plan, is an irritation to anyone trying to build a project.

President Trump believes in commitment to a cause and believes everyone involved agrees to and desires the same outcome. But in his administration, there are staff members who secretly don't want productivity, so they sabotage it, for him and the rest of the country. Thankfully, M&Bs don't find it difficult to free a business of toxic people.

Washington D.C. and Honesty – An Oxymoron

President Trump refuses to build a team of half-hearted, disloyal employees. Who would? Half-hearted means limited results. No billionaire settles for limited results.

This POTUS expects honesty. Without it, there isn't a foundation for people to negotiate deals. #45 doesn't mind disagreements, but if he hires someone to promote his Pro-America agenda, then the new hire should deliver with honor and loyalty, as agreed, for the good of the country.

I notice this M&B loyalty and honor expectation develops another behavior, it's similar to a homing missile. What's the target? Others who fight productivity, lack loyalty or integrity.

Professionally or personally, M&Bs remove these people from positions of authority. It isn't personal. M&Bs do this because they know disloyalty and/or lack of integrity create chaos, and chaos kills. So, they kill the opportunity to promote chaos before it kills productivity.

But D.C. doesn't seem to work this way. They like to reward treacherous people by giving them a different job, in the same broken system. This should concern Americans.

Hacking a New Norm in D.C.

"I discovered, for the first time but not the last, that politicians don't care too much what things cost. It's not their money."
Donald Trump, The Art of the Deal.

President Trump is hacking out a new norm in D.C. His desire is to reestablish the 5 Ps in our country, including our government.

In particular, he:

- **Positions** the U.S. for better trade deals.
- Creates better **Practices** by **Pruning** the old, wasteful ways of government by reestablishing our veteran's healthcare system.
- Uses presidential power to honor our country's **Purpose**, found in the Preamble of our Constitution, "We the People of the United States, in Order to form a more perfect Union, establish Justice, insure domestic Tranquility, provide for the common defence, promote the general Welfare, and secure the Blessings of Liberty to ourselves and our Posterity..."
- Seeks to encourage our **Passion** for our country through increasing economic growth.

By creating tradition, such as being the first sitting president to attend the New York City Veterans Day Parade, he encourages citizens to uphold our country's values.

POTUS #45 will continue to work great deals for the United States. It is disappointing some politicians refuse to negotiate with him because of their own egos. Ironically, they claim Trump has a huge ego. If so, his ego is about making great deals for The People while their egos are about killing them.

God help us.

Final Thoughts

A week ago, I dropped off a photo for custom framing at a framing studio. I went yesterday to pick it up, but the matting wasn't straight. It was a reverse bevel edge, cut by a machine, so it surprised me to see a poor cut.

To me it was noticeable and disappointing. I commented on the flaw to the assistant, but she didn't see it. After running my finger above the slightly curved edge, twice, she still didn't see it. Then I put a straight-edged piece of paper alongside the matting edge. She gasped, then said she's been a framing specialist for years but would never notice a half-millimeter variation.

Her surprise led to curiosity. She asked me what I did for a living. After I explained my work, she understood my need for precision. Our conversation ended with her promising to fix the flaw.

Later that afternoon, I contemplated our conversation, which prompted a realization: these commonalities are now at work in me, but I didn't see this until someone unfamiliar with them questioned me. I learned I could learn the habits of the wealthy and make them my own.

My experience confirmed mindful practice creates naturally subconscious behaviors. I hope this encourages those who doubt they can master the habits of the wealthy. No more wondering, I've given you their strategies so now you can.

What now? Plan!

Invest in yourself the way M&Bs do. They think they're worth it, so should you.

Now you have what the wealthy have, a process to build a "profitable" lifestyle, whether it be with friends, family or finances.

In the next few pages, you will find two charts. One is the 5 Ps and the other, the 13 Cs. Develop a plan to implement these two pages into your daily life.

Strategies:

- Make copies of the pages and post them in areas you frequent.
- Keep a photo of them on a smart phone and study them regularly.
- Find opportunities to practice them.
- Set a reminder on your phone to apply one of the 13 Cs within the hour, every waking hour.
- Create a study group with friends, family, or coworkers. Talk about how to apply the strategies and challenge one another to do so.
- Create a reward system for when you or others implement the strategies.

One way I implement these strategies is ask myself, "What would my client do?" I remember the stories and make my decision as if I'm role-playing them. It helps me get outside my normal way of thinking and play more offensively.

You can use this same strategy. First, categorize a circumstance under the 5 Ps. Then review the stories in the corresponding chapter. Get a feel for the M&B's personality and practice in your mind how he or she resolved the issue. Then ask yourself, "What Would Pepper's Client Do?" W.W.P.C.D.? Next; be that person you imagine.

Act it out every day, and you will become what you role-play.

A journal for your transformational journey.

Honesty. It's healthiest. First be honest with yourself about what you *really* want, the good Wants. Be honest about what keeps you from attaining them. Then start a journal. Why? Because journaling provides miraculous health benefits as well as an opportunity for honest self-reflection.

The benefits of journaling from www.mic.com:

> *These benefits include long-term improvements in mood, stress levels and depressive symptoms. Not only does writing make you less likely to get sick, it also increases chances of fighting specific diseases like asthma, AIDS and cancer.*
>
> *It can even make physical wounds heal faster. A study from 2013 found that 76% of adults who spent 20 minutes writing about their thoughts and feelings for three consecutive days two weeks before a medically necessary biopsy were fully healed 11 days later. Meanwhile, 58% of the control group had not recovered.*
>
> *The study concluded that even one hour of writing about distressing events helped participants make sense of the events and reduce distress… The study found that participants who wrote about traumatic, stressful or emotional events were significantly less likely to get sick, and were ultimately less seriously affected by trauma, than their non-journaling counterparts.*
>
> Science Shows Something Surprising About People Who Still Journal. www.mic.com.

Journal. It can save your life.

PRACTICE, PRACTICE, PRACTICE!

Building success starts today, you're one decision away.
~ Laine

So, you're ready! Get your Wants in order, start a journal, use the charts, build a plan (including a team), role play W.W.P.C.D.? (What Would Pepper's Client Do?), and journal your journey. Remember, every decision matters.

Wishing you all the best riches to your heart, your mind and your pockets!

Laine

THE 5 PS - *M&B success formula*

PASSION:

It's a burning feeling. Sometimes passion is hidden in our values. Know your values and you'll know your passion, try the Kerwin Values Survey to learn more about your passion.

PURPOSE:

Values tell us what is most important to us. Values drive us to act because of that burning feeling (Passion). It may take time to discover purpose, so in the meantime work on the other Ps. They'll establish your success.

POSITION:

Where can you position your passion and purpose in an industry that can pay you well? Research how others change their position, sometimes a copycat strategy is a good start. And volunteer, it can help clarify passion and purpose.

PRACTICE:

Practice while in your position through networking, mentorship, learning and teaching. Become an expert. Create a career path and learn to market yourself, to continually position yourself along your path.

PRUNE:

The 13 Cs are about practicing boundaries. Boundaries are necessary for growth. They protect what is on the inside and keep out what is harmful. Cutting off chaos means you value what's on the inside - **you**.

13 CHAOS ✂ CUTTERS

	CONFIDENCE  Remember the Hero Within	
CONTROL  ***You are the Captain*** Who & what influences you?	**CAUTIOUS**  Behavior + time = trust Plan to prevent.	**CALCULATE** 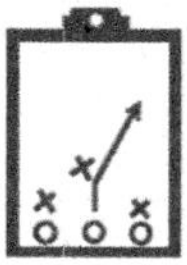 What is a fair trade for your resources?
COST-CONSCIOUS  ***Frux it all!*** Give your dollars a purpose	**CONSISTENT & COMMITTED**  Create routines. Take breaks. Be grateful.	**CLOSURE**  Stop the drama & save your I.Q.
COMPETE  Reduce the stress of captivity. No Mr. mediocre!	**CREATE WIN-WIN**  Who can prosper from meeting your need?	**CORRECT**  Bring clarity and prevent liability.
CLEAR  Turn a bland "goal" into: "I want."	**CONCISE**  Blunt is best for the brain.	**CC&O**  Create a hot spot. Find twofers.

MILLIONAIRE AND BILLIONAIRE BIOS

Phil Knight: Entrepreneur, Co-founder of Nike Inc. Estimated worth: US $33.5 billion.

Oprah Winfrey: Actress, entrepreneur, The Oprah Winfrey Show. Estimated worth Us $3.5 billion.

Richard Branson: Entrepreneur, Virgin Group founder. Estimated worth US $5 billion.

Charles Koch: Grew Koch Ind. From $21 million to $100 billion. Estimated worth US$50.7 billion.

David Koch: Co-owner Koch Industries. Estimated worth US $50.6 billion.

Warren Buffett: Investor, CEO Berkshire Hathaway. Estimated worth US $82 billion.

Donald Trump: Real estate investor, builder. POTUS #45. Estimated worth US $3.1 billion.

Sergey Brin: Co-founder of Google, Alphabet Inc. Estimated worth US $52.5 billion.

Sheldon Adelson: Entrepreneur, casinos and hotels. Estimated worth US $32.8 billion.

Elliot Hulse: Entrepreneur, Strength Camp Gym, social media star. Estimated worth US $2 million.

J.K Rowling: Author and movie producer, Harry Potter series. Estimated worth US $1 billion.

Mark Cuban: Entrepreneur, owner, MicroSolutions and Broadcast.com. Estimated worth US $4.1 billion.

Ray Dalio: Entrepreneur, investor, founder Bridgewater Associates. Estimated worth US $19.4 billion.

Jim Rohn: Entrepreneur, author, motivational speaker. Estimated worth, todays value US $5 billion.

Aristotle Onassis: Entrepreneur, tobacco and shipping. Estimated worth today, US $2.3 billion.

Alice Walton: Financier, philanthropist, Walmart heiress. Estimated worth US $48.7 billion.

Jeff Bezos: Entrepreneur, founder Amazon. Estimated worth US $110 billion.

Ted Turner: Founder, Turner Broadcasting. Estimated worth US $2.2 billion.

Paulo Coelho: Novelist. The Alchemist. Estimated worth US $550 million.

Stefan Persson: Chairman, H&M retail stores. Estimated worth US $17.1 billion.

Carlos Slim: Entrepreneur, telecom. Estimated worth US $62.3 billion.

Larry Ellison: Entrepreneur, co-founder Oracle. Estimated worth US $65.6 billion.

Carl Icahn: Entrepreneur, investor, founder Icahn Enterprises. Estimated worth US $18.5 billion.

Elon Musk: Entrepreneur, inventor. Founder, SpaceX and Tesla. Estimated worth US $19.9 billion.

Bill Gates: Entrepreneur. Founder Microsoft. Estimated worth US $99.5 billion.

Leonardo Del Vecchio: Entrepreneur, founder Luxottica. Estimated worth US $23.3 billion.

Andrew Carnegie: Entrepreneur, railroad, Carnegie Steel Corporation. Estimate worth today, $4.8 billion.

Kathy Ireland: Actress, model, entrepreneur, designer. Estimated worth US $450 million.

Steve Jobs: Entrepreneur, inventor, designer. Apple Co-founder. Estimated worth today, US $23 billion.